A Tawdry Place of Salvation

A TAWDRY PLACE
OF SALVATION
The Art of Jane Bowles

Edited by
Jennie Skerl

Southern Illinois University Press

Carbondale and Edwardsville

Library of Congress Cataloging-in-Publication Data

A tawdry place of salvation : the art of Jane Bowles / edited by
Jennie Skerl.
p. cm.
Includes bibliographical references (p.   ) and index.
1. Bowles, Jane Auer, 1917–1973—Criticism and interpretation.
2. Women and literature—United States—History—20th century.
3. Women and literature—Morocco—History—20th century.
4. Morocco—In literature. I. Skerl, Jennie.
P3552.0837Z89 1997
818'.5409—dc20   96-43454
ISBN 0-8093-2100-9 CIP

The paper used in this publication meets the minimum requirements of American National
Standard for Information Sciences—Permanence of Paper for Printed Library Materials,
ANSI Z39.48-1984. ⊗

Contents

Preface

THE ESSAYS IN this volume explore Bowles's *oeuvre* from a variety of perspectives. My introductory essay analyzes Bowles's writing career and critical reception, placing her within the context of the historical avant-garde and experimental writing. Carolyn J. Allen discusses *Two Serious Ladies* as a text whose narrative tension between modernist content and postmodernist spirit questions stable sexual identities, making the novel an anomalous queer theory text. Stephen Benz's essay on *Two Serious Ladies* and "A Guatemalan Idyll" (a short story that was originally part of the novel manuscript) reveals Bowles's unusual exploration of neocolonial relationships as compared to other American literature set in tropical lands. Both of these essays on Bowles's novel emphasize Bowles's unique angle of vision that enables her to transcend convention and convey prescient critiques of stable sexual identities, cultural assumptions about eroticism, and imperialist attitudes toward the geographical or cultural Other. Together, Allen and Benz reveal a multifaceted work that demands further exploration.

The two essays on Jane Bowles's play, *In the Summer House*, are the most thorough analyses of that work to date, detailing Bowles's portrayal of motherhood and of the mother-daughter relationship that was so original at the time that audiences could not grasp it and also so psychologically complex that the play is still a challenge to contemporary drama and its critics. Peter G. Christensen emphasizes Bowles's complex and original analysis of mothering and her insight into the conflict between a mother's continuing psychological development and society's (and children's) need to reify motherhood. Charlotte Goodman focuses on the complexities of Bowles's exploration of the mother-daughter relationship in the three mother-daughter pairs in the play (one of which is usually overlooked). Her feminist analysis pays attention to the patriarchal context that makes women's relationships with women so ambivalent. Regina Weinreich's essay on Bowles's puppet play, *A Quarreling Pair*, is the first detailed discussion of a work that is often dismissed as having no importance. Turning away from a feminist interpretation of the play's pair of sisters, Weinreich places the minidrama in its surrealist context and explores the metaphorical complexities of its oppositions.

John Maier's discussion of three Bowles pieces written after she moved to Tangier is a challenge to the accepted belief that Bowles's residence in Morocco did not influence or inspire her writing. Maier makes a compelling case for his analysis of how "Everything Is Nice," "The Iron Table," and "Emmy Moore's Journal" show Bowles responding to Morocco's different way of drawing sexual and gender boundaries. Just as Benz praises Bowles for her rejection of neocolonial stereotypes and her openness to engagement with the cultural Other and the consequent revision of the Self, Maier sees a similar responsiveness to the Moroccan culture and the subtle ways Bowles incorporates her experience with a different system of gender relationships into her own analysis of identity, gender, displacement, disorientation, and isolation.

The essays by Carol Shloss and Robert E. Lougy are wide-ranging philosophical overviews of Bowles's *oeuvre*. Shloss explores the images of displacement, homelessness, and transience, the theme of the impossibility of being at home in the world, and the portrayal of alienation as a prelude to transformation. Shloss sees Bowles's fictional treatment of estrangement as having political implications that parallel the philosophical essays of Adorno and Kristeva on the same subject, pointing out that Bowles's most estranged characters are most open to strangers. Shloss devotes her most extended analyses to "Camp Cataract," *Two Serious Ladies*, and "Everything Is Nice." Lougy's essay builds upon his previously published article in developing an overview of Jane Bowles's work, paying most attention to those themes, human relationships, and questions that give her writing the texture, style, and voice so uniquely her own. Lougy finds that Bowles radically problematizes the self and uses the comedy of the grotesque to subvert the illusions of wholeness that screen the individual from her existential dislocation.

The final two essays are studies of Bowles's unpublished work. Gena Dagel Caponi surveys the manuscripts in the Harry Ransom Humanities Research Center, revealing much of interest in the dramatic and narrative fragments and sensitively chronicling the story of Bowles's frustrations as a writer. Caponi's essay adds more detail to our knowledge of Bowles's world view, themes, and images, and to our understanding of her writing processes. Allen E. Hibbard gives us a close analysis of the unfinished *Out in the World*, making a case for it as a postmodern text. Building upon his previously published reconstruction of the work, Hibbard explains how this text problematizes relationships between the sexes, ethnocentric assumptions, the nature and construction of human identity, and the conventional configurations of narrative. Although Bowles thought her fragmentary manuscript a failure, Hibbard argues for its value as a postmodern text that critiques the modernist ideal of the autonomous work of art, challenging us to create an aesthetic that embraces this work. That is the challenge in all of Bowles's work which allies her with the avant-garde: Bowles's writing creates its own world, which alters our vision of our own; her work creates its own aesthetic, which causes us to revise our critical criteria; and her originality produces an idiosyncratic, but authoritative, style.

Throughout this volume, all quotations of Jane Bowles's published works are from

Ecco Press's 1978 expanded edition of her collected works, abbreviated as *Collected Works* or *Works* (1978), and from Black Sparrow Press's 1985 selected letters, edited by Millicent Dillon, abbreviated as *Letters*. Millicent Dillon's 1981 biography is abbreviated as *Life*. See the bibliography for full references to these works. Jane Bowles's unpublished manuscripts are housed in the Harry Ransom Humanities Research Center of the University of Texas at Austin. Gena Dagel Caponi's essay includes a detailed listing of these materials. The bibliography that concludes this volume lists Jane Bowles's published works and all secondary sources consulted by the contributors, including all scholarly criticism of Bowles's work and a generous sampling of reviews.

This book could not have come into being without the ground-breaking work of Millicent Dillon, who has almost singlehandedly brought Jane Bowles's work to contemporary attention and in such a way as to make it more difficult for her to be forgotten again. An NEH Fellowship supported the research that led to this volume. Thanks to Paul Bowles for permission to quote from Jane Bowles's unpublished manuscripts in the Harry Ransom Humanities Research Center. I thank all of my contributors for their cooperation, patience, and continuing dialogue about Jane and Paul Bowles. The editorial advice of Robin Lydenberg also supported the progress of this volume. Thanks go also to Deans Wells and Buchanan for their support of this project, to the reference librarians at West Chester University for their expert assistance, to my colleagues at West Chester for many helpful conversations, and to Sharon Bradbury for her excellent typing service. Thanks as always to John L. Hynes for his constant encouragement and editorial advice.

A Tawdry Place of Salvation

1

Sallies into the Outside World

A Literary History of Jane Bowles

Jennie Skerl

THIS BOOK IS devoted to the art of Jane Bowles. Her works have received high praise from other writers such as Tennessee Williams, Truman Capote, John Ashbery, Millicent Dillon, and Alan Sillitoe, as well as the respect of other artists in the sophisticated bohemia of which she was a part. Yet, in spite of the high esteem of her peers, Bowles has not received sustained critical attention, nor has her contribution to twentieth-century literature been adequately recognized and placed in its historical context. Like many other female experimental writers, Jane Bowles has suffered from critical silence and marginalizing labels—such as cult author, coterie writer, minor talent, underground legend, eccentric, and madwoman—that occur repeatedly in reviews and criticism of her work. Also, like that of many other female bohemian artists, Jane Bowles's work has been overshadowed by fascination with her unconventional life and legend.

Thus, the purpose of this collection of essays on Jane Bowles is to pay attention to the works, not the biography or the myth, in order to understand and appreciate her brilliant, complex *oeuvre*. The essays in this collection examine her work from a variety of critical and theoretical perspectives. This introduction focuses on Jane Bowles's life in letters: her writing career, her published or performed work, and its critical reception. As will be seen, Bowles's originality and power led to a silencing that is a recurrent pattern in the careers of female artists. Her work and its reception, then, can be seen as representative, contributing to the contemporary re-examination of modernism and experimental literature from the perspective of gender.

Jane Auer was born in 1917 to middle-class Jewish parents and was brought up in Woodmere, Long Island, and New York City. Her parents were nonpracticing Jews, and their daughter never displayed any particular interest in Judaism or Jewish identity, except as a source of self-deprecating humor. Her early education included a French governess and attendance at a French school for children in Manhattan. She attended public schools in Woodmere and Manhattan and spent one semester at a private girls' school in Massachusetts. However, in 1932, she developed tuberculosis of the knee and was treated in a Swiss clinic from 1932 to 1934, where her education was completed with a French tutor. Thus, the French influence on her intellectual and literary development should not be overlooked.

As a child, Jane Auer could read and speak French. As a teenager, she studied Proust, Gide, and Céline, powerful precursors in the twentieth-century literary avant-garde and particularly the Anglo-American novel. Proust's novels, of course, have been one of modernism's critical touchstones, defining the *künstlerroman*. Gide's literary rebellion against bourgeois norms, his homosexuality, and his definition of *l'acte gratuit* profoundly influenced younger artists of the 1920s and 1930s, such as Jane Auer's future husband Paul Bowles and their friend in Tangier, William Burroughs. Céline's work is an even more subversive influence in its anticlassical, colloquial, and picaresque style and in its adversarial stance, bred by the horrors of world war, toward conventional social and moral values. Millicent Dillon, Bowles's biographer, reports that Jane Auer actually met Céline on shipboard in 1934 when returning to the United States after leaving the Swiss sanatorium and that this meeting resulted in her determination to become a writer (*Life* 27). She subsequently wrote her first novel in French. (*Le Phaéton Hypocrite* was written in 1935. Never published, the manuscript is now lost.) She also began her second novel, *Two Serious Ladies*, in French before switching to English. This novel shows a familiarity with the artist's quest and its bohemian setting as first articulated by French culture. As an adult, Jane Bowles lived in Paris at times and read contemporary French literature with a particular interest in the postwar existentialist writers. Within this context, her artistic preoccupation with a sense of guilt and alienation, the grotesque and the absurd, and the isolation of the individual are not eccentric but part of the Franco-American intellectual landscape of the 1940s and 1950s. Similarly, her reported comments about wanting to be a religious leader and her interest in Simone Weil (Dillon, *Life* 120, 414) are comprehensible within the French intellectual context.

In 1938, Jane Auer married Paul Bowles, at that time a rising young composer, protégé of both Virgil Thomson and Aaron Copland. Jane and Paul Bowles became a brilliant artistic couple in the sophisticated bohemias and art worlds of New York, as well as in the expatriate art communities of Paris and Mexico. As Gore Vidal remarked,

> Together and separately, they were much admired. During the late thirties and forties they became central figures in the transatlantic (and Pan-American) world of the arts. Although unknown to the general public, the Bowleses were famous

among those who were famous; and in some mysterious way the art-grandees wanted, if not the admiration of the Bowleses (seldom bestowed), their tolerance. (Vidal 6)

In the 1940s, the Bowleses lived at some of the most famous literary addresses in New York: Patchin Place, the Chelsea Hotel, and the house on Middagh Street in Brooklyn inhabited at the time by W. H. Auden, Benjamin Britten, Peter Pears, and Golo Mann. They frequented the Askew Salon, as did other younger American composers, painters, and writers, as well as many émigré French surrealists during the war. Like many other American artists disaffected from the war and wartime society, they joined expatriate communities in Mexico, principally Taxco. Seven years younger than her husband and one day shy of twenty-one when she married, Jane gained full entrée into this world as his wife, but she was respected in her own right as a person and as an artist. Her talent as a writer was recognized by her peers in the art world—a sophisticated and critical audience. After the war, the Bowleses settled in Tangier and became the center of an expatriate scene that rivaled Paris after World War I. They were hardly isolated; in fact, together and separately, they were a magnet for other writers, artists, and bohemian travelers (beats and hippies in later days) who were drawn to Tangier because of them and who often visited, or made the pilgrimage, so to speak. Also, in the early postwar years, both often traveled to New York, London, Paris, and elsewhere.

The bohemian environment in which Bowles lived had a pervasive influence upon her art and her self-concept as an artist. First, bohemia made it possible for Bowles to *be* a writer, to find support and recognition for her work. As a young woman, Bowles was an "original," a lesbian, and a rebel who had the audacity at eighteen to assume the mantle of Céline. Her husband and friends accepted, even admired, her unconventionality and believed in her talent. In this highly competitive world in which contacts and patronage played an important role, Bowles was often generously provided for. Her peers were also generous in their praise for her published work. (They certainly understood her writing better than the reviewers did.) Bowles's practice also shows that she had absorbed the avant-garde concept of the artist and the artwork: the artist's quest, an original vision, a personal style, iconoclasm, and a formalist perfectionism. Bowles's early work was also inspired by bohemia's myth of the modern artist as rebel and seeker risking self-destruction in pursuit of some kind of illumination. This myth informed her first published novel, *Two Serious Ladies*, and the title of the lost novel, *Le Phaéton Hyprocrite*, suggests a similar theme.

Bohemia also encouraged the development of the legend of Jane Bowles, for the avant-garde has long had a tradition of the artist "living up to" his or her art (Shattuck 39). Bowles lived continuously in a milieu of avant-garde culture—one that idealized the rebel and the iconoclastic art that was seen as arising from the vision of the individual genius as well as an unconventional lifestyle that experimented with radical political ideas, sexual freedom, altered mental states produced by alcohol and drugs, and exploration of other cultures. Self-destruction was a risk to be taken in order to achieve the vision that produced art. The legend of Jane Bowles is based on her social success in living up to her art in this way, first as the *enfant terrible* of New York salons, then as the victim of disorder, alcohol, dangerous sexual liaisons, and primitive magic. So strong is this legend that many readers of Bowles's work read it through the legend, focusing on autobiographical interpretations.

During the nineteen years from her marriage in 1938 to her stroke in 1957 at the early age of forty, Jane Bowles produced all of her published work: a novel, *Two Serious Ladies* (written 1938–41, published 1943); a play, *In the Summer House* (written 1945–47, first act published 1947, revised continuously until performance on Broadway 1953–54); a puppet play, *A Quarreling Pair* (written and performed 1945, published 1946); several short stories—"A Guatemalan Idyll" (written 1941–43, published 1943), "A Day in the Open" (written 1941–43, published 1945), "Plain Pleasures" (written and published 1946), "A Stick of Green Candy" (written 1948–49, published 1957); a novella, "Camp Cataract" (written 1943–48, published 1949); a travel piece, "East Side: North Africa" (written 1950, published 1951, later retitled "Everything Is Nice," published as a short story in 1966). During this period, she worked on a second novel entitled *Out in the World*, accumulating a four-hundred-page manuscript in notebooks, fragments of which have been published after her death. She also worked on several plays and stories and collaborated with Paul Bowles on an opera. According to her husband, she was also the author of hundreds of pages of manuscripts now lost (Caponi, *Conversations* 27). Bowles continued to write after her stroke but was never able to complete anything for publication. In the mid-1960s her health declined sharply, and her writing career came to an end several years before her death in 1973. Dillon referred to "fifteen years of unfinished work" from 1949 to 1964 (*Life* 360). Yet, even though Bowles's published output is small, almost every work has received high praise. The novel and the play have been recognized for their originality, power, and wit in experimental, albeit flawed, forms, while the novella and some of the short stories have been pronounced perfect examples of those genres. Many have agreed with Bowles that "Camp Cataract" is her best work, perhaps her masterpiece.[1] Several scholars who have read the unpublished manuscripts have attested to the quality of these fragments, many of which read as self-contained stories or vignettes.

Bowles's small *oeuvre* and currently limited reputation can be attributed to a powerful process of silencing, partly internal and partly external. At the precocious beginning of her career, when she was only eighteen, through the completion of

Two Serious Ladies at the age of twenty-four, Jane Bowles had great confidence in her talent, in the power of her originality, and in her ability to write. She declared herself a writer, and she was always "at work" no matter what the distractions and how little she accomplished from day to day. At the same time, she set very high standards for herself, was a perfectionist, and therefore a slow, laborious writer. Paul Bowles has provided valuable insight into her writing process in his autobiography, in Dillon's biography of Jane, and in interviews. As he said, "It cost her blood to write. . . . Sometimes it took her a week to write a page" (Caponi, *Conversations* 125). In 1948, he was stunned to learn that she had to know how to construct a bridge before referring to one in her novella, "Camp Cataract" (Paul Bowles, *Without Stopping* 287). Also, he reported, she believed each new work had to be totally different from previous works, "begun from scratch," requiring her to develop new subjects, themes, style (Dillon, *Life* 253). This perfectionism was, as her husband pointed out, "a combination of enormous ego and deep modesty" (Dillon, *Life* 254). Her carelessness with her manuscripts exhibits the same psychology. According to Paul Bowles, she lost hundreds of pages over the years, which caused her little overt anxiety at the time, implying a confidence in her ability to replace what was lost and, at the same time, a belief that the lost manuscripts were of little value to others. This slow writing process and the preparation for publication of only a small portion of what was written are evidence of her fear of failure as well as of high standards and the confidence to meet them.

Bowles's letters and notebooks also refer to the guilt produced by writing. According to Dillon's interpretation, Bowles early felt a sense of guilt and sin because of her "difference"—first as a child with an unusual imagination, later as a lesbian (in her youth, she referred to herself jokingly as "Crippie, the kike dyke"), and finally as a writer. The guilt she associated with writing derived from the fact that the substance and style of her work came out of her difference. Hence, her originality and power as a writer were in conflict with the shame and guilt of being different. This guilt as a writer placed her in a paralyzing doublebind: writing made her feel guilty and confirmed her sinful difference; if she did not write, she felt guilty because only her writing justified her difference.

Both Millicent Dillon and Gena Dagel Caponi speculate that Jane's difficult writing process also stemmed from her fear of the irrational forces in her own psyche, a fear of madness which she kept at bay in her everyday life through fantasy games, humor, and absorption in the mundane details of daily life (Dillon, *Life* 93; Caponi, *Paul Bowles* 137). To write, for her, was to court madness by giving free rein to her imagination (another double bind). Her friend and fellow artist, Edouard Roditi, also puts forth a similar theory in his memoir of Jane. He sees her eccentricities as mechanisms to defend herself against her fear of insanity, and her art also as a similar defense, a conscious way to control her irrational fears and exorcise them.

He also sees her drinking as a defense against neurosis and depression. Of course, alcoholism in and of itself can be the source of artistic decline, and this may have been a factor in Jane Bowles's case.

Nevertheless, in spite of the perfectionism, the few publications, the fear of failure, the guilt, the fear of madness, and the drinking, Jane Bowles did work steadily in the early years. According to evidence provided in Dillon's biography, and in the letters of both Bowleses, a progressive writer's block began in the 1940s after the publication of *Two Serious Ladies* and at the time that Paul Bowles began to publish his fiction. It is at this point that the critical reception of Jane Bowles's work becomes an important part of her story as a writer, for the lack of understanding and continuing interest in her work certainly did sap her self-confidence.

Two Serious Ladies was published in 1943 by Knopf. The novel is a female quest narrative that mocks the quest conventions with a playful antinarrative structure. The style and structure are highly original, and the two female protagonists are portrayed in a grotesque mock-epic style that can be compared with only one contemporary—Samuel Beckett, whose early fictions were virtually unknown in the United States in the 1940s.[2] Although the middle of World War II was not a propitious time for such an experimental work, the reviews were not entirely unsympathetic. The critics' mixed evaluations, however, produced a polarized response that has been typical of the criticism throughout Bowles's entire career. While Leo Lerman, in a major review in the *New York Herald Tribune*, praised the novel's wit, psychological perception, and corrosive realism, the *New Yorker* considered it an amusing light impromptu. N. L. Rothman of the *Saturday Review* called the author "undoubtedly clever, and perhaps brilliant," while Edith H. Walton called the novel senseless, at times silly, and accused the author of developing her own brand of lunacy that did not measure up to the fantasies of other comic writers. George H. Freitag found the book to be a sympathetic portrait of lesbianism, whereas Walton's labeling of the women characters' adventures as bizarre, mad, and weird may be a coded homophobic response. All of the reviewers described the creation of a special dreamlike world arising from a unique vision, grotesque irrational characters, and a plotless narrative, yet they differed as to whether these formal innovations were delightful or repulsive, illuminating or just plain odd. Their different responses are common reactions to experimental, unconventional work, particularly in the novel form with its large audience trained to respond to the realistic tradition.

According to Dillon, Bowles had hoped for a popular success and was not cheered by the admiration of a discerning few or of her own friends in the art world. According to Paul Bowles, what depressed her the most was the incomprehension the reviews displayed (Dillon, *Life* 111). On a personal level, her lover Helvetia Perkins, Jane's family, and Paul's family did not approve of the book because of its lesbian content. (The novel was dedicated "To Paul, Mother, and Helvetia.") Bowles's immediate reaction was to say, "*Two Serious Ladies* wasn't any good anyway" (Dillon, *Life* 112), and later she declared it "was after all *not* a novel" (Bowles, *Letters* 63). In *A Room of One's Own*, in her discussion of the difficulty of artistic creation in the face of worldly distractions and indifference, Virginia Woolf points out that the woman artist is doubly discouraged by a climate of actual hostility, whereas a man faces only indifference, formidable in itself. In this context, she wrote compellingly of the effect of criticism on the creative mind: "Unfortunately, it is precisely the men and women of genius who mind most what is said of them. . . . Literature is strewn with the wreckage of men who have minded beyond reason the opinions of others" (58).

It appears that Bowles reacted sharply to reviewers' incomprehension and the failure to attract a wider audience with her first novel. The criticism of *Two Serious Ladies* took Bowles in two new directions: a novel, called *Out in the World*, and a play, *In the Summer House*. In these works, Bowles tackled new genres and labored to develop a plainer style. The novel and the play occupied her for a decade, and, during this time, she complained more and more about the slowness of her writing process and her persistent writing block.

In composing *Out in the World*, Bowles planned to write a more conventional novel. She informed her husband that *Out in the World* would be very different from *Two Serious Ladies*: "classical," that is, nineteenth-century in style and structure, but with the characters representing abstractions (Dillon, *Life* 192; Bowles, *Letters* 5). She worked on this novel for the rest of her active life, compiling over 400 pages of fragments. Dillon speculates in "Jane Bowles: Experiment as Character" that the fragments that Bowles produced were "a mode of expression that was attempting to manifest itself through her but that she could not accept. . . . she took the result to be only failure. . . . had she been able to view this fragmentation as a valid expression of her own narrative vision, the fragmentation could have led her to further development—which may say something about the nature of 'blocks' " (140). Bowles did succeed in creating a plainer style, as shown in the later stories and fragments, but constant work on the unfinished novel increased her self-doubt.

In turning to the drama, Bowles had to learn to write in a completely different genre, one which she believed required a more explicit, direct style than fiction, including a simplification of character and plot (Dillon, *Life* 230). *In the Summer House* was written mainly from 1945 to 1947; however, the play took several years to reach the stage, and Bowles continued to revise it, particularly the last act, until the Broadway production of 1953–54. The time and constant revisions imply that adapting to a new form was difficult. When the play did reach the stage, Bowles was also forced to respond to the demands of those involved in the production, who pressed her for character motivations and an ending that would be acceptable to Broadway audiences (Dillon, *Life* 230–31). Thus, working on this one play absorbed an inordinate amount of Bowles's creative energy for eight years.

Jane Bowles's self-doubt during this period was also increased by the positive critical reaction to her husband's fiction of the late 1940s and early 1950s. Paul Bowles's dozen or so short stories published from 1945 to 1950 attracted much comment and praise. "A Distant Episode" was selected for Houghton Mifflin's *Best American Short Stories 1948.* "Under the Sky" appeared in *Best American Short Stories 1949,* and "Pastor Dowe at Tacaté" was selected for the O. Henry Awards *Prize Stories of 1949,* and also included in *Best American Short Stories 1950.* On the strength of his stories, Paul received a contract for a novel from Doubleday, and this first novel, *The Sheltering Sky,* was a critical and popular success, appearing on the bestsellers list for several weeks in 1950. The novel was soon followed by the publication of his well-received short story collection, *The Delicate Prey.*

Although Jane supported Paul's work and admired his writing, she could not help but feel chagrined by his disciplined work habits and the distinguished body of work he was able to publish in such a short time. But, most of all, she could not avoid invidious comparisons between the critical reception of his work and her own. In a series of letters she wrote to Paul in 1947 and 1948, Jane speaks honestly of the impact of his success on her assessment of her own work. She speaks of her isolation as a writer, of her difference which is incomprehensible to others and which causes her to question her own experience and sincerity. She says that *Two Serious Ladies* is not a novel and that she has no career. In 1947, while at work on *Out in the World,* Jane wrote to Paul:

> I am terribly discouraged and of course the fact that you get these letters from publishers complimenting you on stories is no help to my morale as far as *career* is concerned. I have never once received a letter from anyone about "Plain Pleasures" or the first act of my play or my little *Cross-Section* stories and *Partisan Review* would laugh and probably does at my work. This does not concern me deeply but I realize I have no career really whether I work or not and never have had one. You have more of a one after writing a few short stories than I have after writing an entire novel. All this while, I have been slap-happy, not realizing that publishers did write anybody but now I see how completely unnoticed my work has been professionally. (*Letters* 46)

Nevertheless, she expressed strong commitment to writing her novel.

Reacting against the limited critical response to *Two Serious Ladies* and the silence greeting her subsequent publications, Bowles had great hopes for the success of her play, and with reason, since so many friends in the theater world believed in her dramatic talent. After a repertory production at Hedgerow Theatre in the suburbs of Philadelphia in 1950, and tryouts at the University of Michigan and in Boston in 1953, *In the Summer House* opened on Broadway under the direction of José Quintero, starring Judith Anderson as Gertrude and Mildred Dunnock as Mrs. Constable. (The music was by Paul Bowles.) Again, Bowles's hope for a popular success was dashed: the play closed after two months, although the work did not lack admirers. The actors loved the play and had sharp insights into the characters. In spite of its short run, *In the Summer House* had developed a cult audience that filled the theater at the closing performance, and it was selected for *The Best Plays of 1953–54*, edited by Louis Kronenberger.

In the Summer House* was very widely reviewed. Most critics hailed a new talent even though they thought the play was flawed. The mixed reviews were quite similar to those of *Two Serious Ladies* in recognizing Bowles's unique style and humor, her original female characters, the focus on women's relationships with women, and her stylistic authority, while bemoaning the lack of conventional plot structure, or motivation, leading to charges of lack of substance. Kronenberger's rationale for including the play in *Best Plays* sums up the critical assessment in general: "*In the Summer House* seems on the contrary no play at all, and a far better half than whole; it just happens, at its best, to boast the most individual and expressive writing of the season" (4). Just as the critics of the novel ignored its spiritual quest or its sexual (lesbian) elements and insisted the characters were incomprehensible or crazy, the play's critics barely acknowledged Bowles's analysis of the mother-daughter relationship and accused the author of dwelling on pointless neuroses. The latter charge led the two most influential drama critics of the time to dismiss *In the Summer House*. Although Brooks Atkinson praised Bowles for sensitivity, humor, nuance of mood, and insight into character relationships, he ultimately concluded that the play was an analysis of neuroses with little point or value. Eric Bentley's review, entitled "The Ill-Made Play," saw the play as an example of the current (deplorable) trend in drama for works that are "all atmosphere and no plot," and he also condemned the play as a slight portrait of meaningless neuroses. The general social climate of the early fifties was as inhospitable to a woman's play about mothers and daughters as it was to a woman's experimental *jeu d'esprit* about women seeking spiritual or sexual salvation in 1943. Qualified praise for a first play and a select audience could not compensate Bowles, at this stage in her career, for a work that had occupied her for many years. In an interview with *Vogue*, Bowles observed, "There is no point in writing a play for your five hundred goony friends. You have to reach more people" ("Candidates" 137). (By "goony" she meant "intellectual.") Walter Kerr praised her for this comment in a piece in the *Herald Tribune* that was widely read, embarrassing Bowles, but also confirming to her that plays that are admired only by the literati are not worth writing.[3] Bowles never again completed another work.

Yet she did not give up writing and continued to work on plays and the novel, even though constantly blocked. She said, "I must write, but I can't write" (Dillon, *Life* 277). Even her stroke in 1957 did not stop her writing, although her ability to read and write was impaired. Her letters and the comments of friends indicate that she kept on because her identity as a writer was important to her: it gave her a sense of personal autonomy and the hope of financial independence. She didn't stop writing until her health completely failed in the mid-1960s. Then, she referred to herself as "the dead Jane Bowles." (See Dillon, *Life* 392.)

Ironically, in the mid-1960s, there was a revival of interest in her work. In 1964, *In the Summer House* was performed in an off-Broadway production. Although it closed after a few weeks, it presaged a Jane Bowles resurgence. At Paul Bowles's suggestion, his London publisher, Peter Owen, read *Two Serious Ladies*, was impressed, and published it in 1965. When he asked for more, Paul put together a collection of Jane's short stories, along with his revised version of "East Side: North Africa," transposed into third person and retitled "Everything Is Nice." The collection, *Plain Pleasures*, was published in London in 1966. At the same time, Farrar, Straus and Giroux in New York published *The Collected Works of Jane Bowles* in 1966 with an admiring introduction by Truman Capote and blurb by Tennessee Williams. With Williams calling her "the most important writer of prose fiction in modern American letters," Ashbery asserting her to be "one of the finest modern writers of fiction," and Sillitoe identifying *Two Serious Ladies* as "a landmark in 20th-century American literature,"[4] Bowles might have gained the wider audience she craved if she had been well enough to travel to New York or London to promote her work, well enough to be interviewed, well enough to write or to mine her unpublished manuscripts for publishable pieces.

The republication of Bowles's work in the mid-1960s had the positive effect of attracting wide critical comment, yet it is most striking from a perspective of thirty years later to see the same polarized and contradictory responses in 1966 as had been apparent in the reviews of the play in 1954 and the novel in 1943. The social and literary climate of the 1960s was more open to new subjects or themes, and readers were better able to comprehend the spiritual quests, psychological conflicts, and existential anxiety of Bowles's female characters. But critics were still conservative in their expectation that works conform to generic conventions and still in a quandary about how to classify and evaluate Bowles. In fact, reviews of Bowles's *Collected Works* can be read as a covert debate about the canon and the role of experimental works in relation to the critical construction of modernism. The 1960s were also a male-dominated literary era, and this also influenced the reception of Jane Bowles's work.[5]

Of course, many reviewers commented on the fact that the work they were reading was written a generation previously, but, for most, belatedness was not an issue. Bowles was reviewed as a contemporary, often in group reviews with current writers. The admiration of other well-known writers caused reviewers to refer to her underground reputation, and this provided rationale enough for the reconsideration of her work. (Ashbery's seminal review was entitled "Up from the Underground.") Webster Schott in *Life* magazine aptly remarked, "The return of her work is like the reappearance of a comet" (17). Several called her a neglected genius, but no one asked why she had been neglected, why she was a comet and not a permanent star in the firmament.

Reputation and classification were puzzled over in a variety of ways. How could an *oeuvre* so small, many asked, arouse such extravagant praise in those whose views must be respected? Because of the power of her vision and superior artistry of her style answered many, while others insisted that such a slight output made her a minor writer. The praise of recognized masters and an underground reputation led to the label of coterie writer and also gave rise to some resentment as well: "her work can be easily overvalued" (Samuels 39). Some reviewers found the substance and style of her work to be as slight as her output, and this reinforced the "minor" label. Since Bowles had not created a "masterpiece," but merely possessed a masterly style, she was *only* a stylist. Even Ashbery's review referred to her as a "writer's writer's writer" (5). The focus on size, obscurity, and difference carried a subtext of misogyny.

Many reviewers felt compelled to rank order Bowles's works against each other, but the resulting judgments were in complete disagreement. Each of the following works was rated a great success or a total failure by one reviewer or another: *Two Serious Ladies*, *In the Summer House*, "Camp Cataract," and the short stories as a group, with "Plain Pleasures" and "Guatemalan Idyll" mentioned the most. Reviewers also differed as to whether drama or fiction was her forte. Bowles's originality of style and structure was again the source of a polarized response as different reviewers pointed to the same stylistic traits as the source of effective or ineffective artistry: an idiosyncratic style, an unusual wit, different characters, and unconventional narrative structures. Her works were rated high or low, major or minor, according to whether the reviewer was open to experimentalism, particularly from a female perspective, and whether the reviewer would accord high status to an experimental work.

A few contrasting reviews will give the flavor of the debate. The separate *Times Literary Supplement* reviews of *Two Serious Ladies* and *Plain Pleasures* are good examples of extreme contrast, signaled by the titles, "Two Empty Ladies" and "A Serious Lady." The 1965 review of the novel states that the book is meaningless, with no significant plot, no character motivation, and no theme. The reviewer describes the characters and settings as empty and the style as threadbare, and concludes that the book fails as a book. This dismissive stream of invective is clearly based on certain conventional generic expectations of the novel and a total rejection of any prose fiction that does not conform to the conventions of realism. On the other hand, the 1966 review of the story collection begins with high praise for *Two Serious Ladies* before turning to the stories. This reviewer praises Bowles's character portraits for charity, clarity, respect and admires her style is for its plainness, restraint, understatement, and dignity. This appraisal is based on a positive assessment of Bowles's stylistic control and the pathos of her gallery of grotesques.

The United States reviews of the *Collected Works* by Geoffrey Wagner in *Commonweal* and John Ashbery in the *Times* provide a similar contrast. Wagner's language is abusive, stating that "the book is about nothing" and that Bowles's work is both dated and overrated. He sees her experimentalism as the failed imitation of great modernists such as Joyce. The implied sexism and homophobia in many of the reviews or ratings were blatant in Wagner's review: "Publisher's blurbs about an 'under-ground reputation' usually euphemize minor talents, and the feminine states of semi-hysteria." He also referred to "fairy stories in all senses of the term" (494). Ashbery's review in the *New York Times Book Review* proclaimed Bowles a great modernist writer based on an authoritative creation of a world and skilled stylistic control, concluding that "No other contemporary writer can consistently produce surprise of this quality, the surprise that is the one essential ingredient of great art. Jane Bowles deals almost exclusively in this rare commodity" (30). More representative is the "balanced" review by Stephen Koch in *Book Week*, who praises Bowles's devotion to style as narrative as a successful continuation of modernist experiment, playfulness, and poetic prose. Yet he concludes that she has not produced a masterpiece because her novel is flawed and her stories, by virtue of being short stories, are minor: she is a minor writer even if "one of the best writers around" (13). These reviews outline the major-minor debate and its context of the problem of canonizing the modernists. Jane Bowles cannot be canonized as a major modernist because she is female and gay, because her output is small, because she did not write solely in one genre, because her originality both of vision and style is too different.

Since Bowles's revived work had no ready-made context or label, reviewers often tried to classify her by comparison with other writers: frequently mentioned were Lewis Carroll, Daisy Ashford, Ronald Firbank, Ivy Compton-Burnett, Carson McCullers, Flannery O'Connor, Anton Chekhov, Edward Albee, and Tennessee Williams. Literary movements thought to be relevant were dada, surrealism, American Gothic fiction, and absurdism. Some of these comparisons enabled reviewers to perceive themes such as the individual's isolation, lack of communication, the quest for meaning, and women's quest for identity without men; but often the comparisons were superficial, a reaching for context from a puzzled reader. Furthermore, many reviewers were certain there was no comparison between Bowles and other writers, that she was *sui generis*. Ashbery stated with authority: "it [her work] stands alone in contemporary literature" (5). Standing alone could make her a giant or an eccentric; the combination would be a female monstrosity that the 1960s could only reject and transform into a minor oddity. Better a miniature grotesque on the margins of literature than a threatening female monster with the authority to challenge the boundaries. It would take a postfeminist and postmodernist critical climate to "justify" Jane Bowles.

After the brief 1960s revival, Jane Bowles's comet disappeared again. When she died in 1973, her death went unnoticed by the outside world until Tennessee Williams insisted that the *New York Times* publish an obituary that appeared a month later. Coincidentally, that same year, the writer Millicent Dillon learned of Bowles's work for the first time and decided to embark upon a biography. Another resurgence was about to begin. Black Sparrow Press published *Feminine Wiles* in 1976, a collection of previously unpublished fragments and letters, with an introduction by Tennessee Williams. *In the Summer House* received brief off-Broadway productions in 1977, and again in 1980. In 1978, Ecco Press published an expanded collected works called *My Sister's Hand in Mine* in its Neglected Books of the 20th Century series. Six fragments from Bowles's notebooks were added to the original collected works, along with Capote's original introduction. Virago Press, the English press devoted to neglected women writers, published *Two Serious Ladies* in 1979, with an introduction by Francine du Plessis Gray. Dillon's biography, *A Little Original Sin*, appeared in 1981, and she subsequently published *Out in the World: Selected Letters of Jane Bowles, 1935–1970* in 1985, which was the year this writer first became aware of the work of Jane Bowles. Dutton published a paperback of *Two Serious Ladies* in 1984; Peter Owen republished the *Collected Works of Jane Bowles* in 1984; and Arena republished *Plain Pleasures and Other Stories* in 1985. Beginning in the 1980s, there was also renewed interest in Paul Bowles's work and the postwar expatriate scene in Tangier, which brought additional attention to Jane's life and work.

The commentary upon Bowles's work that appeared from the late seventies on was often still mixed in its evaluations, but the trend was toward a more consistent affirmation of her literary achievement. The influence of the feminist movement encouraged a more sympathetic response and led reviewers to greater understanding of her woman-centered work. Prominent reviews of *My Sister's Hand in Mine* by Francine du Plessis Gray in the *New York Times Book Review* and by Muriel Haynes in *Ms.* included particularly perceptive interpretations of *Two Serious Ladies*. Both Gray and Haynes remarked upon the silence surrounding Bowles's work, noting that many readers had never heard of her in spite of earlier critical acclaim. Gray attributes the silence to the fact that Bowles writes of modern women's independence from men, while Haynes says that she was a victim of her underground legend, which gave her a rarefied reputation. Gray identified Bowles's major theme as "women's relentless search for autonomy and self-knowledge" (3), and defines her independent women characters as "spiritual, nomadic, and asexual" (28), although she speaks openly of the lesbian content. Haynes notes Bowles's radical vision of women as "not emotionally dependent on men, who have no entry into female inner life. Love and its bitter fruits . . . are found in women's relations to one another, as friends, mothers and daughters, sisters, lovers" (35). She notes the ultimate separateness and isolation of all of Bowles's characters. Haynes also comments favorably on Bowles's unconventional narrative structures as an attempt to give language itself narrative force, to give prose fiction the status of poetry.

The British reviewers of the reprinted *Two Serious Ladies*, *Collected Works*, and *Plain Pleasures* mostly commented on her originality and power, singling out either *Two Serious Ladies* or "Camp Cataract" or the short stories as chief example of her mastery of her art. Anita Brookner, however, in a review for *Books and Bookmen*, thought Bowles was overrated and to some degree dated by her absurdist style. She also speculated that the power of the writing stemmed from the author's real madness (22). In spite of the high praise by many, there were still the same reservations and objections in both England and the United States, and, in spite of the assertion of achieved stature, the number of reviews was much smaller than in 1966.

The general affirmation of Bowles's work at this time was counterbalanced, however, by the polarized responses to the biography, *A Little Original Sin*, and the selected letters, *Out in the World.* Here, the self-destructive legend of Jane Bowles aroused revulsion as well as pity, and the negative response to the life led some to a devaluation of her writing. In seeking to analyze Bowles's small output and tortured writing process, it was all too easy to excoriate her for succumbing to bohemian disorder or for choosing to waste her talent. Laurie Stone's review in the *Village Voice* is the prime example of this tendency. There were several joint reviews of the biography, the letters, and the new collected works, which cast the works in the shadow of the legend of waste. The polarization of response is well illustrated by the contrasting views of the librarians' standard review sources. *Booklist* recommended the biography "in libraries where feminist literature is popular. It is recommended only on those grounds" (1383). *Choice* stated, "This biography presents as full a view of this fascinating, tortured woman as one is likely to get, and it should lead readers to her writing. Very highly recommended" (378). *Kirkus* commented, "the book [*A Little Original Sin*] is unlikely to elevate Bowles's status as a rather fey if nightmarishly tormented coterie writer" (710), while *Library Journal* blandly predicted that the new collected works and the biography "should find appreciative readers in academic and large public libraries" (1223). It should be noted, as well, that there was disagreement on the feminist pigeonhole, which as shown above could become another dismissive label. As Susan Jacoby pointed out in the *New York Times Book Review*, "It would be a mistake to wrap up Jane Bowles's life into a tidy feminist parable," noting that Bowles was often linked to other women writers with whom she had little in common as an artist (11). And Jack Collins, in the *Threepenny Review*, asserts that avant-garde is the best context: "the work of Jane Bowles has had to await the understanding of a sophisticated readership in the way Melville's work had to or Kafka's. To call her writing avant-garde is an understatement" (8).

Renewed interest in Jane Bowles prepared the way for a revival of *In the Summer House*, which enjoyed a one-month limited performance at the Vivian Beaumont Theater in Lincoln Center in August of 1993. The production was directed by Joanne Akalaitis and starred Diane Wiest as Gertrude and Frances Conroy as Mrs. Constable. Music was composed by Philip Glass. The production was announced by an article in the *New York Times* by Paul Bowles in which he recalled the final preparations for the first production. The program was accompanied by an insert that consisted of brief memoirs by those who knew Bowles. These tended to present Jane Bowles as "the last great bohemian," a phrase used in the insert's brief summary of her career. The biographical apparatus surrounding this special revival seemed to be a pre-emptive response to the inevitable question, "Who is Jane Bowles?" This production stressed the psychological similarities to Williams, a surreal ambiance, and the centrality of the two mothers: Gertrude and Mrs. Constable. The two *New York Times* reviews summarize the reception. Frank Rich said Bowles was "born to be a heroine for our time" and called the play "unjustly neglected" (C11), while David Richards labeled the play mysterious, elusive, nuts, exotic, cock-eyed (5). They and other reviewers agreed that Akalaitis's staging was in conflict with the play's intimate scale and psychological nuance and that the casting of the young people was weak. The consensus seemed to be that the play was worth reviving and that its mother-daughter theme was contemporary, but that Akalaitis's conception was flawed.

The return of Jane Bowles to public consciousness in the 1980s and 1990s largely repeated the pattern of the 1960s revival in the world of reviews, but the availability of the collected works, the selected letters, and the biography in a post-feminist era generated academic interest for the first time in Bowles's literary history. Her work is beginning to be contextualized and the initial frames are feminism, existentialism, and experimentalism. The insights of feminist literary criticism have influenced many of Bowles's critics, in that the feminist perspective "makes sense" of Jane Bowles. *In the Summer House* has been discussed in two critical overviews of American drama: *The American Woman Playwright* (1981) by Judith Olauson and *Feminist Theories for Dramatic Criticism* (1990) by Gayle Austin. Both of these scholars discuss the mother-daughter relationship as Bowles's focus, and Austin points out the originality of this theme in the American dramatic canon. In 1987, Mark T. Basset published a perceptive analysis of "A Stick of Green Candy" as a story of a girl's realization that she must give up the childhood innocence of her imaginative world for a diminished role in an adult world organized by men. Also in 1987, Gray included her earlier feminist piece on Bowles in a collection of essays. Andrew M. Lakitz's essay on *Two Serious Ladies* in Laura Doan's *Old Maids to Radical Spinsters* (1991) sees the novel as an attempt at female self-definition by rewriting the role of the spinster. Robert E. Lougy's 1987 essay is an overview placing her work in a European, existential context and making a case for the importance of her small *oeuvre* by virtue of her success in creating a world that resonates with the modern condition. Kathy Justice Gentile's 1994 essay on *Two Serious Ladies* and "Camp Cataract" analyzes those works as examples of female existentialism that challenge the masculinist construction of this philosophy. Millicent Dillon published two critical pieces in the eighties, one on Bowles's sense of exile and one on the value of the fragmentary forms in her unpublished notebooks. The latter essay appeared in Ellen G. Friedman and Miriam Fuchs's important book on experimental women writers: *Breaking the Sequence: Women's Experimental Fiction*, which gave Bowles a permanent place among "second-generation" experimental women writers in the 1930–60 period. Friedman subsequently included Jane Bowles in her 1993 PMLA essay, "What Are the Missing Contents? (Post)Modernism, Gender, and the Canon." This essay claimed Bowles for a postmodern aesthetic in which women fiction writers have taken a leading role. Kathleen Wheeler's *"Modernist" Women Writers and Narrative Art* (1994), a study of twentieth-century women writers of experimental fiction, includes a detailed analysis of Bowles's subversion of the narrative conventions and ideologies of realism, firmly placing her in the modernist historical context. Growing interest in Jane Bowles has also led scholars to the unpublished writings in the Humanities Research Center at the University of Texas. Allen Hibbard's careful piecing together of Bowles's unfinished novel, *Out in the World* in his 1994 *Library Chronicle* essay conveys the ambitious scope, complexity, and postmodern quality of this fragmentary work.

Serious criticism and historical understanding of Bowles has only just begun, and perhaps a postfeminist, postmodernist era has at last provided the stage for a lasting appreciation of her work and a sustained critical dialogue about her contribution to modern literature. This introductory essay has placed her in the context of the international avant-garde and experimental writing. To this writer, these contexts render Bowles's work more accessible, while also providing some insight into the silencing process that makes the trajectory of her career similar to that of many other women writers: a brilliant debut, the admiration of other writers, critical neglect, a decline in productivity, and possibly a belated revival or series of revivals. Reputation as "a writer's writer" and the overshadowing of the work by biography, legend, or relationship with a male writer or artist is also a typical pattern. The careers of Djuna Barnes, Jean Rhys, and Jean Stafford parallel Jane Bowles's story.

In many ways, the reception of Jane Bowles's work by reviewers is typical of the reception of experimental writing by women. Polarized responses reflect the critics' open or closed attitudes toward experimentalists in narrative forms where the conventional expectations are strong and where taboos against female rebellion or difference are even stronger. The rejection of Bowles's work as too strange has partly stemmed from a refusal to see her as a writer of the avant-garde, a reaction typical of the invisibility of women in the experimentalist tradition that Friedman and Fuchs discuss. As pointed out by Shari Benstock, Marianne DeKoven, and Christine Brooke-Rose, the avant-garde has been a male-dominated phenomenon that, for all it transgression of bourgeois norms and revolutionary formal experiments, has ignored the contribution of female artists, many of whom have been more radical in their innovations and who have served as precursors to more well-known male writers. As has been seen in the preceding survey of the reception of Bowles's work to date, the process of canonization of modern writers has relegated Bowles—along with other women experimentalists such as Stein, Barnes, or Nin—to the margins of the margins of the modernist canon: "minor" avant-gardists who are themselves less important than those who occupy the modernist pantheon.

The critical silencing of Bowles's work reinforced her internal doubts and conflicts and, combined with her experimental focus on innovation, resulted in a small body of completed, published work, which is also generically diverse. Bowles's small but varied *oeuvre* causes her to be automatically designated a minor writer. Yet the power and craft of her work challenge that label and the assumptions behind it. The high praise of other writers attests to a value that has nothing to do with quantity, productivity, or careerism. Those who admire Bowles's work find each work and each genre attempted rich enough and unsettling enough to reward sustained attention and therefore to make a lasting contribution to modern literary history.

Notes

1. Jane Bowles wrote to Paul Bowles in 1948, "I *know* that it's the best thing I've ever done" (*Letters* 95).
2. The parallels between the two are interesting. Beckett was an Irishman who settled in France and ultimately became a bilingual writer. The fiction he wrote in the 1940s, like Bowles's work, reflects

the existential sensibility of the era without referring to specific existential philosophies. Both writers powerfully portray unresolved dualities and conflicts.

3. Walter Kerr's *Herald Tribune* article was later collected in *Pieces at Eight* (New York: Simon and Schuster, 1957) 154–56. Kerr confirms Bowles's belief that the theater requires explicitness and simplification: "The theater is . . . cruder than some other arts need be; it is cruder in the sense that it is more direct, more concrete, more expansive, more explosive" (156).

4. Williams's and Sillitoe's praise appeared on the dustjacket of Peter Owen's edition of *Two Serious Ladies*, and both statements are frequently quoted. John Ashbery's comment is from his review of the *Collected Works*, "Up from the Underground," *New York Times Book Review* 29 January 1967: 5.

5. Charlotte Goodman has pointed out in her biography, *Jean Stafford: The Savage Heart*, that the American literary world of the period 1950–70 was an aggressively masculine one in which women writers were deprecated or ignored: only one work of fiction by a woman writer received the National Book Award during those twenty years (226).

2

The Narrative Erotics of
Two Serious Ladies

Carolyn J. Allen

*T*WO SERIOUS LADIES is a queer little novel. It's not just that the characters sometimes refer to each other as queer to suggest both their ventures outside the heterosexual and their odd, quirky sensibilities. For the contemporary reader, the novel's combination of modernity's preoccupation with the psychological and postmodernity's attention to surfaces also make it a peculiar read. In what follows, I try to account for that peculiarity by teasing out the novel's narrative erotics as they function both structurally within the text and hermeneutically as a reading effect. I argue that the narrative tension between modernist content and postmodern spirit destabilizes sexuality so that the novel resonates as an anomalous queer theory text; that is, it questions stable sexual identities and easy assumptions about sexual pleasure and speaks to the complexities of erotic investments across class and racial difference.[1]

The brief opening scene sets the narrative in motion by presenting one girl's fascination for another as sensuous, even erotic, but strangely so since it depends on a parody of Christian baptism. Christina Goering, the first of the two serious ladies is, in this opening, thirteen, an outsider disliked by other children with "an active inner life" and "the look of certain fanatics who think of themselves as leaders without once having gained the respect of a single human being" (Bowles, *Works* [1978] 3). Especially since Christina's first name points to the religious nature of her fanaticism, it is difficult not to read her equally telling last name as an echo of Nazi fanatic Hermann Goering whether or not Bowles intended the coincidence.[2] Such a reading makes Christina's mind-set suspicious from the first. Since she's unpopular, she's often alone and "in the habit of going through many mental struggles—generally of a religious nature." However, she prefers to be with other people and organize games. "These games, as a rule, were very moral, and often involved God" (4). She particularly envies her sister's friendship with a younger girl, Mary. She imitates the two of them by going into the woods to gather flowers but "each time, fearing that she would not return with enough flowers to make a beautiful bouquet, she so encumbered herself with baskets that the walk seemed more a hardship than a pleasure" (4). One day she convinces Mary to be her audience while she dances before her in a short underslip: " 'Now don't take your eyes off me,' she said. 'I'm going to do a dance of worship to the sun. Then I'm going to show that I'd rather have God and no sun than the sun and no God.' " Later in the scene she plays a game with Mary called "I forgive you for all your sins." She commands Mary to take off her dress, then puts a burlap sack over her head, ties her with a cord, and leads her to a stream near a woods. There she pushes Mary into the mud, carries her against her will into the water, and submerges her. She ends the cleansing by saying, "Come darling, now you can stand up," returns with Mary to the house, and, declaring to herself, "the game is over," leaves Mary to dry herself with a towel (5–8).

I begin with this opening because its details set up the particular workings of the novel's erotics: they focus on women, they involve marked differences in power, they are largely parodic and seldom dyadic. The sequence introduces Christina by suggesting her preoccupation with games of morality. Because it is the opening scene and thus sets up what follows, it becomes part of the novel's enabling conditions for a reading of the narrative dynamics. Even before this sequence other such enabling conditions provide a context for reading an erotics invested initially in desire between women.[3] Some conditions are biographical. At the time she married Paul Bowles in 1938, Jane Auer had had affairs only with women; her brief sexual life with Paul was over by 1940 and during the writing of *Two Serious Ladies* she was passionately involved with Helvetia Perkins (Dillon, *Life* 80, 88). Even as a child, she was called by boys' names, and after her father's death, she sometimes requested that she be called Sidney after him (Dillon, *Life* 19, 35). She occasionally referred to herself as "Crippie, the kike dyke" mocking her stiff leg, her ethnicity, and her sexuality with typically mordant wit. She remained emotionally close to Paul, all the while having long-term relationships, brief affairs, and all-consuming obsessions with women throughout her life.

Like the biographical context, the novel's title, its dedication, "To Paul, Mother, and Helvetia," and its three-part structure enable a reading of its narrative erotics. The novel begins with Christina Goering's story, in which we briefly meet the second serious lady, Mrs. Copperfield, then moves to Mrs. Copperfield's narrative, and returns finally to Miss Goering's tale in which Mrs. Copperfield appears again at the last moment. Originally, it was to be *Three Serious Ladies* (Dillon, *Life* 105), but even when one story was cut, it was structured in three sections—appropriately since its erotics, like Jane Bowles's life, is never just about two women but rather about triangles, jealousies, and sexual fluidity.[4]

With these enabling conditions in mind, we can return to the opening scene in which the erotics begin. Christina's fascination with Mary depends on Mary's friendship with her sister, Sophie. The three-person dynamic at play here continues throughout the novel as Christina, now an adult and called in the narrative Miss Goering, lives with Arnold and Lucy, travels to the mainland with Arnold and Arnold's father, leaves Andy to meet with Arnold's father, and finally abandons Andy to go off with Ben. These emotional triangles prove devastating to everyone involved except Miss Goering who is so focused on her own pleasure that she is oblivious to the pain she causes. The opening scene also suggests something of how Miss Goering's particular psyche will be textually portrayed: she encumbers herself with baskets so that walking in the woods is more hardship that pleasure. This emphasis becomes in subsequent scenes pleasure in hardship and introduces Miss Goering's attention to her own discomfort as the mechanism of self-pleasuring. Her dance to show she'd rather have "God and no sun" and the parody of baptism in her seemingly sadistic game with Mary set up the connection between religious discourse and perverse pleasure that informs the rest of the novel. The erotics of the opening scene make possible both a modernist reading of *Two Serious Ladies* in which Christina's psychosexual subjectivity is one focus and a more postmodernist one in which parody undercuts any serious attempt to read individual moral struggle as central.

Certainly when *Two Serious Ladies* first appeared, reviewers stressed its psychological character. *Book Week* called it a "truly psychological novel, a continuation of where *The Well of Loneliness* left off, a little masterpiece of character analysis" (Freitag 3). *Saturday Review* said it was "a kind of psychotherapy acted out in fable. When these ladies talk, they do not speak the formal, reserved thought which they might recognize as their own, but utter instead long and curiously involved ideas that can come only from the unconscious" (Rothman 20). *The Herald Tribune Weekly Book Review* mentions its "all-inclusive psychological perception and corrosive realism" (Lerman 10). Such reviews encourage a modernist reading of the novel, one that privileges attention to its characters' inner lives. In this reading, the opening scene suggests the reader might expect some future, more overtly sexual "dancing" from that early performance of one girl for another and the perversely erotic baptism that follows. But as it turns out, the erotics of Miss Goering's narrative center finally on Christina herself so that the suggestion of an erotic between women gives way to a study in moral masochism, a kind of autoerotics in which Christina Goering gives herself pleasure through actions designed to produce unpleasure.

In this modernist reading, Christina Goering's autoerotic adventures in parts one and three of the novel bracket, or if you like, center, the erotic exchange between women in part two. Miss Goering's narrative recounts her continuing attempts to set a "morally correct" course for herself by designing seemingly unpleasurable actions. Often related to a manipulation of her upper-class position, these actions produce the promise of pleasure through denial and risktaking that destroys the people closest to her. She sells her large, handsome house to move to a more "tawdry" location on a gloomy island that is filled with third-rate goods, marred by fields of rusted out cars, and permeated by the smell from nearby glue factories. When even this smaller house becomes too cozy, she designs trips to the mainland where she allows herself to be picked up by increasingly sinister men. In the process of pursuing this "course of salvation," as she calls it, she abandons her companion Lucy Gamelon, deserts Arnold, Arnold's father, and Andy, the three main male characters, all of whom declare they care for her, and ends up alone in the closing moments of the novel. In one reading of this narrative, Miss Goering's masochism structures her narcissistic behaviors and suggests the connection argued by Freud between sadism and masochism. In a second reading, all this psychoanalytic apparatus is so severely undercut by the parodic tone, comic juxtapositions, and flat surface of the prose that the novel, like its characters, takes on the "waning of affect" that Jameson argues is characteristically postmodern (*Postmodernism* 10). The tension between these two readings and the anomalous text that results gives *Two Serious Ladies* part of its defining queerness.

I have borrowed from Freud the term "moral masochism" to describe Miss Goering's tendency to seek out unpleasant situations and potentially dangerous liaisons. "Moral masochism" appears in the last of Freud's extended treatments, "The Economic Problem of Masochism" (1924), to describe a condition in which the ego experiences an unconscious sense of guilt and seeks punishment not from another person but from the superego within or from parent-substitutes, including Fate; like other kinds of masochism, it brings sexual pleasure. A modernist psychoanalytic reading of Miss Goering's actions narrativizes the directions of that pleasure first by making concrete the connection between sadism and the subsequent guilt that appears in moral masochism as a need for suffering and then by representing it as autoerotic.

Christina Goering's baptism of Mary evidences sadism both in its gesture as a will to power and in its implicit eroticism. Christina is "very much excited" and "very much agitated" as she leads Mary to "purification" (6,7). She asks Mary to assure her that sin tastes bitter in her mouth, a narrative detail in keeping with the scene's emphasis on the sensuous. Her eyes shine as she buries Mary deeper in the mud and forces her into the water. When the baptism is over, she addresses Mary as "darling," but shortly after feels ill and "deeply troubled" (7,8). She leaves Mary shivering in a towel, and the narrative cuts away immediately to the adult Miss Goering now living with her companion, Miss Gamelon. The remainder of her narrative continues with what might be read as attempts at expiating her guilt through seeking ever more uncomfortable positions in life as a course of moral salvation.

This abrupt textual move from the sadistic child to the masochistic adult shifts the modernist erotics in a second, more crucial direction. Miss Goering's moral masochism continues in her adulthood as a narcissistic autoeroticism in which she is the subject and the object of her own pleasure. The sadistic eroticism of the baptism becomes the masochistic pleasure of self-generated discomfort as, in Freudian terms, the ego seeks punishment from the superego. Her narrative plays out a further feature of Freud's text: "[Moral] masochism creates a temptation to perform 'sinful' acts which must then be expiated by the reproaches of the sadistic conscience . . . or by chastisement from the great parental authority of Destiny. In order to provoke punishment from this last representative of the parents, the masochist must do what is inexpedient, must act against his own interests, must ruin the prospects which open out to him the real world, and must, perhaps, destroy his own real existence" (169–70). It is this last, this tendency to ruin her prospects, that Christina Goering embodies in her decisions to seek positions of discomfort and a version of fate that she sometimes blames: "She felt for one desolate moment that the whole thing had been prearranged and that although she had forced herself to take this little trip to the mainland, she had somehow at the same time been tricked into taking it by the powers above" (144). In planning her course of salvation, Miss Goering acts as a moral masochist and gets from her own actions the pleasure in pain that attaches to masochism as an (auto)erotic practice.

But while this modernist psychoanalytic reading works to narrativize the connections suggested more generally in Freud's texts between sadism and moral masochism as autoerotic pleasure, it does not capture the queer spirit of *Two Serious Ladies.* Miss Goering never accounts for her motives. Her most frequent assertion about various acts in her course for salvation is simply that they are necessary. The first of these occurs in the crucial opening scene with Mary:

> When Mary arrived in the tower, Christina asked her if she would not like to play a very special game with her. "It's called 'I forgive you for all your sins,' " said Christina. "You'll have to take your dress off."
> "Is it fun?" Mary asked.
> "It's not for fun that we play it, but because it's necessary to play it." (6)

Similarly, when Christina decides to leave the island to test herself on the mainland, she tells Arnold, "It's not for fun that I am going, . . . but because it is necessary to do so" (124). In his formulation of moral masochism, Freud suggests that hidden guilt prompts the ego to seek punishment from the superego within. In *Two Serious Ladies,* motivation for Christina's actions in the erotic "cleansing" of Mary and subsequent masochistic self-denials and risktakings remain an aporia in the text. She is simply introduced from the beginning as a child troubled by unspecified "horrible ideas" who likes to play moral games involving God. This lack of motivation clashes with attempts in the spirit of modernism to establish a depth of self for Christina and prompts a more postmodern reading of the novel.[5] At the same time, the repeated assertion that she acts not for fun but from necessity suggests a connection between that early scene and her later adult actions and promotes a reading of Christina's autoerotic maturation more in keeping with modernist interest in the psychological development of the character. Indeed, the tension between the two readings—a modernist insistence on maturation and a simultaneous postmodernist refusal of motive—itself mimics the erotic tension of Christina's actions.

In a further turn, there is something parodic about her attempts to deny herself and to put herself in dangerous situations in the name of her course of salvation. Take the only scene in which she even comes close actually to having sex. Thinking about Andy's request that she tell him what she likes sexually, she muses that:

> until recently, she had never followed too dangerously far in action any course which she had decided upon as being the morally correct one. She scarcely approved of this weakness in herself, but she was to a certain extent sensible and happy enough to protect herself automatically. She was feeling a little tipsy, however, and Andy's suggestion rather appealed to her. "One must allow that a certain amount of carelessness in one's nature often accomplishes what the will is incapable of doing" she said to herself. (154)

She acknowledges that her attempts to be morally correct by subjecting herself to danger haven't really succeeded in the past. And comic circumstances thwart her in this scene as well. While trying to seduce her, Andy plays a recording of the "Washington Post March," then shows her pictures of previous dates, whom he finds nice-looking, but who seem to Christina "terribly unattractive and plain" (156). She suddenly feels weary, pleads tiredness, tucks Andy into bed and departs. The comic failure of this "moral excursion" parodies Christina's attempt at salvation through moral masochism. And the emptiness of her moral gesturing contrasts to Andy's story of his own failed love affair, told just before his seduction attempt. Andy's is the only intratextual story narrated by one of the characters, and though it too is ultimately comic, it functions as a counter to the narrative focus on Miss Goering's little schemes to inconvenience herself. Andy's is a traditional closed narrative in which he accounts for his present isolation by explaining the origins of his plight and its eventual outcome. He tells how he lost his sweetheart Mary because he met Belle, a woman with no arms or legs, ate "the apple of sin" and began to obsess about what "the rest of her" would be like. Sex with her gives him syphilis and ends his relationship with Mary. He finishes his queerly comic story by describing how, after his guilt makes him avoid his mother by bowling all day, he spends a day with her watching a Fourth of July parade. When the flag goes by and the band plays "Yankee Doodle," his guilt overcomes him and he accepts his "status as a skunk": " 'Citizen Skunk' happens to be a little private name I have for myself. You can have some fun in the mud, though, you know, if you just accept a seat in it instead of trying to squirm around" (152). At least his exile in "No-Man's Land," as he terms the mainland destination of Miss Goering's excursion, is motivated by his guilt over his sexual curiosity, and his guilt is narrated in the text. His origin story gives his textual presence an illusion of developmental depth that emphasizes by contrast how Miss Goering's "mental struggles" and "moral games" are a characterlogical given from the opening moments of the novel.

Andy's presence also brings to the fore the narrative of class that functions as Miss Goering's venue for acting out her course for salvation. Here is their exchange following his assertion about fun in the mud:

> "Well," said Miss Goering, "I certainly think you could pull yourself together with a bit of an effort. I wouldn't put too much stock in that flag episode either."
> He looked at her vaguely. "You talk like a society lady," he said to her.
> "I am a society lady," said Miss Goering. "I am also rich, but I have purposely reduced my living standards. I have left my lovely home and I have moved out to a little house on the island. The house is in very bad shape and costs me practically nothing. What do you think of that?"
> "I think you're cuckoo," said Andy, and not at all in a friendly tone. He was frowning darkly. "People like you shouldn't be allowed to have money." (152–53)

Throughout, class privilege functions as a weapon of power for Miss Goering so that her playing with moral masochism depends on economic manipulation. The opening sentence introduces not her but her parents by marking their class and ethnicities: "Christina Goering's father was an American industrialist of German parentage and her mother was a New York lady of a very distinguished family" (3). For all that the novel's early readers found it a writing out of the psyche, it is equally, though perhaps less obviously, an account of how psychosexual games call forth, even depend on, the specifics of class differences rather than on a universalized "psyche." Christina Goering can punish herself by choosing less elaborate surroundings only because her money allows her that choice; she can take in Lucy Gamelon and Arnold and his father because she controls the purse strings. She seems drawn to Andy because he has fallen on hard times and is at once a little frightening and a "terrible burden" (53). Her class position becomes part of the novel's erotics because it permits her to act without restraint in designing her course of salvation.[6]

Andy's last reference to "fun in the mud" recalls the early narrative description of Christina's baptism game, also played with a "Mary." In one sense, all Christina Goering's attempts at setting herself a masochistic course for moral salvation turn out to be versions of "trying to squirm around." In a postmodernist reading, the very grandness with which she proposes them dooms them rhetorically to failure and parodies both the idea of salvation through abnegation and moral masochism as a source of pleasure. The novel's ironic closing mocks her futile attempts. Not only is she quite alone, having been abandoned by the last and most threatening of the men she picks up, she cannot connect her self-absorbed life and rhetoric of moral correctness with the "new sadness" that comes over her as Ben drives off: instead, she is thwarted by her own lack of insight: " 'Certainly I am nearer to becoming a saint, . . . but is it possible that a part of me hidden from my sight is piling sin upon sin as fast as Mrs Copperfield?' This latter possibility Miss Goering thought to be of considerable interest but of no great importance" (201).

The closing recalls Freud's comment about the moral masochist: "the masochistic trend of the ego remains as a rule concealed from the subject and has to be inferred from his behaviour" (169). Certainly Miss Goering's blindness is the subject of narrative ridicule. At the same time the ending might also be said to participate in the "self-ironizing" that Terry Eagleton identifies with postmodernism: "There is, perhaps, a degree of consensus that the typical postmodernist artifact is playful, self-ironizing and even schizoid; and that it reacts to the austere autonomy of high modernism by impudently embracing the language of commerce and the commodity. Its stance toward cultural tradition is one of irreverent pastiche, and its contrived depthlessness undermines all metaphysical solemnities, sometimes by a brutal aesthetics of squalor and shock."[7] In fact, much of this particular description of the "postmodern artefact" describes the narrative of Christina Goering, with its "contrived depthlessness," even including its embracing the language of commodity and commerce. Recent discussions of parody and pastiche by Fredric Jameson and Judith Butler, as well as Eagleton, debate the status of the original being mocked and the possibility of laughter as a result. The status of the parodic in the novel, like the narrative itself, is open to a double reading. It captures Jameson's modernist emphasis on the production of laughter that ridicules the "normal" original with which there is also some sympathy, however secret ("Postmodernism" 113). But it also can be read as a postmodern pastiche (or a parody in Butler's sense) in which the original is also a copy, since both moral masochism and baptism may be thought of as "copies" in which repetition at once establishes their meaning and empties them of stable content (Butler, *Gender Trouble* 138, 139). The tension between these kinds of doubled reading possibilities, like that between modernist maturation and postmodernist motivelessness, contributes to a hermeneutic erotics that gives Christina Goering's story its queer tone.

The "sins" of Mrs. Copperfield in the middle, framed section of *Two Serious Ladies* occupy a more singularly modernist space. Like the acts of Christina Goering they initially involve a triangular erotics, but unlike the first serious lady's comic/parodic moral masochism, they constitute a more traditional narrative of choice, a modernist presentation of problem and resolution. At the same time, the unfolding of Mrs. Copperfield's story continues the novel's focus on dynamics between women begun in the earlier scenes. Mrs. Copperfield travels to Panama with her husband, to "penetrate into the interior" as he so phallically puts it (18), and, after much interior struggle of her own, decides to leave him for Pacifica, a Panamanian woman with whom she has fallen in love. Reading this story as one introduced by Miss Goering's relationships with women indicates how a lesbian erotics is enabled in part by reader expectation based both on conventions of lesbian fiction and on textual desire put into play by ordered events of the narrative. From the novel's opening, the flow of events constructs what might be called a "lesbian reading effect," that is, a desire to find desire between women functioning in the text. "Lesbian erotics" implies the mutual and constitutive workings of this extratextual reading desire and intratextual narrative events as they focus on women's emotional and sexual investments with each other.[8] In *Two Serious Ladies*, a specifically lesbian erotics operates only intermittently. "Lesbian" is never a position of stable identity but rather a component of what I have argued is the "queerness" of the novel. Because Mrs. Copperfield's narrative in part two is structured as a problem resolved by choice, and because she chooses Pacifica over Mr. Copperfield, the second part of the novel might be read finally as a specifically lesbian narrative. But such a reading is an effect of the preceding narrative events, and the actions that follow in part three undo any certain sense of *Two Serious Ladies* as a novel of lesbian identity.

Christina's opening encounter with Mary suggests that an erotic between women will be part of what follows. And indeed, it is followed immediately by a scene in which the adult Christina meets Lucy Gamelon who the next day moves in with her to be her "companion." A trace of that eroticism remains for the reader as Christina and Lucy begin their life together. But even as they enact the contemporary lesbian joke about moving in after only a day's acquaintance, they counter readerly expectations of an overtly realized sexual life together. At their first dinner, "Miss Goering began to feel a little tipsy. She looked dreamily at Miss Gamelon, who was eating her second helping of chicken cooked in wine." But any sense that romance might be in the air disappears in the next sentence: "There was a little spot of grease in the corner of her mouth" (11). A similar qualification of erotic possibility occurs earlier in Christina's dance for Mary:

> One very sunny afternoon Sophie went inside for her piano lesson, and Mary remained seated on the grass. Christina, who had seen this from not far away, ran into the house, her heart beating with excitement. She took off her shoes and stockings and remained in a short white underslip. This was not a very pleasant sight to behold, because Christina at this time was very heavy and her legs were quite fat. (5)

In both scenes, attention to what the narrative judges as "not very pleasant" or to a presumably antierotic detail (that spot of grease) momentarily thwarts readerly envisioning of a potential romantic dynamic. But the extratextual enabling conditions of Bowles's own sexuality and the broader textual play on the potentially erotic circumstances of the baptism and of single women living together continue the possibility of a lesbian reading. The temporary denial of the erotic by the antierotic detail may in fact tease out the expectation so that textual repression of overt eroticism contributes to the heightening of readerly desire. When Arnold moves in with Miss Gamelon and Miss Goering, the tension is queered not only because the couple is now a threesome but also because Arnold moves back and forth in his affections between the two women without ever "courting" either of them. The arrival of Arnold's father and his attentions to Christina add a generational complication made comic by his "second-childhood" romanticism. As Miss Goering's narrative moves forward, the textual refusal to make any of the multiple sexual possibilities overt contributes to readings, both modern and postmodern, that foreground her attempts at moral masochism because they contrast the absence of dyadic sexual relation to the narration of autoerotic denial, however parodic.

Miss Goering's masochistic narrative is, however, interrupted by the story of Mrs. Copperfield. The erotic potential between women established in part one by Christina's baptism of Mary and by Miss Gamelon's moving in with Christina, now Miss Goering, gets its fullest play in the account of Mrs. Copperfield's decision to leave her husband for Pacifica. This decision, in turn, sets up the continuation of Christina Goering's story in part three and heightens the contrast between Mrs. Copperfield's erotic need and Miss Goering's parodic failure. But given the queer reading possibilities the whole novel opens, this binary contrast does not convey the anomaly of the closing erotic in which the parodic tone of Miss Goering's narrative may be said to infect the seeming resolution of Mrs. Copperfield's decision. Consequently, in the best queer postmodern fashion, nothing is concluded.

At the end of part one, Miss Goering informs Miss Gamelon and Arnold of her decision to move to a less grand house; part two quickly moves to another kind of triangulation. When Mr. and Mrs. Copperfield stroll in the red-light district of Colón, a black prostitute addresses not Mr. Copperfield, but his wife: "You come along with me, darling, and you'll have the happiest time you've ever had before. I'll be your type. Come on" (41). So begins the erotics of Mrs. Copperfield's narrative, a three-person story imbued from its opening by racial and class dynamics. The prostitute starts to pull Mrs. Copperfield by the hand away from her husband, who protests. Then "the Negress caressed Mrs. Copperfield's face with the palm of her hand. 'Is that what you want to do, darling, or do you want to come along with me?' " (42). Another version of this threesome repeats even before Mrs. Copperfield meets Pacifica. An older, muscular woman, who seems to Mrs. Copperfield "A West Indian type" and who is "almost a giantess" offers "both of you for a dollar" (43). Mr. Copperfield declines and when the two women are alone, the black woman hugs "little

Mrs. Copperfield" to her in a kind of dance: "Mrs. Copperfield put her cheek on the woman's breast. The smell of the theatrical gauze reminded her of her first part in a school play. She smiled up at the Negress, looking as tender and as gentle as she was able" (44). They are interrupted before anything more happens. This brief encounter, in which a threesome becomes a twosome, suggests also a kind of maternal power relation, complicated by differences in race, class, and ethnicity, that provides in miniature the queer dynamic of part two.

The contexts for this dynamic have been established in the opening pages of the section before the Copperfields go out for their walk. It is clear there is tension between them. When they first arrive in Panama, they speak, but neither responds to the other. Mrs. Copperfield meets a woman on the boat and asks if she might visit her in Panama. The woman declines and comments on Mrs. Copperfield's "beautiful husband." " 'That doesn't help,' said Mrs. Copperfield, but no sooner had she said this than she was horrified at herself" (36). The Copperfields' troubles are apparent in other ways as well. Mr. Copperfield prefers a cheap hotel; Mrs. Copperfield a more comfortable one. When he is threatened by not getting the hotel he wishes, "he was like a baby and Mrs. Copperfield was obligated to comfort him" (37). More important, they differ temperamentally. She describes him in a brief passage that helps establish not just their difference but her need: " 'My husband is a man without memory.' She felt an intense pain at the thought of this man whom she liked above all other people, this man for whom each thing he had not yet known was a joy. For her, all that which was not already an old dream was an outrage" (40). Her attachment to the past suggests in brief what becomes central to her attraction to other women: somehow, they recall for her an old dream. These early scenes with her husband establish her ambivalent relation to him. She likes him, but liking him isn't quite enough.

One other early passage sets up the particulars of Mrs. Copperfield's attractions to women. The woman Mrs. Copperfield meets on the boat puts into a play the racial discourse that continues throughout part two. This woman's vitriolic racism separates her from the Copperfields:

> "Now remember," she said to Mrs. Copperfield, "the minute you get to your hotel, stretch yourself out and rest. Don't let them drag you through the streets, no matter what kind of a wild time they promise you. Nothing but monkeys in the streets anyway. There isn't a fine-looking person in the whole town that isn't connected with the American Army, and the Americans stick pretty much to their own quarter. The American quarter is called Cristobal. It's separated from Colon. Colon is full of nothing but half-breeds and monkeys. Cristobal is nice. Everyone in Cristobal has got his own little screened-in porch. They'd never dream of screening themselves in, the monkeys in Colon. They don't know when a mosquito's biting them anyway, and even if they did know they wouldn't

lift their arm up to shoo him off. Eat plenty of fruit and be careful of the stores. Most of them are owned by Hindus. They're just like Jews, you know. They'll gyp you right and left." (36; Bowles omits the accent in Colón)

Her distinction between Colón, a city with a largely black population, descendents of the builders of the United States-financed railroad, and Cristobal, home to the American military stationed to run the Panama Canal, continues the narrative use of geography as trope. While Panama itself is no longer a colony, the occupation of the Canal Zone makes colonized subjects of its Panamanian residents. The racism of the description frames not only the Copperfields' decision to stay in Colón but also Mrs. Copperfield's move to the Hotel Las Palmas in the heart of the "red-light district."

Like Miss Goering's decision to move to less grand quarters, Mrs. Copperfield's move marks the power differences of the narrative's erotics. Instead of Miss Goering's unconscious pleasure in singular self-abnegation, Mrs. Copperfield finds relational connection to various Panamanian women who differ from her by racial ethnicity and class. Her position as a white colonizer to their "otherness" as colonized forms a part of their erotic engagement. The opening encounters with "Negresses" are followed by the story of Mrs. Copperfield's decision to leave her husband for Pacifica. She makes that decision after rejecting the advances of Peggy Gladys, whom Mrs. Copperfield decides is Malayan, but who later describes herself as half-Irish and half-Javanese. The racial specificity of the Negresses and Peggy Gladys makes the ambiguity of Pacifica's racial ethnicity particularly striking. She is described first as "an intelligent-looking girl with sharp features and curly hair," and later as "a Spanish girl." In the final pages of the novel, Miss Goering notes that she is "fairly attractive," but that "her hair was far too wiry for her own taste" (196). This last comment would seem to link Miss Goering to the racist woman on the boat and further undercut her futile attempts at keeping a "moral course." By contrast, Mrs. Copperfield chooses the possibility of life with Pacifica over staying with her husband, and prefers a life among the colonized racial "others" of Colón to the dubious comforts of the American quarter. At the same time, however, the erotics of part two are built in part on a power difference between Mrs. Copperfield and the prostitutes she favors, including Pacifica. She is privileged by her money, like Miss Goering, and by her whiteness as well. Descriptions of Colón share an eroticizing of the exotic, and none of the women of color is given any individual subjectivity. They are powerful physically, and provide Mrs. Copperfield with a strength that she thinks of as a dream. But part of their attraction for Mrs. Copperfield and thus part of the lesbian erotics of the novel depends on their otherness; they are taboo not only because they are women but also because they are not white. That they are prostitutes makes the erotic depend as well on the old stereotype of women of color as commodified sexuality. At the same time the choice of Pacifica, whose mixed race makes her "whiter" than the other women encountered suggests that covert attachment to whiteness is also functioning in the text. So while the novel offers a critique of overt racism, it also eroticizes social and economic power dominances in a colonized country and privileges "Spanish" over "West Indian" color. Such dynamics, operating as they do out of textually covert race and class privilege, mark the novel as "white" and deny the claim of any single representation of a "lesbian erotic" to universality.[9]

These power differences are not, however, foregrounded in Mrs. Copperfield's story. Rather, the erotic would seem more directly to depend on Mrs. Copperfield's desire to be protected, even taken care of, in exchange for (covert) economic advancement. Early in the section, before she goes out in Colón with her husband, she suggests something of this need to be "watched over":

> "Now," she said to herself, "when people believed in God they carried Him from one place to another. They carried Him through the jungles and across the Arctic Circle. God watched over everybody, and all men were brothers. Now there is nothing to carry with you from one place to another, and as far as I'm concerned, these people might as well be kangaroos; yet somehow there must be someone here who will remind me of something . . . I must try to find a nest in this outlandish place." (40, ellipsis in the original)

This passage differentiates her from Miss Goering who, as the girl Christina, dances in her slip for Mary because she wants to show why she would rather have "God and no sun"; Mrs. Copperfield becomes instead in this passage, one who finds "sun and no God." (In fact, in another use of geography as trope, these two modalities might be said to divide one serious lady's world from the other's.)[10] Her dismissive and racist remark about kangaroos catches her by the time the section is over, since "the nest" she finds is with Pacifica, one of "these people," who turns out to be "someone who will remind me of something."

While this "something" is never explicitly spelled out, some of the scenes between them outline a possibility. In their first conversation Pacifica says she likes women very much but that she is always in love with "some nice man." Mrs. Copperfield says instead: "I once was in love with an older woman. . . . She was no longer beautiful, but in her face I found fragments of beauty which were much more exciting to me that any beauty that I have known at its height" (49). Her earlier maternal attraction to the older black prostitute and this memory of a former love come together in her relation with Pacifica, whose strength and competence are particularly evident one day when they decide to go swimming together. Given Mrs. Copperfield's stated fear of drowning, her willingness to acquiesce to Pacifica's suggestion is in itself a mark of Pacifica's power. As usual in the novel, details refuse the possibility of an idyllic day as lovers together. Pacifica begins the morning drunk, the beach itself is rocky and uncomfortable, Pacifica has a fever blister. Nevertheless, the scene is pivotal in a lesbian reading. Pacifica swims Mrs. Copperfield out into the ocean. She is "breathing like a bull," but her touch is light as she supports Mrs. Copperfield: "Mrs. Copperfield felt happy and sick at once. She turned her face and in so doing she brushed Pacifica's heavy stomach with her cheek. She held on hard to Pacifica's thigh with the strength of years of sorrow and frustration in her hand" (97). At that moment she recalls a recurring dream in which she is being chased by a dog up a hill. At the top is an eight-foot-tall mannequin made of flesh. When she puts one of the mannequin's arms around her in a dance, they roll together down the hill "locked in each other's arms":

> Mrs. Copperfield loved this part of the dream best; and the fact that all the way down the hill the mannequin acted as a buffer between herself and the broken bottles and little stones over which they fell gave her particular satisfaction. . . . She was trembling and exhausted as one is after a love experience. She looked up at Pacifica, who noticed that her eyes were more luminous and softer than she had ever seen them before. (98)

This is as explicitly erotic as the novel gets. As a consequence, the scene takes on added weight. In addition to its echo (and reversal) of Christina's "baptism" of Mary in that other world where there is God but no sun, this scene functions as the deciding one in Mrs. Copperfield's decision to permit her husband to travel on without her.[11] Read as the culmination of the scenic series where Mrs. Copperfield interacts with Panamanian women, the episode emphasizes her desire to be protected in a world without God by a stronger woman who can also teach her and keep her safe as the heart of her longing.

That desire contrasts sharply with her lack of enthusiasm about caring for her husband ("He was like a baby and Mrs. Copperfield was obligated to comfort him" 37) and especially with her response to Peggy Gladys in the closing pages of the section. Just as the scene with the older West Indian woman introduces the fuller relation with Pacifica, the scene with Peggy Gladys brackets it by contrast. She is only sixteen and "feels like a child" (106), is thinly built, and has plenty of money given to her by a kind of sugar daddy. In addition, "she had the bright eyes of an insatiable nymphomaniac" (101) and laments the death of her mother as she tries to take care of Mrs. Copperfield. She is, in short, unlike the women to whom Mrs. Copperfield is attracted, not personally powerful nor financially needy and thus cannot exchange strength, protection, and experience for gifts of silk stockings and elaborate kimonos. Her sexual aggression separates her as well from Pacifica who never directly interacts with Mrs. Copperfield sexually in the narrative. The dynamic between Mrs. Copperfield and the Panamanian women in the novel depends not on sexual desire but on an eroticized and racialized maternal nurturance. Little Mrs. Copperfield doesn't want to be a mother; she wants to have one.[12]

Even after swimming, with Pacifica protecting and teaching her, her decision to leave her husband is full of ambivalence. She realizes that in staying with Pacifica "she was only interested in duplicating a dream" but worries that "in so doing she necessarily became the complete victim of a nightmare" (107). Finally it is a letter from Mr. Copperfield that pushes her over the edge. Imperious in its announced intention to outline her faults, frequently imperative in voice, it describes obliquely (and opaquely) a never-specified "first pain" that he counsels her to stop circling around. As a man with no memory, he seems unable to understand her dream for that elusive "someone who will remind me of something" and urges instead that "a ship leaving port," presumably heading for future adventures, "is still a wonderful thing to see" (111). In the last lines of the section she has crushed this letter and run from the room to find Pacifica.

Her departure concludes the tracing in part two of Mrs. Copperfield's growing awareness that she needs to leave her husband and be with Pacifica. For the moment, in the novel's middle section, a problem has been solved, a realization reached, a decision made. Another triangle of characters opens the third section, and still another closes the novel. But what in Mrs. Copperfield's Panamanian story is a traditionally modernist interior, psychosexual struggle to choose one love over another plays out in the conclusion of Miss Goering's story as a self-enclosed eroticism and becomes at the novel's end an assertion of sexual and emotional fluidity among both men and women. The narrative solution of the middle section is undone and left open at the novel's conclusion. Though part three opens with Miss Goering, Miss Gamelon, and Arnold all living together, it quickly moves to follow Miss Goering alone on her course of salvation. Miss Gamelon and Arnold end up living together in a third house with a third woman, and Mrs. Copperfield and Pacifica return without Mr. Copperfield to the United States.

In the final scene of the novel, Mrs. Copperfield brings Pacifica to meet Miss Goering. Like the opening story of Christina and Mary, the closing episode emphasizes the particulars of an erotic. But unlike the perverse baptism of one girl by another, the dynamics of the last scene play out what has become the dominant queer erotic in the novel, an exchange of power between women with a potential male lover hovering on the sidelines. The closure implied by Mrs. Copperfield's choice of Pacifica has reopened to admit both the new man and Miss Goering's never ending search for new ways to make herself happily unhappy. No sooner does Mrs. Copperfield arrive with Pacifica than the Panamanian departs to meet her newest boyfriend. Mrs. Copperfield is increasingly upset, and her good spirits revive only when Pacifica returns and the boyfriend disappears. The tone of the ending is at least partly comic. The meditative notes of interior psychological struggle that sound often in Mrs. Copperfield's section fade, and she becomes subject to narrative mockery bordering on ridicule. She is treated, that is, as comically as Miss Goering:

> "I'll tell you," said Mrs. Copperfield, leaning over the table and suddenly looking very tense. "I am a little worried—not terribly worried, because I shan't allow anything to happen that I don't want to happen—but I am a little worried because Pacifica has met this blond boy who lives way uptown and he has asked her to marry him." . . .
>
> Mrs. Copperfield leaned back and stared intently into Miss Goering's eyes.
>
> "I am taking her back to Panama as soon as I am able to book passage on a boat." . . .
>
> "Perhaps you'd better wait and see whether or not she really wants to marry him."
>
> "Don't be insane," said Mrs. Copperfield. "I can't live without her, not for a minute. I'd go completely to pieces."
>
> "But you have gone to pieces, or do I misjudge you dreadfully?"
>
> "True enough," said Mrs. Copperfield, bringing her fist down on the table and looking very mean. "I have gone to pieces, which is a thing I've wanted to do for years." . . .
>
> "You will contend," she continued in a very clear voice, "that all people are of equal importance, but although I love Pacifica very much, I think it is obvious that I am more important."
>
> Miss Goering did not feel that she had any right to argue this point with Mrs. Copperfield. (197–98)

The use of adverbial intensifiers like "very," "dreadfully," "intently" together with the repetition of "a little worried—not terribly worried . . . a little worried"; "gone to pieces . . . I have gone to pieces"; and "equal importance . . . more important" undercut Mrs. Copperfield's pronouncements and make her sound not very important, not one to take seriously. She has, in addition, textually "gone to pieces," her humanist, "seeking" self decentered by Pacifica's sexual fluidity and Miss Goering's narrative proximity so that by the novel's end she occupies a more nearly postmodern (queer) subject position.

In the closing moments, Pacifica finally speaks for herself and verbalizes for the first time the nature of the power exchange (maternal protection for economic advancement) implicit in the much more psychological language of part two with its dream sequence and interior discourse:

> "What a baby your friend is! I can't leave her for ten minutes because it almost breaks her heart, and she is such a kind generous woman, with such a beautiful apartment and such beautiful clothes. What can I do with her? She is like a little baby. I tried to explain it to my young man, but I can't explain it really to anyone." (200)

But the parodic language associated with Miss Goering's narrative has already infected this scene and its voicing of the erotic dynamic between women, so that Mrs. Copperfield becomes a copy of Miss Goering in her self-importance and her disregard for others. At the same time, however, there is one further textual spin in which the lesbian reading effect, the desire to find desire between women, of the novel's opening makes a final brief appearance:

> Mrs. Copperfield returned and suggested that they all go elsewhere to get some food.
> "I can't," said Miss Goering, lowering her eyes. "I have an appointment with a gentleman." She would have liked to talk to Pacifica a little longer. In some ways Pacifica reminded her of Miss Gamelon although certainly Pacifica was a much nicer person and more attractive physically. (200)

Miss Gamelon's discursive reappearance is brief but reintroduces a textual space of lesbian desire earlier waived in favor of autoerotic absorption. Instead, Miss Goering rushes off to her next moral risk only to find it impossible to take because she has been abandoned.

Finally, the novel provides its own commentary on the queer erotic and textual direction I have been discussing: " 'How amusing,' said Mrs. Copperfield," when Miss Goering tells her a an odd story about a partially torn-down building where rain had come in where a wall had been, spotting the wallpaper, " 'or perhaps it was depressing' " (17). Her inability to decide whether the tone of the tale was amusing or depressing captures the queerness of *Two Serious Ladies*. It is at once amusing in its parody of moral masochism and depressing in its depiction of all erotic connections as at best transient and incomplete. Or perhaps it is depressing for the reader inclined to modernism and the struggles of the humanist self and amusing to the more postmodernist reader who delights in the play of surfaces and the seemingly open fluidity of erotic possibilities. Or maybe after all, the interposition of the amusing and depressing, surface and depth, comic and serious that results from the novel's refusal to take to heart any binary set of erotic arrangements demands that all its readers learn to read more queerly.

Notes

1. By "queer theory" I mean various antifoundational inquiries stressing intersections and boundary crossings between and among marginalized sexualities and positions of race, class, and gender. As "theory," these inquiries critique stable identities ("gay," "lesbian," "bisexual," "transsexual," "heterosexual") and emphasize instead provisional identifications and shifting erotic and emotional

investments. They resonate with recent feminist poststructuralist articulations of difference and domination (understood both psychoanalytically and socially) at the same that they reclaim and assert the the power of radical sexual "otherness." For discussion of queer theory, its relation to lesbian and gay studies, and the importance of racial difference in an understanding of queer sexuality, see De Lauretis. For queer theory as an emerging field of academic study, see Warner. For queer theory as an intervention into identity politics, see Duggan and Stein. For queer theory's intersections with once and future versions of feminism and gender, see Butler, "Against Proper Objects." For queer desire as a modality of pleasure, see Grosz 207–27. For "the singularity of queer desire as theory," see Probyn 9.

2. Dillon quotes Paul Bowles as saying Jane used the name purposefully to recall Goering as a ridiculous figure, but might not have joked about it in 1938 had she known about Nazi atrocities (*Life* 99).

3. For a working out of the Foucauldian formulation "enabling conditions" to which I am indebted, see Cummings. She defines enabling conditions as "the set of available discourses, contemporary events, communal norms, institutional context, and other sociohistorical factors which make it possible for a sexual representation to appear when, where, and in the form that it does" (795).

4. The third "serious lady" appears as a minor character in Bowles's story, "A Guatemalan Idyll." She cut the third section, which is set in Guatemala, at Paul Bowles's suggestion, apparently to help tighten the novel's structure. Another fragment of the third section appears as "A Day in the Open" in her *Collected Works* (Dillon *Life* 107).

5. For "depth models" of modernism, including Freud, see Jameson, *Postmodernism* 12.

6. The seemingly superfluous story of Andy's encounter with three businessmen emphasizes that he fails to win their support for his real estate project both because he is of the wrong economic class and because he seems to be living with Miss Goering, who is not his wife.

7. Terry Eagleton, "Awakening from Modernity," *Times Literary Supplement*, 20 Feb. 1987, quoted in Harvey 7–8.

8. For further discussion of lesbian erotics as involving emotional as well as sexual dynamics, see Allen.

9. It is difficult in the context of reading *Two Serious Ladies* not to think of Jane Bowles's own later complicated relations with various Moroccan women in a similar context of race and class power differences.

10. I thank Deborah Woodard for first suggesting this idea to me.

11. Millicent Dillon, in her reading of the novel, also points out the repetition involved in these two scenes. She discusses Jane Bowles's biographical connections to the novel and argues that cutting out the third "lady" leaves Mrs. Copperfield and Miss Goering "deadlocked together in sin" (*Life* 102, 107).

12. "Have" in both the senses implied by the sentence that I echo here from one of Freud's discussions of identification: "It is easy to state in a formula the distinction between an identification with the father and the choice of the father as an object. In the first case one's father is what one would like to be, and in the second he is what one would like to have." (See *Group Psychology* 38.)

3

"The Americans Stick Pretty Much in Their Own Quarter"

Jane Bowles and Central America

Stephen Benz

G IVEN THE PROXIMITY of Central America to the United States, and given the widely perceived importance of the region for United States interests, it is somewhat surprising that American writers have rarely used Central America for background or setting in their fiction. In contrast, the colonial situation has inspired a number of significant works in British literature (Forster's *A Passage to India*, Orwell's *Burmese Days*, and Cary's *Mister Johnson*, to name a few). Yet a parallel neocolonial involvement in Central America has led to only a handful of romances by popular American writers such as Richard Harding Davis and O. Henry.[1] Before the 1970s, Central America figured prominently in only one exceptional American novel: Jane Bowles's *Two Serious Ladies*.[2]

The focus of this essay is on the image of Central America that emerges in the Panama section of Bowles's novel and in her short story "A Guatemalan Idyll." In these works, Bowles presents the reader with an idiosyncratic, almost surreal picture of Central America, one that has almost nothing to do with a realistic depiction of the place and its peoples. Initially, this portrayal seems wildly off the mark, and one could argue that the Mrs. Copperfield section of *Two Serious Ladies* is only incidentally situated in Panama. One could even argue that Bowles "gets it wrong" when she writes about Central America. There is, after all, little in the novel or the short story of the kind of local color that we associate with fiction set in exotic foreign lands. While Bowles seems uninterested in offering a faithful and realistic (or even stereotypical) depiction of the place, she does explore and challenge some deeply rooted truths about the encounter between North Americans and Central Americans—that is, the imperial encounter between the powerful and the powerless, between Self and Other. While Bowles's writing is less superficially realistic than even a hackneyed travel book, it is, on the essential issue of neocolonial relationships, more intriguing and indeed more truthful than most American literature set in tropical lands.

Initially, Jane Bowles was not attracted to Latin America. On a whim, she decided to travel to Mexico with her future husband Paul, but found the experience so disturbing that she fled back to the States alone. A honeymoon trip to Central America was the idea of the more adventurous Paul Bowles. It appears that Jane had mixed feelings on this trip: although certain places, like the Panamanian port of Colón, clearly intrigued her, she was always uncomfortable in the wilder areas, such as the rain forests and cattle ranches that the couple visited. For years, she could not speak about her most unusual experience in Central America—a wild escapade in and escape from a Guatemalan brothel. Yet it is clear that the trip through the region profoundly affected her imagination and her art; it is worth noting, for example, that Central America appears more often as a setting for her work than either France or Morocco—countries she lived in for much longer periods of time.[3]

When Bowles decided upon Panama as a setting for *Two Serious Ladies*, she was contributing, whether she knew it or not (and probably she did not), to a fairly well-established subgenre of American writing on the tropics, a subgenre that includes the small body of work on Central America. While she was probably not consciously aware of the conventions that distinguish this subgenre, her work clearly repeats many of them. Therefore, before exploring what is unique about Bowles's work, it is worthwhile first to review the ways in which *Two Serious Ladies* and "A Guatemalan Idyll" fit the tradition.

There are several motifs that appear again and again in American writing on the tropics.[4] There is, in an American traveler's initial southward journey, an attraction to the tropics, an eager anticipation of their paradisiacal associations. Usually, this association is fanciful, dependent on a number of geographical clichés, such as a hot sun, exotic flora and fauna, and a dreamy atmosphere. Even when reality does not quite correspond to these fancies, the traveler will usually insist upon them— exaggerating them, if need be—for a little while after arrival. So it is with the narrator of Melville's *Typee* as he anticipates his arrival in the Marquesas:

> The Marquesas! What strange visions of outlandish things does the very name spirit up! Naked houris—cannibal banquets—groves of cocoa-nut—coral reefs—tatooed chiefs—and bamboo temples; sunny valleys planted with bread-fruit trees—carved canoes dancing on the flashing blue waters—savage woodlands guarded by horrible idols—*heathenish rites and human sacrifices.* (5, emphasis in original)

In *Two Serious Ladies*, Mr. Copperfield dutifully plays the role of the paradise-seeking American abroad. From the moment that land is sighted, he eagerly searches the tableau for the clichés that will confirm his arrival in the tropics. From the boat, he sees "green trains loaded with bananas" (Bowles, *Works* [1978] 35), and as soon as he arrives on land he goes out to buy a papaya (40). Mr. Copperfield, we learn, is "delighted to be in the tropics at last" (39). His delight, focused on the most banal of expectations, marks him as a typical American visitor to Central America. Likewise, the vision of the traveler in "A Guatemalan Idyll" is drawn to clichéd images. For him, Central America is "old grilled windows," volcanos, and other tourist "points of interest": " 'I should think,' he said, 'that these old buildings were your point of interest here, aside from your Indians and their native costumes" (Bowles, *Works* [1978] 328).

Closely related to this motif of tropical expectations is the convention of the arrival—that moment when, the traveler being thrust into a strange new land, sensations and impressions are most intense. The arrival may produce a number of conflicting reactions. Travelers may ignore the evidence around them and persist in their hope for a tropical paradise. These travelers, like Mr. Copperfield, remain blind to everything but the clichés mentioned above, clichés that seem to proliferate around them, as when Mr. Copperfield takes a bus out to see the jungle with its "enormous trees" and "tangled undergrowth" (65).

Other travelers are, upon arrival, overwhelmed by the strangeness all about them. A certain irreality informs their vision, forcing upon them a strong sense of displacement and sometimes an irrepressible dread. Helen Sanborn, a young woman writing in 1886 about *A Winter in Central America and Mexico*, put it this way:

> I wondered if I were in fairy-land; but then there were no fairies, for the inhabitants of this land dwelt in mud huts and were dark enough to be goblins. I felt like pinching myself to see if I were awake or dreaming, and said to myself, "Who am I?" "Where am I?" "Can this be part of the same earth on which I dwell?" Every moment now was bringing us to stranger and stranger sights, and I wondered with something of apprehension as to what lay before us, and how we should fare when we came to penetrate this land and mingle with this uncivilized people. (27)

And almost a century later, novelist Joan Didion described similar sensations in her travel narrative *Salvador*. The country of El Salvador, she felt, was "a state in which no ground is solid, no depth of field reliable, no perception so definite that it might not dissolve into its reverse" (3).

In *Two Serious Ladies*, Frieda Copperfield shares in these sensations as she walks along a street in Colón, Panama: "Mrs. Copperfield's forehead was burning hot and her hands were cold. She felt something trembling in the pit of her stomach. When she looked ahead of her the very end of the street seemed to bend and then straighten out again" (41).

Another reaction upon arrival, perhaps the most common in American discourse on the tropics, is simple disappointment, especially when the traveler realizes that the shabby reality of the place invalidates all paradisiacal expectations. The focus in this case is usually on the natives and their productions—buildings, huts, streets, and so on (a favorite adjective for describing these productions is "miserable"), although sometimes the tropical environment itself disappoints the visitor because "paradise" turns out to be hot, disease-ridden, and quite a bit more desolate than expected. Ephraim Squier, an American diplomat who in 1855 published the first American fictional narrative set in Central America, covered all sides of this disappointment in his *Waikna*. First, his narrator, an artist who has eagerly anticipated stunning panorama and spectacle in the tropics, sights the coast of Nicaragua: "The approach to the coast, near Bluefields, holds out no delusions. The shore is flat, and in all respects tame and uninteresting" (56). And then the narrator sees his first Central Americans: "There was a large assemblage on the beach, when we landed, but I was amazed to find that, with few exceptions, they were all unmitigated negros or Sambos (i.e. mixed negro and Indian)" (58).

Bowles's characters are nowhere near as crass as Squier's, but Mr. Copperfield feels some of the same disappointment as he and his wife take a taxi through Colón shortly after arrival. To Mr. Copperfield, Colón looks "like a city that is being constantly looted" (38). Despite this reservation, Mr. Copperfield prefers, for the most part, to express delight, rather than disappointment, at the shabbiness of the place, concluding that "This is the sort of thing I love" (42). The traveler in "A Guatemalan Idyll" is unenthusiastic from the moment of his arrival in a Guatemalan town. The place appears "dismal" and "monotonous" to him. He regrets his decision to stay in the country an extra week. He has to force himself to "brace up."

For most Americans, disappointment and dread quickly lead to a third attitude: resistance. This resistance constitutes a major motif in American literature on the tropics. The excitement the travelers feel in approaching the tropics having dissipated, they quickly establish a set of defenses based on "Yankee" values. These they steadfastly maintain in the face of what they perceive to be tropical corruption. The narrator of O. Henry's *Cabbages and Kings*, a short story sequence set in a fictional Central American country, explains the attitude: "Thus in all the scorched and exotic places of the earth, Caucasians meet when the day's work is done, to preserve the fullness of the heritage by the aspersion of alien things" (616).

Upon their arrival in Panama, still flush with the excitement of a tropical tour, the Copperfields receive the same advice from another American, an old Panama hand:

"There isn't a fine-looking person in the whole town that isn't connected with the American Army, and the Americans stick pretty much in their own quarter.

The American quarter is called Cristobal. It's separated from Colon. Colon is full of nothing but half-breeds and monkeys. Cristobal is nice. Everyone is Cristobal has got his own little screened-in porch." (36; Bowles omits the accent in Colón)

Though advised to "stick pretty much" in the American quarter, the Copperfields eventually ignore the advice and begin to wander around "dangerous" Colón. This is where Bowles's novel begins to depart from the conventions typical of American narratives set in the tropics. In order to understand this departure, we need to examine how Bowles treats relationships between Americans and Central Americans. Such relationships are rare in most travel narratives on Central America; usually, any kind of encounter between natives and Americans occurs only on the most basic level (typically a commercial one), a level in which the power structure is clearly defined and the native exists merely to receive orders, perform a service, or assist the American in some way. For example, Richard Harding Davis, who wrote about the American military involvement in tropical countries in the novels *Captain Macklin* (Honduras) and *Soldiers of Fortune* (Cuba), rarely extended that involvement to include the natives themselves. The players in his novels were always the American, British, or French mercenaries who fought against each other for the spoils of the tropical country. Indeed, the Latin Americans have almost no voice in Davis's works, other than when they are made to attend obsequiously upon the Americans, or perhaps to display some egregious effrontery for which an American quickly punishes them (sometimes an entire mob of natives, raising Cain, is subdued by a single Yankee).[5]

This pattern is repeated in other works as well: Americans do not wish for and do not experience any significant encounter with tropical peoples. And this includes sexual encounters—a somewhat surprising fact since, as Edward Said notes in *Orientalism*, the tropics (whether the Orient or Latin America) are often perceived as places "to look for sexual experience unobtainable" at home (190). Resistance means shunning these encounters and their attendant dangers. Rather than subject himself to these dangers, the traveling or visiting American sets up a sort of screen, just as the Americans in Bowles's Colón sit inside their screened porches, to protect himself (and the masculine is appropriate here) from the debilitating effects inherent in such encounters. He sees the place and its peoples only through this screen.

Jane Bowles challenges the pattern. The issue residing at the core of her work is the relationship between the Self and the Other; *Two Serious Ladies* and "A Guatemalan Idyll" re situate this issue in a tropical context, and the result is a unique textualization of the problematics inherent in the encounter between Americans and native Central Americans. In textualizing this encounter, Bowles details two distinct ways of dealing with tropical peoples, and it is the tension between these two ways that gives the Panama section of *Two Serious Ladies* its startling atmosphere of anxiety, dread, and dereliction.

   The first way of dealing with tropical peoples is that of the typical Yankee tourist—in this case, Mr. Copperfield and the traveler in "A Guatemalan Idyll." Initially,
Mr. Copperfield appears more outgoing than his wife. He is certainly the more en-
ergetic tourist, always willing and eager to seek out new experiences, whether buy-
ing a papaya, walking around the city, or going out to see the jungle. His first action
in the narrative—studying—is indicative of his approach to the place: "Mr. Copperfield was studying the shore line" (34). For him, Central America is a place of spectacle, a *tableau vivant* for him to observe, to study, and to define according to his
culturally specific criteria. At various points in the novel, he declares Panama to be
"beautiful," "amusing," and "of some interest." He emphasizes that Panama and the
rest of Central America are places that can be known ("codified," to use Edward
Said's term) through study and observation, an attitude derived from Western empiricism. "I've found out a lot about the various countries in Central America," he
says. But what he finds out is strictly (and superficially) factual, the sort of guidebook
information obtainable by any tourist. In other words, Central America is "of some
interest" not as a place but as a congeries of characteristics and clichés ("Imagine
red and blue Guacamayas flying over the cattle," he says to Frieda) that give definition to a superficial Panama, the one that a guidebook student like Mr. Copperfield
expects to find. For Mr. Copperfield, the place itself is unimportant; it can be, and
is, obliterated by the images that Copperfield's imperial vision assigns to it, a vision
prepackaged by Frommer or Baedecker. When Mr. Copperfield tells his wife, "I just
think you'll be missing a good deal by not seeing Central America," he emphasizes
knowledge through the passive means of sightseeing. But seeing does not necessarily mean meeting or encountering, so ultimately his knowledge, like his encounters,
remains superficial. As for the people of Panama, he believes that "it would be easy
to know what they were like in a very short time" (63).
   Like so many American tourists, Mr. Copperfield and the traveler in "A Guatemalan Idyll" practice a sort of resistance to things native. Although they profess an
interest in and (in the case of Copperfield) even a love for the tropics, they remain
aloof, steadfastly avoiding any possibility of experiencing the place on a level more
meaningful than the merely touristic. Whenever there is the possibility of an encounter, Mr. Copperfield backs off. For example, on his initial walk through Colón,
several people accost him and Mrs. Copperfield. He does not, however, wish for
any kind of engagement with them and makes excuses for getting away. Ultimately,
Mr. Copperfield is like the tourists that his wife writes about in her journal:

   Tourists, generally speaking . . . are human beings so impressed with the importance and immutability of their own manner of living that they are capable of
   traveling through the most fantastic places without experiencing anything more

than a visual reaction. The hardier tourists find that one place resembles another.
(45)

This description perfectly summarizes Mr. Copperfield's experience in Panama: it is nothing more than "a visual reaction." His is an imperialist experience, one that is controlled and delineated by what Edward Said calls "*positional* superiority, which puts the Westerner in a whole series of possible relationships . . . without ever losing him the relative upper hand" (7). Mr. Copperfield avoids any relationship that might cause him to lose this superiority. Similarly, the traveler in "A Guatemalan Idyll" carefully avoids contaminating contact: "He had been warned that the natives would cheat him and he was actually enraged every time they approached him with their wares" (328).

Mrs. Copperfield, however, does not avoid these relationships; indeed, she cultivates them. Her interest lies in experiencing something beyond a "visual reaction" to "fantastic places." She therefore represents a second way of dealing with tropical peoples, one that no other character in American narratives on the tropics undertakes. Granted, Mrs. Copperfield is by no means an enthusiastic traveler. She shirks most of the experiences that her husband so eagerly embraces, and she is not interested in the jungles, or the seedy hotels, or the cattle farms that he finds so amusing. In fact, she seems to loathe the whole idea of a trip to Panama. She is unable to suppress "a rising feeling of dread" as they go through the usual tourist motions. Moreover, she "hated to know what was around her because it always turned out to be even stranger than she had feared" (59).

But for the most part, Mrs. Copperfield's feelings of dread and fear are associated with nature. When it comes to people, Mrs. Copperfield is quite open and willing to engage herself. In other words, she is the exact opposite of Mr. Copperfield, who finds nature and place "amusing" or "of some interest," but refuses any significant interaction with people.

Mrs. Copperfield is not only willing to interact, she is also willing to abandon the pretense of positional superiority. Unlike other Americans in the tropics, including her husband, Mrs. Copperfield does not raise a screen between herself and the native people, but rather is vulnerable to their influence. She seems unable to assert any sort of superiority. The contrast is apparent as she walks through Colón with her husband and comes across some "little one-story houses" outside of which are seated groups of women. Curious, Mrs. Copperfield walks up to the window of one house and looks inside. Then she turns her attention to the woman seated out front:

> She sat on a stool with her elbows resting on her knees, and it seemed to Mrs. Copperfield, who had now turned to look at her, that she was probably a West Indian type. She was flat-chested and raw-boned, with very muscular arms and

shoulders. Her long disgruntled-looking face and part of her neck were carefully covered with a light-colored face powder, but her chest and arms remained dark. Mrs. Copperfield was amused to see that her dress was of lavender theatrical gauze. There was an attractive gray streak in her hair. (42–43)

To this point, Mrs. Copperfield's observations parallel those of most American tourists. In fact, a common convention of American narratives is to include an up-close study of a particular native. Usually, such a study, written in an amused or shocked tone, is included in the arrival motif (the customs official, as the first native one meets, is often singled out for this detailed description). Mrs. Copperfield observes, as Americans are wont to do in these descriptions, the grotesqueness of the native's body, particularly the darkness of the skin (emphasizing difference), and the comical clothing worn by the native (emphasizing ignorance and a lack of sophistication).

But Mrs. Copperfield abruptly departs from the tradition. Rather than recoiling from the grotesqueness of this native, she seems rather attracted to her. Her inclination is to embrace the native's difference rather than to reject it. As soon as the native woman speaks to the Copperfields ("Both of you for a dollar"), Mr. Copperfield decides it is time to get away (" 'Frieda,' he said, 'let's walk down some more streets' "). His wife, however, wishing to assert her independence and drawn in a way that he cannot possibly understand to this woman's otherness, decides that she wants to talk with the woman. After Mr. Copperfield leaves, Frieda goes into the little room with the woman, and thus abandons her positional superiority. Indeed, the normal relationship between a white American and a dark Panamanian is abruptly reversed, and Mrs. Copperfield submits to the reversal:

> She took both Mrs. Copperfield's hands in her own and pulled her off the bed. "Come on now, honey." She hugged Mrs. Copperfield to her. "You're awful little and very sweet. You *are* sweet, and maybe you are lonesome." Mrs. Copperfield put her cheek on the woman's breast. The smell of theatrical gauze reminded her of her first part in a school play. She smiled up at the Negress, looking as tender and as gentle as she was able. (43–44)

This pattern—Mr. Copperfield rejecting encounters while Mrs. Copperfield becomes further involved—is repeated several times in *Two Serious Ladies*. When, for example, the American couple first meets Pacifica, Mr. Copperfield engages in only superficial conversation and then decides that he is tired and wants to return to the hotel. Mrs. Copperfield, "much too nervous," prefers "to spend a little more time" in Pacifica's company, and goes with her to the Hotel de las Palmas.

Mrs. Copperfield's relationship with Pacifica is her most serious encounter with a Panamanian. She abandons her husband in order to spend time in the company of this young prostitute, but it is not clear what exactly she hopes to get out of such a relationship. Even though Mrs. Copperfield is wealthy and American—both attributes of power in Panama—she cannot assert her will and clings desperately to Pacifica. Once again, the normal power structure is inverted: Pacifica dominates and Mrs. Copperfield almost meekly follows. The most important scene of the novel, in this regard, occurs when Pacifica takes Mrs. Copperfield to a secluded beach. Pacifica immediately undresses and enters the water. Without the slightest qualm, she can stand naked in front of Mrs. Copperfield while the American woman tries "to decide whether or not to remove her own clothes" (95–96).

The situation on the beach reiterates the inversion that has taken place in the power structure. Normally in American travel literature on the tropics, native nakedness is seen as a sort of weakness and an indication of inferiority. A common scene, for example, has the American traveler, fully clothed, observe and describe naked native women bathing or washing clothes. The tone of such passages ranges from derision to incredulity, but in all instances it is evident that the clothed have, by implication, power over the naked—somewhat like the armed have power over those without weapons.

Once again, Bowles subverts the convention. In *Two Serious Ladies*, it is Mrs. Copperfield who feels weak and embarrased by the Panamanian's nudity:

> When at last Pacifica grew tired of splashing about in the water, she stood up and walked towards the beach. She took tremendous strides and her pubic hair hung between her legs sopping wet. Mrs. Copperfield looked a little embarrased, but Pacifica plopped down beside her and asked her why she did not come in the water. (96)

When Pacifica talks Mrs. Copperfield into removing her clothes, the American woman's nakedness brings her further under the control and will of the Panamanian. She is intensely aware of the inferiority of her own body: "Mrs. Copperfield undressed. She was very white and thin and her spine was visible all the way along her back. Pacifica looked at her body without saying a word. 'I know I have an awful figure,' said Mrs. Copperfield" (96). Pacifica then leads her into the water, and in a dramatic moment Mrs. Copperfield's dependency on Pacifica is made evident. She cannot swim, and must surrender completely to the other woman:

> Pacifica started to swim, dragging Mrs. Copperfield along with her. As she had only the use of one arm, her task was an arduous one and she was soon breathing like a bull. The touch of her hand underneath the head of Mrs. Copperfield was very light—in fact, so light that Mrs. Copperfield feared that she would be left alone from one minute to the next. (97)

This is the critical moment of their encounter. Mrs. Copperfield, having surrendered completely to Pacifica, feels "happy and sick at once" and has to beg Pacifica: "Don't leave me." The Panamanian has complete control of her. Here Bowles has succeeded in creating a moment unmatched in other American tropical narratives, a moment in which an American's wealth and whiteness lose value and positional superiority is given up in favor of total submission to the Other. Perhaps Laura, in Katherine Anne Porter's "Flowering Judas," comes close to such a moment—when for example she accedes to Braggioni's request that she clean his guns. But Laura has control of the situation in a way Mrs. Copperfield clearly does not, and Laura never completely yields. Frieda Copperfield is certainly unlike other traveling Americans—fictional or nonfictional—in Central America, and her experience there is both more profound and more disturbing than the experiences recounted and reiterated in dozens of American texts.

Compare, for example, Mrs. Copperfield's experience with that of another Bowles character, the anonymous traveler in "A Guatemalan Idyll." This American traveler, a man, has a Central American encounter every bit as disturbing as Mrs. Copperfield's, but unlike her, he dismisses the experience as unimportant. Even though a Guatemalan woman has seduced him, he never really surrenders to her, and in the end decides to reject any serious implications in his encounter with the tropical peoples. While the sexual experience takes Mrs. Copperfield to the edge of vulnerability, for the traveler it is merely "one of those things that you don't want to remember next morning" (339). For him, it is just another meaningless experience, the kind that travelers are unfortunately subjected to when forced to leave home:

> "Well," he told himself, "there is no use making myself into a nervous wreck. What is done is done, and anyway, I think I might be excused on the grounds that: one, I am in a foreign country, which has sort of put me off my balance; two, I have been eating strange foods that I am not used to, and living at an unusually high altitude for me; and three, I haven't had my own kind to talk to for three solid weeks." (350)

The traveler easily rejects any possibility of profundity in his experiences. "I sure have been giddy in this place," he says, "but the bad dream is over now" (357). Guatemala—"a crazy Spanish country"—has meant nothing to him, and upon departing he can declare simply, "I don't think I will come back here again" (358).

Mrs. Copperfield, by contrast, must return. At the end of *Two Serious Ladies* she announces that she cannot live without Pacifica, "not for one minute," and that she is therefore returning with the prostitute to Panama. For Mrs. Copperfield, Panama comes to represent the fulfillment of some deeply felt and urgent need. She looks past the surface of the place, past the abject and frightening reality that initially presented itself to her, and she embraces the "dangerous" world that she has found there.

Bowles, too, embraces that world. Panama represents, in her imagination, something similar to what Africa represented in the work of one of Bowles's favorite authors, Céline. In *Le voyage au bout de la nuit*, Céline depicts an African colony, Bambola-Bragamance, in which whites have reached a state of decadence in their colonial excesses. They are lost derelicts who "melt worse than butter" in the tropical climate. In many ways, Bowles's work is also about the dereliction of whites in the tropics, but it is a dereliction with a twist: not only do the characters revel in it, they actually seem to benefit from it. This, at any rate, is Mrs. Copperfield's view:

> "True enough," said Mrs. Copperfield, bringing her fist down on the table and looking very mean. "I *have* gone to pieces, which is a thing I've wanted to do for years. I know I am as guilty as I can be, but I have my happiness, which I guard like a wolf, and I have authority now and a certain amount of daring, which if you remember correctly, I never had before." (197)

Happiness, authority, daring: these are the qualities she gains by going to pieces in the tropics. "Going to pieces" in this context means several things, including escaping her staid husband and taking up with a female lover. It also means foregoing the resistance that typifies the usual American traveler's experience in Central America. Her happiness and her authority—and, one presumes, her freedom—result from her willingness to push through the screen, to enter into Pacifica's world, without the resistance that Mr. Copperfield or the traveler or Celine's characters exhibit.

The ultimate success of Mrs. Copperfield's venture is ambiguous. She may succeed only in discovering that she too is displaced and coming undone in a derelict demimonde. On the other hand, there may be for her a happiness of sorts in the nutty life of Colón; if there is, it is a happiness that depends upon fleeting and all too fragmentary moments of human contact. It is a happiness that can only be gained by risking an encounter with the Other. Bowles suggests that such an encounter is both threatening and comforting. For Mr. Copperfield, the threats are too much; he follows in the tradition of American travelers whose initial enthusiasm for the tropics soon wanes. His interest in Panama is superficial. Ultimately, his presence is artificial, he sees only what he has expected to see, and his tour is designed to confirm those expectations.

Mrs. Copperfield, on the other hand, becomes involved in the way that an ordinary tourist like her husband will not. Unlike other Americans, she does not "stick pretty much" in her own quarter. She seems to recognize, albeit implicitly, that on the imperial frontier established systems of difference, based on positional superiority, can be abandoned without undue harm. She discovers, through an encounter with an unfamiliar Other, an unfamiliar Self. Mrs. Copperfield's discovery constitutes Jane Bowles's intriguing contribution to American discourse on Central America.

Notes

1. I will not speculate here on just why this is so, but it does seem clear that neocolonialism, predicated on the capitalism of multinational corporations, has never attracted creative minds into its ranks the way that British colonialism sometimes did.

2. Recent works by Joan Didion, Robert Stone, and Paul Theroux contribute to the subgenre, of which Bowles's novel is the precursor. Also, it should be noted that I have not mentioned Paul Bowles's Central American novel, *Up Above the World*, which is one of his weaker works. Several of his Central American short stories, however, are important contributions.

3. The details of this intriguing journey of two fine writers are covered in Millicent Dillon's *A Little Original Sin* and Christopher Sawyer-Lauçanno's *An Invisible Spectator*.

4. Apart from literature set in Central America, a somewhat larger body of works takes other parts of Latin America, especially Mexico, for a setting. We can also include Melville's tropical works, such as *Typee*, some of Twain's travel writing, and the works of several contemporary writers, such as Paul Theroux. Many of the recent Vietnam novels also share these conventions.

5. A convention that has been amply reiterated in Hollywood movies, e.g., *Indiana Jones* and *Rambo*.

4

Family Dynamics in Jane Bowles's •
In the Summer House

Peter G. Christensen

THE EXPLORATION OF RELATIONSHIPS between women, particularly those between mothers and daughters, that we find in Jane Bowles's play, *In the Summer House*, comes to us from a period when this subject was either ignored because deemed insignificant or viewed negatively in the misogynistic social climate of the time. No doubt the subject was also neglected during the 1950s because few contemporary plays by women were produced then. Given this cultural silence on mothers and daughters and the exclusion of the female playwright's perspective from the stage, it is not surprising that audiences had a difficult time understanding *In the Summer House*.

Even a comparison of Bowles's play with the two other well-known plays by American women from that period emphasizes Bowles's originality in both subject matter and style. Dorothy Parker and Arnaud d'Usseau's *The Ladies of the Corridor* and Lillian Hellman's *The Autumn Garden* show more conformity to the prevailing norms of American theater: characterization, plot, and values are more conventional and less ambiguous than in Bowles's play. Although both Parker's and Hellman's plays share Bowles's concern with family issues, they focus more on the mother-son relationship, a pattern characteristic of some of American theater's most famous works: *The Glass Menagerie, Death of a Salesman, A Long Day's Journey into Night*. Neither Parker nor Hellman focuses solely on mothers and daughters as does Bowles. Parker's and Hellman's styles are also more conventional than Bowles's, for Bowles relies a great deal on unresolved ambiguity in both character and action, challenging the audience to create a narrative logic that avoids reduction to common clichés. The result is a play of psychological complexity and emotional intensity without easy resolution of conflict.

In particular, Bowles's audience is forced to create a scenario that explains the relationship between a mother and a daughter by filling in a story around clues that are given in the play's five scenes. In order to do so, Bowles challenges us to exam-

49

ine our predispositions toward the issues of mothering that have been structured by social norms. Although the 1950s provided audiences with few tools to question conventional attitudes toward motherhood, the postfeminist 1990s has greater resources.

Vivien E. Nice's *Mothers and Daughters: The Distortion of a Relationship* provides an essential overview of some of the inhibiting views about women as mothers that need to be cleared away. We should first note that there is much more writing from the point of view of daughters about mothers than the reverse. Thus it is immediately striking that Bowles has concentrated on the mother, Gertrude, rather than the daughter, Molly, in the play.

Second, our society tends to give value to those qualities seen as masculine, such as assertiveness, independence, and rationality (5). So a fair evaluation of dependency and relatedness is difficult to achieve. It is important that we keep this bias in mind as we consider whether Molly's desire at various times to stay with her mother is supposed to be seen as immature or regressive.

Third, psychoanalytical theories have had a misogynistic slant which is not always apparent on the surface. According to Nice:

> The misogynistic theory which underlies much mental health and child abuse work has also been central in interpretations of the mother-daughter relationship. A core belief that adult mental health has its origins in the earliest relationship between mother and child accounts for this centrality. Even where feminists have sought to interpret the theory, there has often remained a mother-blaming, mother-hating emphasis . . . which seems to suggest that mothers are to blame for perpetrating women's oppression and that the answer lies in an increase in father involvement in early child care. (7)

Considering that *In the Summer House* depicts a family with an absent man, Gertrude's husband/Molly's father, we must be careful that we do not assume that Molly would have been better off if she had had a father. Nor should we take it for granted that her decision to marry Lionel represents in part the desire for the love of a man that was denied to her in childhood.

Fourth, Nice points out that the idea of emotional "ambivalence" is used to pathologize the mother-daughter relationships in which women have feelings of both love and hate. Nice writes that ambivalence is not accepted as normal because society fosters an idealized, unrealistic, and potentially damaging view of the mother as all-loving and all-giving:

> The daughter is seen as having ambivalent feelings toward her mother, feelings of both love and hate which are interpreted as unhealthy and which are seen as causing the daughter problems in her relationship with her mother. To a lesser

extent the mother is considered to hold ambivalent feelings towards the daughter in her desire to hold onto her daughter and to push her away. (11)

One can guess that some of the reviewers shared in this fear of ambivalence when the
play was first produced, for the claims that it was deranged, neurotic, and morbid
(Dillon, *Life* 218) seem predicated on the feeling that mothers and daughters should
not have the feelings that are demonstrated in the play.

Fifth, we tend to forget that motherhood should be considered a developmental
process in the life cycle of women. The power of the daughter to transform the life
of the mother is often ignored. Citing Nancy Mairs's essay, "On Being Raised by a
Daughter," Nice reminds us that we tend to assume that adulthood signifies completion and forget that "the spurts of growth and sluggish spells of childhood never
cease" (15). To be the mother does not mean to be in control pure and simple. In
Bowles's play the mother does change, and she is clearly not in control of the situation with Molly in the last act. One might constructively compare this situation
to that in the earlier play, *The Glass Menagerie*, by Bowles's friend and supporter,
Tennessee Williams. Williams shows a mother trying to get her daughter to take
action, but the mother is a fully formed character who is not growing in an interac-
tive relationship with her daughter.

Finally, patriarchal social and economical constraints are overlooked when we
expect mothers to be all-nourishing. We pay little attention to the social construction of motherhood that leads to isolation of the mother from other women, depression, and economic hardship. *In the Summer House* places Gertrude's economic
problems in clear view, as she has tried to raise money by taking in boarders and is
turning to an unsatisfactory romance with Mr. Solares at the play's beginning to
insure her financial security. This economic reality takes part in prompting Molly to
marry as well.

We have suggested that much of the psychological interest of the play comes
from its ability to engage us in examining our assumptions about mothers and
daughters. The play has no thesis, but it helps us realize that, although there are no
ready answers to problems between mothers and daughters, greater problems are
often created by assuming from the start unrealistic relational models and developmental processes and by failing to understand the mother's viewpoint.

Certainly the first scene can be interpreted so that Gertrude is the bad mother
that Americans were warned against in the post World War II era by such authors
as Philip Wylie in his *Generation of Vipers*. Indeed, according to Beverly Birns and
Niza ben-Ner, the 1950s may well have been the peak period for mother-bashing.
In this conservative decade, "as mothers were told of the joys of housewifery, they
were also vilified for providing either too little or too much love" (58). Thus we must
ask if Gertrude is accurately described as a "bitch" by Mrs. Constable (Bowles,

Works [1978] 248) and whether she incarnates the "witch" of Lionel's imaginings (284).

Gertrude's famous opening harangue cues us in on her bad habits. She knows how to substitute verbal violence for physical violence, calling out, "If I believed in acts of violence, I would burn the summer house down" (208). She criticizes her daughter, implying that Molly's apparent laziness is contributing to their economic insecurity. Molly's physical traits are turned into moral failings, as when Gertrude says, "Don't you think you could correct your walk?"

Gertrude is a cold-hearted person in her courtship of Mr. Solares, for money seems to be her only consideration. She is already plotting to keep his sister at a distance. Gertrude's references to lecturing her previous husband on "letting his father's interest go to pot" (209) may show her to be a nag who drove her husband to seek refuge by socializing with other men away from home.

Alienated and depressed, Gertrude recognizes that "a shadow passed over my life and made it dark" (210). However, she is unwilling to face the depth of her depression. So she forces herself into a better mood by sitting with the lights switched on at night and drinking fizzy water.

Strongly identified with her father, Gertrude portrays herself as a forceful individual like her father. She tells herself that she was her father's favorite when it is obvious to the audience that she is living in a fantasy. In contrast, Gertrude identifies Molly with mockery, "an underhanded Spanish trait of yours you inherit from your father" (213).

Gertrude closes by implying that Molly secluded in the garden house is like the snake in the Garden of Eden, for Molly has turned paradise into hell (213). Gertrude threatens to get rid of Molly by sending her to business school when she herself marries Mr. Solares. After Molly's departure to get ready for company, Gertrude declares that "Nature's the best company of all" (214).

Such a tongue-lashing would initially appear to show Gertrude in the worst light possible and push us toward extending all our sympathy to Molly as the play develops. However, when Molly first shows anger at Vivian's attempts to attract her mother's attention and then weeps at the prospect of leaving her mother on the double wedding day, we realize that our initial impression is incomplete. If Gertrude is a bad mother, why is Molly so attached to her? Also, why does the play begin with Gertrude's harsh treatment of Molly and then shift to show Gertrude declaring that she loves Molly so much that she does not want to lose her? Have we judged Gertrude unfairly or has Molly learned to love her oppressor? And if we ask if they are caught up in codependency, we risk assuming the bias against motherhood that Nice has warned us against.

We can continue to see Gertrude as the villain: Gertrude takes an arrogant at-

titude toward Mr. Solares's relatives (1, i), fails to create an adequate distance between herself and the intrusive Vivian (1, ii), patronizes the grieving Mrs. Constable
(1, iii), and finally tries to blackmail Molly into staying with her on her return from
Mexico by suggesting that she knows that Molly has murdered Vivian. As Molly
makes her escape to a better life with her husband, Gertrude is left retreating into
the past, saying, as the curtain falls, "When I was a little girl . . . "

If we experience *In the Summer House* in this fashion, then it is possible to see
it as part of the status quo of mother-bashing in our society. Millicent Dillon implies
that we should sympathize with Lionel in trying to get Molly away from Gertrude,
for what "is clear . . . is that he is the only one who understands Molly" (*Life* 230).
In the unfinished novel, *Out in the World*, according to the Dillon biography,
Andrew faced the same issue of getting away from his mother (*Life* 230). Is Gertrude
so bad that we should compare Gertrude to Violet, the monstrous mother, in
Tennessee Williams's *Suddenly Last Summer*?

In one of the few scholarly discussions of the play, Judith Olauson in *The American Woman Playwright*, also takes a harsh view of Gertrude, although she stresses
the ironic humor in the play. She reads the close of the last scene as follows:

> Regaining possession of Molly is the solution to [Gertrude's] dilemma, she
> thinks, but Molly's dependence on her mother's strength has been destroyed,
> and their relationship ends with Molly following her husband and with
> Gertrude's final admission of her true feelings of jealousy toward her sister and
> hatred for her father. The depths of the never-realized relationships between
> father and daughter and mother and daughter are made evident by implica-
> tions that both Gertrude and Molly, out of their separate jealousies, caused the
> deaths of the individuals who threatened their illusions, Vivian and, presumably,
> Ellen. (86)

There seems to be some jumping to conclusions here. We never know definitively
what part Molly played in Vivian's death, and we should not conclude from Gertrude's
statement, "I know what it's like to wish someone dead," that she had a role in killing
her sister (295).

Furthermore, should we not give Gertrude the benefit of the doubt and believe
that she has learned something in Mexico? She realizes that she had betrayed herself
and emotionally abandoned Molly. She tells Lionel and Mrs. Constable:

> I don't know why I got frightened, why I married again. It must have been . . . it
> must have been because we had no money. That was it . . . We had so little
> money, I got frightened for us both . . . I should never have married. Now my
> life's lost its meaning . . . I have nightmares all the time. [. . .] I've lost Molly.
> My life has no meaning now. It's their fault. It's because I'm living their way. (282)

Despite the fact that Gertrude has never been kindly disposed toward Mr. Solares's sister and his other relatives, the fact remains that they can be a trivial and unreflecting lot, satirically treated since the first scene. Gertrude does realize that she has only been caught up in their world because of her monetary problems. We need a more complex view of the play that will recognize the better side of Gertrude and the economic problems she faces in raising Molly.

Does Lionel really offer Molly a better alternative than Gertrude? First, it is certainly possible that they are not engaged in a sexual relationship, and it is not even entirely clear whether Molly is heterosexual or not. She may have married Lionel because her mother was leaving her. Second, for a person who has a vague ambition to become a religious leader, he is easily swayed by his brother's offer to take part in selling barbecue equipment back in St. Louis. Third, Lionel apparently assumes that as the husband he can make the decisions as to where they are going to live. Whereas Molly is willing to stay with Lionel and her mother is close proximity, Lionel sets the condition that Molly must make a choice between himself and Gertrude. Even Gertrude is willing to risk letting Molly choose. Furthermore, Molly wants to be free because, as she says, "You've all changed" (233). Presumably Lionel, with his sudden career change in mind, has also become unrecognizable.

A more reasoned consideration of the action should not assume that Lionel is necessarily better for Molly than Gertrude is. If Molly did have a hand in Vivian's death, then it suggests that Gertrude has an instinctive knowledge about her daughter's actions that indicates the ability to identify with her emotionally. And, despite the fact that one of Gertrude's worst actions is to suggest to Mrs. Constable that Molly murdered Vivian, Mrs. Constable's claim that nothing happened only reinforces the retreat from reality that has always been one of Molly's problems. Mrs. Constable herself has retreated into alcoholism after her daughter's death and has little hold over the outside world. In contrast, Bowles writes the final action so that one can believe that, in the last moment, Gertrude comes to a better understanding of reality. Gertrude says, "Go," and Molly leaves. Gertrude may realize that her emotional blackmail was a terrible means of trying to keep her daughter. The final line, "When I was a little girl," may show her attempting finally to be honest about her difficult relationship with her father.

The alternative of assuming that Molly had nothing to do with Vivian's death leaves us with a Gertrude who has probably projected her own murderous feeling toward Ellen onto Molly. However, Dillon's interviews with Paul Bowles make it more likely that we are to assume that Bowles felt Molly did play a role in Vivian's death because Bowles believed that sins in theater plots needed to be clearer than those in fiction (*Life* 230). Even so, it is not clear that such extratextual information should have any part in our interpretation of the play.

Our response to the play is inextricably connected with our attitude toward ambivalence. When Molly leaves the garden house to get ready in the first scene, she does not get into a fight with her mother or act as if she has been maltreated. In fact, she has insisted at one point, "I would never mock you" (213), and the stage direction is given as "tenderly." Molly is prepared to accept her mother's behavior, suggesting that Gertrude must have a much better side or that she is in uncommonly bad spirits, perhaps even taking out all the hostility she feels for Mr. Solares on her daughter. Her furious knitting (212) may also indicate that thinking of her mother and sister has put her in a bitter state.

It is only in the third scene that another possible reason for Gertrude's anger is suggested. She feels so dwarfed by Molly's love for her that she deliberately tried to alienate her to make breathing room for herself. Here we are reminded of the fact that the mother is not always the person leading the relationship. Gertrude says:

> But I was right, there's something heavy and dangerous inside you, like some terrible rock that's ready to explode . . . And it's been getting worse all the time. I can't bear it any more. I've got to get away, out of this garden. That's why I married. That's why I'm going away. I'm frightened of staying here with you any more. (253)

Molly may be placing on Gertrude the hope that she can provide for all her wants and needs. As Vivien Nice notes, women can identify with the "idea of the 'little girl' within, the needy child who wishes to be looked after. . . . It is then only a short step to believing that this 'little girl' exists because we were not loved enough by our mothers" (8). Or, as Adrienne Rich puts it, "Few women growing up in patriarchal society can feel mothered enough; the power of our mothers, whatever their love for us and their struggles on our behalf, is too restricted" (243). To think of Molly as a needy little girl keeps us biased against Gertrude. If we sympathize with needy Molly and accuse Gertrude of bad mothering, we fail to adopt the broad perspective we need to see that both women are reacting to social situations that defy easy mastery.

The other two mother-daughter relationships stand in marked contrast to that of Gertrude and Molly. Mrs. Fula Lopez, who seems to be without a husband, has no major disagreements with her daughter Frederica. The latter is a likable young woman who offers Gertrude a bouquet of flowers when she is in great distress after her final confrontation with Molly. Frederica shares in her mother's acceptance of day-to-day pleasures of life, moving through existence unreflectively but with enthusiasm. Frederica does not engage in a psychological struggle to escape from her mother's influence. They share a similar world view. Maturation does not necessitate abandoning the mother.

Certainly Vivian's relationship with her mother is more troubled. Mrs. Constable is more self-effacing than Gertrude, as we can see from her willingness to live apart from her. She tells Mrs. Lopez:

> My daughter likes her freedom, so we have a little system worked out when we go on vacations. I stay somewhere nearby but not in the same place. Even so, I am the nervous type and I would like Mrs. Eastman Cuevas to know that I'm at the Herons . . . You see my daughter is unusually high spirited. She feels everything so strongly that she's apt to tire herself out. I want to be available just in case she collapses. (225)

We learn more about this relationship when Vivian tells Lionel that she had tried to run away before unsuccessfully. Now she fantasizes a future with Lionel, and even with Molly, declaring, "she has to escape from her mother too" (237). Since Vivian appears to have a crush on Gertrude, whom she admires, she replies that it is natural for daughters to escape from their mothers. Thus the relationship between Molly and Gertrude is placed between the poles of Vivian's desire to escape her mother and Frederica's willingness to stay close to hers.

Bowles's exploration of mother-daughter relationships led her to write a thesis-less psychological play about the troubled interaction of mother and daughter. In contrast, Dorothy Parker's *The Ladies of the Corridor* avoids such complex characterizations and offers a clearer thesis: American women are socially conditioned to devote their adult lives to mothering, and, when their children leave home and their husbands die, they are left without the emotional resources to forge a new life.

Parker took the Hotel Volney in Manhattan, where she lived, as the model for the Hotel Marlowe (Meade 347). Female companionship in this environment is represented in the play as a fate worse than death. To become one of the "ladies of the corridor" and have nothing to do but talk to other women is not presented as a possible starting point for deeper sustaining friendships but the situation widows and divorced women are forced into *faute de mieux*. Her play has no big confrontation scenes between women such as that between Gertrude and Mrs. Constable, because Parker is not much concerned with interactions among women.

The Ladies of the Corridor has a number of plots rather than a single one, but the most important character is Lulu Ames, a recent, relatively young widow who has come from Akron to Manhattan without any definite reason other than that her son's family lives there. The question raised is whether she will find a better fate than becoming one of the ladies of the corridor, like Mrs. Gordon, Mrs. Lauterbach, and Mrs. Nichols. In what Parker thought of as the relatively happy ending, she chooses solitude over female companionship. These women seem emotionally dead compared to Gertrude, Mrs. Constable, and Gertrude's Mexican in-laws. The rejection of a women's world is equated with rising above loneliness in Parker's value system. Even so, Parker had originally wanted to conclude with Lulu joining the ladies of the corridor, an ending she found more realistic and pessimistic. (The alternate ending can be found as an appendix to Arthur F. Kinney's edition of *The Coast of Illyria* [195–210], Parker's play about the Lamb family.)

Whereas *The Ladies of the Corridor* confronts the damage that is constantly done to American women by forcing them to devote their whole lives to their families at the expense of an education and a career, the only solution offered is for a woman to learn to survive entirely on her own in her career without the possibility of emotional support from other women. Thus Constance Mercer, the widow who has found worthwhile employment, has the good fortune and enterprise to be chosen to go on a trip to Europe for job advancement, an experience that she will handle through her own variety of rugged individualism. Lulu ruins her love affair with Paul Osgood and treats him terribly almost as if she seeks a perverse kind of triumph. She has finally faced life's essential loneliness and despair, as if she were accepting the truth of life rather than the unnecessary outcome of a perverse, self-fulfilling prophecy. In contrast, anguish in Bowles's play is based on the idea that people do need to interact and that solitude does not necessarily bring epiphany.

Parenthood in *The Ladies of the Corridor* has absolutely no appeal, as we can tell by looking at the play's three other mothers. The most unfortunate one is Mrs. Lauterbach, who seldom sees her daughter in Oswego. Whether her daughter is fond of her or whether circumstances are more to blame is never clarified, but in either case Mrs. Lauterbach invests her emotions in the hope that she will be asked by her daughter to visit for the family holidays. As she tells Mrs. Gordon:

> I wrote asking if I could come up to Oswego to see them over Thanksgiving. Now I'm kind of scared. I think I'll wait for the morning mail, because there might be a letter from them asking me to come. If this got there first, it'd make me look pushing. (6)

At the end of the play, a year later, she is going to go to Oswego for Thanksgiving. However, she still admits that she was fearful of opening her daughter's last letter, for it might have indicated a change of plans. In this situation, the daughter has the ability to make all the important final decisions because the mother is no longer a central part of her life. In *In the Summer House*, Gertrude, as mother, is not reduced to passively acting to meet her daughter's conditions.

In contrast to Mrs. Lauterbach, Lulu Ames, the second mother, appears to be better off, for her son lives in New York City. However, since she has not indicated that she will be moving, her daughter-in-law, Betsy, does not feel that her husband, Robert, should make any sacrifice of his business socials so that they can be with Lulu. In the course of the play Robert and Betsy move to the suburbs and have a second child. They have effectively excluded Lulu from their lives. Still, Lulu's life was not very fulfilling before this turn of events. Recalling her life to her son, she comments:

> It isn't all a horror story. There were nice things, you know. When you were a baby, and then when you were a little boy before you went away to school. After that there were other things. Oh, hope for instance; and then a sort of inertia, I suppose. And then, every day, of course, all the puttering little errands that make you think you're doing something. The days were slow, but the years went quickly. (20)

Although Lulu has some insight into her life, she is unable to learn how to avoid making future mistakes. Parker presents a situation in which the wife discovers that togetherness has just been a facade disguising loneliness, whereas Bowles shows Gertrude as a woman who had been left on her own by her first husband, a man who liked to have jolly times with other men. Consequently, she became a more assertive person than a passive Lulu.

In the course of the play Lulu falls in love and has an affair with a much younger man, Paul Osgood, recently divorced. However, she is never able to overcome the anxiety that she looks ridiculous with a man whom she knew vaguely when he was a small boy. Smitten by unwarranted jealousy and the bad effects of too much time on her hands, she never manages to capitalize on her insights into her nonproductiveness:

> Look, Bob, would you honestly feel any better if I was taking a course in art appreciation at Columbia? Or did you have in mind something nobler? Such as volunteering to run the switchboard in a hospital? . . . Bob, there really isn't a thing I can do. And because I know I can't, I've come to believe that I don't want to. And by now I believe that very firmly. (53)

Not surprisingly, romance is the last refuge for a woman suffering from such passivity. This declaration of independence from meaningful activity probably serves to assert her independence from her son, since it may also be directed at him as an indication that she believes his suggestions are just a means of getting her out of the way as a potential nuisance to his wife. The conflict between mother and son here shows lack of relationship rather than the intensity of bonding as seen between mother and daughter in *In the Summer House.*

Parker makes clear that Lulu's inertia comes from both her own failings and the social constructions of the time. Lulu is able to tell her friend Connie what is wrong with her generation of women:

> I guess there's something lacking in a lot of women; nobody's ever one of a kind. We were told you grew up, got married, and there you were. And so we did, and

so there we were. But our husbands, they were busy. We weren't part of their lives, and yet we never learned how to be alone. It's different with girls now. (97)

Here Lulu finds an improvement in a world in which learning how to be alone is the path to existential wisdom. In contrast, in Bowles's play, Molly's problems with Lionel come from the fact that they try to work out a viable relationship within marriage. Molly does not assume Lionel has nothing to offer her.

For all her faults, Lulu is still a more likable figure than the play's third mother, Mrs. Nichols, an invalid who is looked after by her son, Charles. Enormously domineering, she thrives on emotional blackmail. Some years before, her son had been dismissed from a position as a teacher of young boys when a student had accused him of making sexual advances. Mrs. Nichols had paid the boy's parents to settle out of court. Since that time Charles has spent his days going to the zoo and his evenings working on a stamp collection with his mother. When he finally applies to teach English to young boys again, his mother threatens to expose his past. So Charles abandons his pursuit of a job. It is hard to interpret Charles's passivity to his mother and his general listlessness. On the one hand, he may be attracted to young boys, for he has not made any other job applications in years. Or he may be so depressed as a closeted gay man that he cannot take the initiative to look for other work. The child attached to the parent is here presented as an object of scorn rather than as a person deserving understanding, as is the case with Bowles's Molly.

Lillian Hellman in *The Autumn Garden* does not cast Parker's cold eye on motherhood, but she does not show Bowles's deep concern with it either. The character for whom she has the most sympathy, Sophie Tuckerman, a poor relative taken into her Aunt Constance's household, desires to go back to her mother in war-ravaged Europe, although her mother cannot offer her any of the finer things in life, perhaps not even food and security. Nevertheless, Sophie gets her wish, and in so doing she calls into question what has consistently been taken as the theme of the play, the human inability to overcome habit, routine, and inertia (see Bryer passim). The key lines are delivered by Colonel Griggs, one of the many mediocre middle-aged people in the play:

So at any given moment you're only the sum of your life up to then. There are no big moments you can reach unless you've a pile of smaller moments to stand on. The big hour of decision, the turning point of your life, the someday you've counted on when you suddenly wipe out your past mistakes, do the work you've never done, think the way you've never thought, have what you've never had— it just doesn't come suddenly. You've trained yourself for it while you've waited—or you've let it all run past you and frittered yourself away. (490)

Actually, Sophie's sudden grasping of an opportunity to return to her mother exposes this lament as another self-deception in a lifetime of excuses. Contrary to Colonel

Griggs, Hellman really believes that with will power one can break out of the past. Ironically, *In the Summer House* shows more of this suspicion that we cannot escape the past than does *The Autumn Garden*.

Sophie breaks away from the South even though she has not been in training: she makes no small stands as they come along. Now suddenly she abandons her engagement to Frederick Ellis. Sent to New Orleans to her maternal Aunt Constance in 1944 to escape the devastation of Europe, she has imagined that she has been unable to act. Caught in an upcoming arranged marriage to the indifferent Frederick Ellis, she confides to Ned Crossman, a weary, alcohol-soaked, middle-aged loser:

> Did I want to come? I have no place here and I am lost and homesick. I like my mother. I—Every night I plan to go. But it is five years now and there is no plan and no chance to find one. Therefore I will do the best I can. (429)

When an unusual opportunity comes her way, Sophie departs from character and takes it. She blackmails Nina, the wife of the mediocre artist Nick Denery, who has just compromised her reputation by falling asleep on her bed while in a drunken, flirtatious state. She does not want charity, so she insists on blackmail as more honorable. What interests Hellman here is not a daughter's bond to an offstage mother but the triumph of youth over age and of Europe over America. In the late 1940s America is in sad decline; the future of the world lies in repairing a world in obvious ruins. America, the autumn garden, must be escaped if one is to live. Unlike Bowles's summer house, which is both a real place and a symbol of Molly's conflict with her mother, Hellman's garden is far less real than symbolic, even less real than Chekhov's cherry orchard.

In contrast to Sophie's offstage mother, we have Frederick's mother, Carrie Ellis, a domineering woman, unwilling to let him go, but not a monster mother like Mrs. Nichols. Their problems come to a head over Frederick's friendship with Payson, a young avant-garde author of ill repute, who seems to be treating homosexuality in his novels (402). Frederick wants to break his agreement to escort his mother to a party in order to proofread one of Payson's manuscripts instead. Carrie tells him that he must not back out on her. Later she becomes upset that Frederick plans to sail to Europe with such a scandalous author. However, Frederick is dumped by Payson, and the voyage together never materializes. Consequently, Hellman does not have a climactic confrontation between mother and child. Instead, Frederick, a person who remains attached by art and by family ties to American decadence, serves as a counter-example to Sophie.

As we look back over the three plays for our conclusions, we find that four interesting points of comparison emerge. First of all, Bowles begins with the assumption that parent-child relationships should turn into adult-adult relationships, but Parker and Hellman do not. There would be no plot of *In the Summer House* if we began with the idea that a mother nurtures her daughter up to a certain age and then just lets her go, as is the case with various species of animals.

Parker, on the other hand, assumes that the end of the nurturing period closes the real relationship. Lulu can offer her son and her grandchildren nothing of any real vitality, and Mrs. Lauterbach's daughter's letters cannot be held up as models of personal interaction. In addition, Charles and Mrs. Nichols have only the stamp collection in common, in this case, not a symbol of a shared curiosity but of something filling in dead time together.

For Hellman, the lack of interaction of adult parents and children has its roots in the sense of Chekhovian failure that animates the play. The people in the older generation have failed to live up to either their talents or their dreams. They wallow in pettiness, false illusions, and alcoholism. The question is whether the youth can escape from their fossilized, autumnal world. Sophie recognizes her duty to her mother and the hard times she is facing, but if she actually has a deep relationship with her mother, Hellman does not allow her to give voice to it.

Second, although each play is dramatically enlivened by suspicions of homosexuality, only Bowles is able to treat this problem with adequate complexity and understanding, probably because she had the capacity to love others of her own sex. The lack of romance between Molly and Lionel is not a blot on Molly and neither is her complex attraction to her mother. So if we choose to think that she may be lesbian, we are not stuck with the pernicious stereotype that she is unable to mature and find heterosexual romance. Perhaps because of her own marriage to Paul, Jane Bowles had the intelligence to see that shared interests and compatibility are more important than romance in a marriage. If Molly's marriage has no sexual component, it is not less valid.

Parker, unfortunately, falls into the trap of furthering the stereotype of the domineering mother keeping her gay son in tow, a presentation which is not far from the old psychoanalytic idea that the domineering, even castrating, mother actually caused the son to be gay. The only twist that Parker allows on this idea is the possibility that the mother hates the son for being gay and thus dominates him out of her contempt.

Hellman never entertains this type of overt homophobia, but she is also without Bowles's understanding. If we decide that Payson is gay, which does fill in a narrative hole in the most concise way, then we are back in a world in which decadent older gay authors flirt with callow gay-ish youths and eventually abandon them to their mothers or marriages of convenience. However, in fairness to Hellman, we must state that, through the conversation of Frederick and Sophie, she also recognizes that compatibility is more important to a marriage than romance.

Third, Bowles has chosen for her heroine a woman whose money problems are more visible than the mothers in the other plays. Gertrude has economic decisions to make that Lulu Evans and Mrs. Nichols do not. She can and does do damage to her relationship with her daughter by remarrying for a sense of economic security.

The damage done by Mrs. Nichols in *The Ladies of the Corridor* is entirely separate from the feeling that she will not be able to survive if Charles leaves her for work or to make his own life. She clearly knew how to invest her money, and this shrewdness is presented as an extension of bossiness, not of prudence. Lulu also has no financial needs, as we see from the fact that she never discusses an actual job. Working seems well out of her imaginative realm. In Parker's world, only financial problems would keep her in the orbit of her son's family, since she has no contribution to make to his life.

In *The Autumn Garden*, real financial need functions differently for mothers and daughters than in *In the Summer House*. Although we know that Sophie's mother is economically needy, we do not know if she has been pressuring Sophie to return, and one tends to doubt it, since she did send her over to America. This offstage mother remains a shadowy figure of self-sacrifice. And whereas her decision to separate from her daughter should not be mocked, it leaves Hellman in the position of opting not to question the limitations of that role of sacrificial victim.

Fourth, Bowles has written a play in which the problems are too complicated to be solved by willpower. Obviously, it takes us nowhere in interpreting *In the Summer House* to say that all the characters should resolve to be more kind to one another and not repeat past mistakes. Even if they did, the problems of mothers and daughters and husbands and wives would still be very disturbing because complex relationships cannot be worked through in this fashion.

Parker, however, suggests that massive applications of willpower can improve life. Lulu could resolve not to be a possessive lover because she could resolve to lead a life that is not wholly devoted to romance. And she watches Constance Mercer, the good example, decide to improve her life and self-image by taking the legitimately frightening trip to Europe for her job. Could Mrs. Nichols choose to be better to Charles? It is hard to say. She does not seem to need his love. He fulfills her need for dominating someone.

Hellman, through her comments on *The Autumn Garden*, authorized a reading whereby Colonel Griggs's speech is the theme: a life of lethargy paralyzes the will, and then it is too late to act. Although there is a problem with this reading, since Sophie's sudden action seems to prove it false, in any event the "autumn garden" is a world without Bowles's psychological complexity. One can tell what one should have done, so mistakes are clear. On the other hand, what Gertrude should have done is not at all apparent.

Although Bowles has written the best of the three plays, it does not mean that the other plays are weak. Instead, analysis shows that Bowles makes the most use of narrative gaps for the audience to fill and in so doing creates an ambiguity that provides a deep emotional response. The need for the audience to forego a clearly announced thesis makes the play distinctive for its time. On a thematic level, Bowles again seems more contemporaneous to us. Because of the gains made by the feminist movement, fewer women will end their lives as Parker's "ladies of the corridor." Also inadequate, but for other reasons, is Hellman's image of America as the "autumn garden" that Sophie leaves behind. It seems too genteel in the 1990s to capture the violence, poverty, and despair Americans face. In contrast, the "summer house," a contested emotional space in the lives of a mother and daughter, has not lost its relevance.

5

Mommy Dearest

Mothers and Daughters in Jane Bowles's *In the Summer House* and Other Plays by Contemporary Women Writers

Charlotte Goodman

For we think back through our mothers if we are women.
—Virginia Woolf, *A Room of One's Own*

The first knowledge any woman has of warmth, nourishment, tenderness,
security, sensuality, mutuality, comes from her mother. That earliest enwrapment
of one female body with another can sooner or later be denied or rejected,
felt as choking possessiveness, as rejection, trap, or taboo.
—Adrienne Rich, "Motherhood and Daughterhood"

THANKS IN PART to the efforts of feminist scholars, the history of the American theater has begun to undergo a transformation. Following the recent publication of bibliographies and anthologies of plays by women, critics have now undertaken the task of describing the characteristic themes, forms, and language of women playwrights and of constructing a history of dramatic literature by women.[1] The process of reclaiming the works of American women, however, is still far from complete. Moreover, while such plays by American women as Susan Glaspell's *Trifles*, Lorraine Hansberry's *Raisin in the Sun*, Marsha Norman's *'night, Mother*, and Beth Henley's *Crimes of the Heart* have been included in college play anthologies during the last decade, most of the contributions of women playwrights to the American theater remain unfamiliar to readers of dramatic literature and to the average theatergoer alike.

Until its recent revival at the Vivian Beaumont Theater during the summer of 1993, a virtually forgotten play by an American woman writer that has just begun to receive scholarly attention is the play I wish to discuss here: Jane Bowles's *In the Summer House.*[2] First produced in New York in 1953 under the direction of José Quintero, this haunting drama about three pairs of mothers and daughters featured Judith Anderson and Mildred Dunnock in leading roles. It was briefly revived in New York in 1964, 1977, 1980, and 1993. Directed by Joanne Akalaitis and starring Dianne Wiest, the latest production, like the earlier ones, received mixed reviews, though one reviewer pronounced *In the Summer House* to be "a play whose time has boldly arrived."[3] As I shall argue, *In the Summer House* certainly deserves to be better known than it is to date. Mixing realism and surrealism, comedy and melodrama, the lyrical and the mundane, Jane Bowles considers in this play one of the most important relationships in women's lives: the complex and frequently conflict-ridden relationship of mothers and daughters, whom Bowles depicts as alternately seeking to maintain the vital emotional bonds between them and to separate from one another.

To date, Bowles's play has been compared frequently to Tennessee Williams's *The Glass Menagerie.* Like *In the Summer House,* Williams's play dramatizes the relationship between a domineering mother and a reclusive daughter. The fact that Paul Bowles composed the incidental music for both Williams's play and that of Jane Bowles established an auditory link between these two works; moreover, Williams himself suggested a connection between his work and that of Jane Bowles when he named the gazebo on his property at Key West "Jane Bowles's Summer House."[4] However, although the relationship between Amanda and Laura Wingfield in Williams's play does bear some resemblance to that of Bowles's Gertrude Eastman Cuevas and Gertrude's daughter Molly, the primary focus in Williams's play is the relationship of a son to his mother and sister. As I shall suggest, a more apt comparison can be made between *In the Summer House* and the ever-growing corpus of plays by women that focus principally on the difficult dynamics of the mother-daughter relationship. As Judith E. Barlow points out, *In the Summer House* presents a "radically unsentimental view of maternity," one that contrasts markedly with the representations of motherhood that abounded in the plays, magazines, and television shows of the fifties (xxii). Among the plays about mothers and daughters with which I shall compare Bowles's play are Lillian Hellman's *The Little Foxes* (1939), Shelagh Delaney's *A Taste of Honey* (1958), Tina Howe's *Painting Churches* (1983), Wendy Wasserstein's *Isn't It Romantic?* (1983), and Marsha Norman's *'night, Mother* (1983).

In the Summer House dramatizes a time of emotional upheaval in the life of the mother-daughter pair whose relationship takes center stage: Gertrude Eastman

Cuevas and her adolescent daughter, Molly. Bowles's Gertrude, an improvished widow who has been reduced to taking in occasional boarders, is about to marry again; and Molly is devastated by the impending separation from her mother. Gertrude's way of dealing with Molly's separation anxieties is to marry her daughter off to the first eligible man who appears at the beach house in Southern California where Molly and her mother now are living: a young man named Lionel who is a waiter in a nearby restaurant.

The economic dependency of middle-class mothers and daughters on men in a patriarchal society where women are supported financially by fathers and husbands is evident in the first scene of Bowles's play. Symbolizing his function as economic provider, Mr. Solares, Gertrude's fiancé, leads an entourage of his servants on-stage and directs them as they lay out a lavish picnic he has provided for Gertrude and Molly. To underscore his function as economic provider for the women in his household, Bowles has Mr. Solares's widowed sister, Mrs. Lopez, who also appears on-stage in this scene, mention that he has bought her fifty-nine dresses. Molly will, at the very least, be well fed as a result of her own marriage, for, even though Lionel's job as a waiter in the Lobster Bowl is a menial one, it is also one that can guarantee plentiful food for Molly. And just as Mr. Solares is in charge of the women in his own domain, so will Lionel take charge of Molly. Bowles suggests this symbolically by having Lionel first appear bearing an oversized cardboard figure of Neptune, King of the Sea. While the figure of Neptune is used by Lionel to advertise the Lobster Bowl, this emblem also functions as a signifier of Lionel's own power. Although he is awkward, unassertive, and unsure of himself, Lionel will succeed nevertheless in wresting Molly from her mother's grasp by the end of the play.

Yet despite the fact that Bowles's opening scene shows how the mother seeks solvent males to support herself as well as her daughter, Bowles also suggests that mother and daughter remain emotionally dependent on one another even after both have been separated by their respective marriages. As Gayle Austin has observed, a psychoanalytic feminist theorist such as Nancy Chodorow who emphasizes the importance of the pre-Oedipal period in female development provides a useful paradigm for interpreting the dynamics of the mother-daughter bond in this play.[5] Chodorow postulates that mothers simultaneously push their daughters away, encouraging them to marry, and seek to maintain their pre-Oedipal connection with their daughters, while daughters try desperately to separate from their mothers but also cling to them. In the most recent production of Bowles's play, the importance of the pre-Oedipal period was emphasized visually by the setting and also by the sound effects that the director, Joanne Akalaitis, introduced in Act One. Though neither of these elements is specified by Bowles herself, the setting, a dilapidated garden on the coast of Southern California, was dominated in this production by a large, muscular, twisting root resembling an umbilical cord; moreover, the sound of the sea, alternately soothing and conveying a threat of engulfment, provided an aural reminder of the amniotic fluid in which the fetus is carried.

During the first act, Molly appears to be more dependent on Gertrude than Gertrude is on her. Molly clings to her mother, even though Gertrude endlessly harangues her about her appearance, her lack of drive, her persistent withdrawal into the womblike vine-covered summer house on their property, where, like a young child, Molly spends her days reading comic strips and daydreaming. But despite her overt hostility to Molly, Gertrude also verbally expresses how important Molly has been to her. Admitting that she had wanted to leave Molly's father before Molly was born, "To give it all up . . . start out fresh" because Molly's father lacked ambition and drive, Gertrude nevertheless maintains that Molly became all-important to her. "All my hopes were wrapped up in you then, all of them. You were my reason for going on, my one and only hope," she asserts. Gertrude's ambivalent feelings about Molly, however, are suggested by Bowles's stage directions, which indicate that Gertrude "knits furiously" as she utters these words (Bowles, *Works* [1978] 209).

Act One concludes with the double wedding of Gertrude to Mr. Solares and Molly to Lionel. Gayle Austin, author of the most extensive and insightful discussion of *In the Summer House* to date, points out that, when we see Molly and Gertrude dressed in their bridal gowns at the wedding reception that celebrates both of their marriages, we seem to be witnessing two brides who have married one another, for their grooms are not visible. "This," says Austin, "is the oedipal scene Freud could not envision: the daughter's desire to marry her first love object, her mother" (70). Distraught as she contemplates her imminent separation from Gertrude, Molly begs her not to leave. Until this moment Molly has succeeded in repressing the fact that the wedding heralds her coming separation from her mother and has stuffed herself with food at the wedding feast, but she is now overcome with grief. Admitting that she could not picture what it would be like when her mother left, she cries, "I thought so long as we were here we'd go right on being here. So I just ate right along with the others like you say" (251). In Act Two, Molly will again remind the audience that she is still "wedded" to her mother when she takes out her bridal dress to wear to her mother's birthday celebration.

Nancy Chodorow has observed that even though mothers and daughters recognize their need to separate, both also are "convinced that any separation between them will bring disaster to them both" (135). The mutual dependency of mothers and daughters as well as the shifting dynamics of the relationship between them is dramatized in Bowles's play as mother and daughter reverse their positions. By the end of *In the Summer House*, it is Gertrude who pleads with Molly not to abandon her. Gertrude's marriage to Mr. Solares has proven to be a mistake. Acutely disliking the "pandemonium" of Mr. Solares's household, one that is filled with "old, ladies, babies, men, little girls, everyone jabbering," and "a dirty, noisy parrot, trailing around loose," she announces that she is "never going back." One of the unpleasant incidents at Mr. Solares's house that she describes was the moment when he had said that men should never have given women the right to vote and she had slapped him (277–78). Now clasping her daughter "greedily" to her breast and begging Molly to leave Lionel, Gertrude offers to loan Molly a nightgown Molly always had loved, one with "different colored tulips stitched around the neck" (287). Though Molly ultimately decides to remain with Lionel, she admits to Gertrude that she too has longed to return home and to abandon her life with Lionel at the Lobster Bowl. "After a while I could sit in that booth, and if I wanted to I could imagine I was home in the garden . . . inside the summer house," Molly says wistfully. Seizing upon this confession, Gertrude tries to lure her daughter back by informing her that she has already given orders to have the summer house rebuilt for Molly (289).

As Millicent Dillon, Bowles's biographer, points out, Bowles was unsure whether to emphasize at the end of the play the impulse of both mother and daughter to separate or their equally strong need to remain connected. While Molly opts for separation rather than connection in the published version of the play as well as in the productions that have been mounted thus far, in another version of the play Gertrude drags Molly away, while in yet another version, Molly, tormented by her conflicting need to separate and to remain with her mother, runs out and kills herself (*Life* 229). According to Dillon, Bowles struggled endlessly with the play's conclusion, taking ten years to complete her writing of the play (192). The difficulty Bowles encountered in choosing how to conclude the mother-daughter struggles is understandable given the fact that she was attempting to dramatize the ambivalent feeling that the mother-daughter relationship generates in both the older and the younger woman.

Complementing Gertrude and Molly are two other mother-daughter pairs: Mrs. Lopez, the widowed sister of Mr. Solares, and her daughter Frederica; and the widowed Mrs. Constable and her daughter Vivian, who have come to California for a vacation. The former are the most convivial mother-daughter pair in the play. Although Bowles does not indicate Frederica's age in the script, her behavior and her relationship to her mother suggest that this prepubescent girl represents the pre-Oedipal period in female development, for she is still firmly attached to her mother. The first time Frederica speaks, she speaks in "a scarcely audible voice," virtually repeating the very words her mother has just uttered (219), and, in Act Two, we see Mrs. Lopez and Frederica kissing one another as Frederica insists, "I want to be with my mother" (230). Mrs. Lopez's behavior in Act One, however, suggests that she, like Gertrude, is wont to behave aggressively to her daughter on occasion: as the stage directions indicate, she gives Frederica "a terrific shove" at one point (223) and pokes her at another (228); moreover, just as Gertrude does to Molly, Mrs. Lopez continually orders Frederica about.

Of the three mothers in the play, the least assertive is Mrs. Constable. Dominated by her adventurous, outgoing, loquacious daughter, Vivian, Mrs. Constable admits that Vivian has insisted they occupy rooms in different places. "My daughter likes her freedom, so we have a little system worked out when we go on vacation," she says, "I stay somewhere nearby but not in the same place" (225). After Vivian is either pushed off a cliff by Molly or falls off a cliff—the event occurs offstage and what actually transpired is never made clear by Bowles—Mrs. Constable, in mourning for her "bird," Vivian, clings instead to Molly and Lionel. Frequently inebriated after her daughter's death, the bereft Mrs. Constable now chooses to spend her days near Molly and Lionel at the Lobster Bowl, surreptitiously observing them as they play cards each night. Nevertheless, even though Mrs. Constable adopts Molly as a surrogate daughter after Vivian's death, it is Mrs. Constable who ultimately urges Molly to leave California with Lionel, thereby recognizing Molly's need to separate not only from Gertrude but from her as well.

Jane Bowles's portrait in *In the Summer House* of the relationships between women is not a positive one for the most part. Perhaps it was Molly's statement, "I don't like girls" (234), as well as the rivalry among the women characters in the play, that led one reviewer of the 1980 production to observe that *In the Summer House* verges on being misogynistic (Dace 78). Yet I would argue that rather than indicting women for the way they behave towards one another, Bowles is criticizing a patriarchal society that pits woman against woman, making them rivals for the attentions of more powerful men instead of accomplices in the struggle to subvert the hegemony of patriarchy. Gertrude, for example, vividly recalls how her beloved father, her "model," her "ideal," used to play with the "long golden curls" of her sister, and, though Gertrude doggedly maintains that she herself was her father's "true love," she says during a moment of reverie that her father once took her "frail and delicate" sister to a hotel, leaving the jealous Gertrude behind (212). At the end of the play, revealing how jealous of her sister she had been, Gertrude confesses that, like Molly, she "knows what it means to wish someone dead" (295). The failure of fathers to nurture their daughters adequately is suggested by a compelling symbol Bowles introduces in a dream that Gertrude recounts. Situated in a "cold room" with her father, Gertrude is given a box of macaroons by him for Molly. However, when Molly begins to eat a macaroon, Gertrude realizes that it is "hollow, just a shell filled with dust," and she hears her father laughing at her (281).

Mr. Solares, like Gertrude's father, also pits one female against another. He pushes ahead of his sister, Mrs. Lopez, in his hurry to greet Gertrude, "squeezing his sister's arm rather painfully against the gate post" (214); and in Act One, Scene ii, when Mrs. Constable arrives, Mr. Solares, in Gertrude's presence, invites Mrs. Constable to dinner, prompting Gertrude, who had previously turned down his invitation to eat chop suey with him at a restaurant, to say, "Perhaps I might try chop suey with you, after all." Overhearing what Gertrude has said, Mrs. Lopez chuckles, "Now you want to go eat chop suey because he's talkin to the other lady. You be careful, Senora Eastman Cuevas, or you gonna lose him" (243).

Like Gertrude, Mrs. Constable and Molly see other women as rivals. Mrs. Constable confesses to Molly:

> My husband never loved me.[. . .] They belonged to each other, my husband and Vivian. They never belonged to me . . . ever . . . But I couldn't admit it . . . I hung on hard to the bitter end. When they died . . . Nothing was left . . . no memories . . . Everything vanished . . . all the panic . . . and the strain . . . I hardly remember my life. They never loved me . . . I didn't really love them . . . My heart had fake roots. . . . (263)

Recognizing, in turn, how destructive female rivalry can be, Molly says to Lionel, "A lot of people want to yank you out and get in themselves. Girls do anyway." Then she observes, "I haven't got anything against men. They don't scheme the way girls do . . . " (235). This observation expresses a profound mistrust of women on Molly's part. Bowles's play, however, also demonstrates why men do not have to "scheme" the way women do: less dependent financially and emotionally than any of the women in the play, both Mr. Solares and Lionel appear less vulnerable than the female characters. The only female character who seems to be as autonomous as the two male characters is an outspoken waitress at the Lobster Bowl named Inez. Belonging to a different social class than Gertrude or Vivian Constable or Mrs. Lopez, Inez is a "spirited but a little coarse" (266), self-supporting woman who swears like a man and has the stamina to prepare three hundred oyster cocktails in a day. She asserts her desire to "everybody to be going his own independent way," and emphasizing her own laissez-fair attitude, she tells Mrs. Constable, "I'll bet you wouldn't find ten men in this town as democratic as I am" (270).

With the exception of the independent, working-class Inez and the female servants, however, the other women in the play frequently appear to be rivals, not only for the attentions of men but for the attentions of other women. Vivian arouses jealousy in Molly when she courts Lionel's favor by telling him that she would like to sell her grandmother's jewelry and open a restaurant with him, although Molly is much more perturbed by the attention Vivian lavishes on Gertrude than on Lionel. Just before Vivian's fall from the cliff, Molly says angrily to Vivian:

> The day you came I was standing on the porch watching you. I heard everything you said. You put your arm around my mother, and you told her she had beautiful hair, then you saw my summer house and you told her how much you loved it. You went and sat in it and you yelled, Come out Molly. I'm in your little

house. You've tried in every way since you came to push me out. She hates you. (238)

Even though Molly is almost a grown-up when she utters this speech, her attachment to her mother remains a dominant force in Molly's life, causing Molly to feel threatened when Vivian begins to flatter Gertrude. Vivian maintains that she and Molly both need to escape from their mothers (237); yet as soon as Vivian meets Gertrude, she immediately begins to court the favors of this older woman whom she wants to adopt as a surrogate mother.

Jane Bowles once observed about the summer house, a key symbol in her play:

> The people in my play are all covering up something about themselves. Each of them has her summer house. A summer house is a flimsy construction with no foundation. It is an invention of those who seek reality, a sanctuary, a haven from the terrors which haunt them. (Qtd. in Sievers 402.)

I believe that the play was an "invention" that served to give voice to the "terrors" haunting Bowles herself. An only child like Molly, Vivian, and Frederica, Jane Bowles, like the three daughters in her play, experienced the death of her father when she was still a child. Moreover, rivalry among women, a recurring motif in the play, was a phenomenon very familiar to Bowles, who spent a great deal of time during her childhood in the company of her mother's sisters, the progeny of Austro-Hungarian Jewish immigrants. Inevitably, the sisters' children would be compared to one another. "When the aunts wanted to explain us to strangers," one of Bowles's cousins wrote, "they always said, 'Jane is smart and Mary Jane is pretty' " (Dillon, *Life* 8). No doubt *In the Summer House* also encoded the jealousies and feelings of competition that Bowles observed in the group of Arab women with whom she had become intimate in Tangier during the years when she was writing this play. The most crucial relationship in the play as well as in Bowles's own life, however, was the mother-daughter relationship, one characterized alternately by the desire to separate and the need to connect. According to Millicent Dillon, those who witnessed the interactions between Jane Bowles and Bowles's mother, Claire, observed that Claire was "doting and possessive, adoring and ambitious for her" (*Life* 22). However, also anxious to lead her own life, the widowed Claire hired a governess to look after Jane, sent her away to boarding school, and after Jane developed tuberculosis of the knee following a fall from a horse, put her in a sanitarium for two years in Switzerland, during which time Claire herself lived in Paris, though she visited Jane frequently. Mother and daughter were reunited after Jane returned to America. During that time, Jane lived with her mother, who hired a beautician to do their hair and nails twice a week and carefully supervised Jane's choice of clothes (*Life* 32).

Often reclusive and dependent like Molly, Jane on occasion could also be out-

going, even manic, like Vivian Constable. Bowles spent many hours at home read-
ing in bed during her adolescence, but she also began to frequent lesbian bars in
Greenwich Village and to develop crushes on female torch singers. Although
Bowles informed her mother that she was a lesbian, when Bowles's mother decided
to marry again, she nevertheless began to pressure Jane to find a husband as well.
Jane Bowles later wrote about this period in an autobiographical fragment:

> Like all mothers she hoped I would marry a man who would take care of me.
> By the time I was twenty she had become extremely nervous, because she
> wanted to get married herself. (Dillon, *Life* 48)

Thus Jane Bowles's mother was relieved when Jane and Paul Bowles announced that
they had decided to get married. Though he was hardly the nice Jewish young man
that Claire Bowles had hoped her daughter would marry, he solved Claire's problem
about what to do with Jane. Claire's marriage took place one month after Jane's did.
The marriage of the Bowleses, both of whom were bisexual, was highly unconventional, however, for both of them had numerous homosexual relationships even
though they remained married to one another. During the period when she was writing
her play, Jane Bowles, in fact, was emotionally involved with Helvetia Perkins, a
woman approximately her mother's and Gertrude's age, who prodded Jane to choose
between herself and Paul Bowles, just as Molly is forced to choose between her
mother and Lionel. In 1943, Jane Bowles dedicated her novel *Two Serious Ladies* to
the three important figures in her emotional life at that time: "Paul, Mother, and
Helvetia."

I summarize these biographical details to suggest the autobiographical under-
pinnings of *In the Summer House*. Anxious to fictionalize the autobiographical material, however, Jane Bowles took great pains to create an elaborate plot that included multiple mother-daughter pairs and the melodramatic possibility of a fatal
accident motivated by jealousy. This plot, I would argue, served the function of
providing a screen to conceal the autobiographical elements in her play, a play
written and performed while her mother was still alive. Nevertheless, even though
she avoided blatant self-exposure by replicating the mother-daughter pairs and by
making no direct allusions in the play to two important facets of her own identity—
her Jewish heritage and her lesbianism, one can detect many parallels between her
own life and the experiences of all three mothers and daughters in the play. A
mother who nags her reclusive daughter to "correct her walk" (208); the almost
simultaneous marriages of a mother and daughter; the daughter's marriage to someone connected to the Lobster *Bowl* (emphasis mine); the heated emotions, whether
of love, hatred, or jealousy among the female characters; even the speech of Inez,
the tough waitress—all have their analogues in Jane Bowles's own life. Like Gertrude, Jane Bowles briefly lived in Mexico with her husband. Moreover, the seaside

Southern California setting of the play mirrors the landscape that Jane Bowles observed daily from the room she occupied in the Bowles's small house in Tangier during the years when she was working on the play; in this household, the Arab women who had become part of her entourage communicated with one another in their own language, just as the three Mexican servants of Mr. Solares converse among themselves in Spanish.[6]

In 1953, when *In the Summer House* was first produced, it seemed an anomaly, for relatively few well-known plays or novels or short stories at the time dealt with the relationship of mothers and daughters. "We have heard the story of fathers and sons, of mothers and sons, even of fathers and daughters, but who has sung the song of mothers and daughters?" Cathy N. Davidson and E. M. Broner wrote in 1980 in the forword to an anthology of essays they edited, *The Lost Tradition: Mothers and Daughters in Literature* (xi). Since the publication of that groundbreaking volume, a great many literary and scholarly works by women have explored the mother-daughter relationship. In the theater, however, relatively few plays have dealt with mothers and daughters. Referring to the "vortex of mother/daughter dynamics" as "the last, dark continent to be explored in dramatic material," Kathleen Betsko has called this subject a "hot potato" (Betsko and Koenig 50), perhaps alluding to the reluctance of many women playwrights to express openly on stage the conflicts between mothers and daughters. Jane Bowles, no doubt, would have concurred about the difficulty of dealing with the relationship of mothers and daughters in a play, for she struggled many years to find a dramatic form adequate to express her own ambivalent feelings about her mother and the various other mother-daughter dyads in which she was involved during her lifetime, sometimes playing the role of daughter and sometimes that of mother. A similar ambivalence about the relationship of mothers and daughters is also evident in the plays of other contemporary women playwrights who have explored the "dark continent" of mother-daughter dynamics in their plays. Among the playwrights whose plays about mothers and daughters one might compare with *In the Summer House* are Lillian Hellman, Shelagh Delaney, Tina Howe, Wendy Wasserstein, and Marsha Norman.

Lillian Hellman's *The Little Foxes* presents the most antagonistic mother-daughter pair in this group of plays. Clever, assertive, calculating, Regina Giddens on the surface appears to represent the archetypal "terrible mother," an aggressive harridan who seeks to manipulate her sensitive, ailing husband and her idealistic adolescent daughter, Alexandra. Yet, as I have argued elsewhere, Hellman's portrait of Regina is much more complex than would appear on the surface.[7] Like Jane Bowles's Gertrude, Hellman's Regina is victim as well as victimizer: disinherited by her father, who left his fortune to her brothers, Regina schemes to obtain the money that will allow her to live her life as she wishes to live it. When her marriage fails to provide her with the financial autonomy she seeks, she is willing to abandon any moral scruples she might have in order to triumph over those men—her father, her brothers, and her husband—who have sought to curb her power. Like Bowles's Gertrude, Regina controls her daughter during the first part of the play, though she insists she has always had Alexandra's best interests at heart. "You're young, you shall have all the things I wanted. I'll make the world for you the way I wanted it to be for me," she tells Alexandra (223). Like Molly, however, Alexandra ultimately asserts that she intends to separate from her mother, thereby causing the balance of power to shift from mother to daughter, just as it does in *In the Summer House*. Hellman's ambivalence about Regina is similar to Bowles's ambivalence about Gertrude: both playwrights create domineering mother figures whose energy is fascinating though potentially destructive to their daughters' well-being.

Yet another embattled mother-daughter pair are Helen and Jo in Shelagh Delaney's *A Taste of Honey*. Left without a husband to support her and her daughter Jo, Helen is tired of living in one decrepit rooming house after another in a rundown Lancashire town; like Gertrude, Helen decides to marry a relatively affluent though somewhat unappealing man who will provide for her. Jo, a sensitive young woman like Molly, then tried to make a life of her own, moving to a flat with a homosexual young man who becomes a surrogate mother for her. Like Gertrude, Helen, whose marriage has proven to be a mistake, reappears at the play's conclusion and attempts to forge a new connection with her daughter. Both Bowles and Delaney initially show the mother to be more forceful than the daughter. Two survivors, Gertrude and Helen berate their daughters for being impractical dreamers. At the end of *A Taste of Honey*, however, Helen, like Gertrude, seems more vulnerable than she did in Act One; as she speaks to Jo about her own difficult childhood and thwarted dreams, Helen emerges as a more sympathetic character than she appeared to be initially.

It is no surprise that the emergence of the women's movement of the 1970s gave rise to a plethora of literary and scholarly works that explored the mother-daughter relationship. By 1983, when Tina Howe's *Painting Churches*, Wendy Wasserstein's *Isn't It Romantic?*, and Marsha Norman's *'night, Mother* all were produced, many other works about mothers and daughters had also been published. Like Jane Bowles's *In the Summer House*, what the theoretical studies of mothers and daughters as well as the plays by Howe, Wasserstein, and Norman all describe is the emotional complexity of the mother-daughter relationship: one that expresses both love and hatred, resentment and affirmation, the need to connect and the need to separate.[8]

While the mothers are the more dominant and articulate figures in the plays of Bowles, Hellman, and Delaney, the daughters, more assertive than either Bowles's Molly, Hellman's Alexandra, or Delaney's Jo, emerge as the most important characters in the plays of Howe, Wasserstein, and Norman. In fact, one might be tempted to say that these three more recent plays provide a forum for the daughters to voice their grievances against their mothers: Howe's Mags, an artist, bitterly recalls how her mother had once destroyed a work of art the ten year old Mags had created out of melted crayons, and she explodes in anger against her mother several times during the course of the play; Wasserstein's Janie accuses her mother of forever meddling in her life; and Norman's Jessie, an epileptic, criticizes the way in which her mother has dealt with Jessie's illness. All three playwrights also present in a negative light the calculating maneuvers of the mothers to find husbands for their daughters. However, as is true of *In the Summer House*, by the end of these plays we are afforded an understanding of the mothers' plight as well. Howe's Fanny Church describes her feelings of abandonment because her husband, a celebrated poet, has neglected her; now, confronting old age herself, she must assume the arduous role of caretaker for her senile husband. Wasserstein's Tasha Blumberg expresses how hurt she feels because her daughter Janie never seems eager to see her or Janie's father. And after Norman's Jessie convinces her mother that she is really intent on committing suicide, Mama evokes our sympathy when she tells Jessie how much she needs her and insists that she will forever feel she has failed Jessie if Jessie actually carries out her plan to kill herself. As is true of Bowles's Molly, all three daughters assert their right to shape their own destinies by the time the curtain falls, but the mothers succeed in arousing our sympathies as well.

In his 1962 critical study of contemporary American drama since World War II, Gerald Weales described *In the Summer House* as a play that seems to "belong to no particular group," calling it "a genuine stray" (224). Although Weales agreed with those reviewers who found Bowles's play "strangely attractive (225), he did not seem to know what to make of it.[9] Neither did Walter Kerr, who applauded Bowles's "evocative language" and "fresh, bold, patently truthful" characterization, but criticized the failure of her characters to demonstrate "the power of choice and the exercise of will" (*How Not to* 134). As I have suggested, however, Bowles's achievement can best be appreciated if her play is examined in the context of other plays by women whose objective it is to dramatize the ambivalent, oscillating feelings generated by the mother-daughter relationship. Seeking an appropriate dramatic form that would allow her to speak publicly about the central conflicts in her life but also to avoid the pitfall of flagrant self-exposure, Bowles created a play that is quirky, idiosyncratic, original. Far from being a "genuine stray," Bowles's *In the Summer House*, nevertheless, has much in common with other plays by contemporary women playwrights that examine the mother-daughter relationship. Such plays express the mutual emotional dependence of mothers and daughters, explore the tensions that divide them, describe the often painful process of separation, and dramatize poignant moments of connection as mothers and daughters confide their fears and longings to one another.

Notes

1. See, for example, Gayle Austin, *Feminist Theories for Dramatic Criticism* (Ann Arbor: U of Michigan P, 1990); Judith E. Barlow, ed., *Plays By American Women 1930–1960* (New York: Applause Theatre, 1994); Judith E. Barlow, ed., *Plays by American Women: The Early Years* (New York: Avon, 1981); Helen Rich Chinoy and Linda Walsh Jenkins, eds., *Women in American Theatre: Careers, Images, Movements* (New York: Crown, 1981); Honor Moore, ed., *The New Women's Theatre: Ten Plays by Contemporary American Women* (New York: Random, 1977); Judith Olauson, *The American Woman Playwright: A View of Criticism and Characterization* (Troy, NY: Whitson, 1981); June Schlueter, ed., *Modern American Drama: The Female Canon* (Cranbury, NJ: Associated University, 1990); Victoria Sullivan and James Hatch, eds., *Plays By and About Women* (New York: Random, 1973).

2. The most extensive discussions of *In the Summer House*, to date, appear in Gayle Austin, *Feminist Theories for Dramatic Criticism* 67–72, and Judith Olauson, *The American Woman Playwright: A Review of Criticism and Characterization* 81–88.

3. Jan Stewart, "Into the Ocean of Family Alienation," *Newsday* 2 August 1993: 45.

4. Donald Spoto, *The Kindness of Strangers: A Life of Tennessee Williams* (Boston: Little, 1985) 162.

5. For a comprehensive survey of the contributions of feminist psychology to the understanding of mother-daughter bonding as it is depicted in dramatic literature, see Chapter 4 of Gayle Austin's *Feminist Theories for Dramatic Criticism*.

6. In Tish Dace's negative review of a 1980 revival of the play (*Soho Weekly News* 4 June, 1980: 78), she says that the Spanish characters are caricatures. On the contrary, I find Bowles's treatment of these Mexican women to be quite unusual, in that when they speak among themselves, they speak in their own tongue, often expressing anger or annoyance. I wish to thank Peggy Boyers, who translated for me the passages in the play that are written in Spanish.

7. See Charlotte Goodman, "The Foxes' Cubs: Lillian Hellman, Arthur Miller, and Tennessee Williams," in June Schlueter, ed., *Modern American Drama: The Female Canon* 130–42.

8. For the most extensive bibliography to date about theoretical discussions of the mother-daughter relationship see Mickey Pearlman, ed., *Mother Puzzles: Daughters and Mothers in Contemporary American Literature* (New York: Greenwood, 1989).

9. Opening in New York on 29 December 1953, *In the Summer House* ran for less than two months. Though the reviewers' response to the play was mixed, most found the language and characterization in it memorable, and Louis Kronenberger included it in his *Best Plays of 1953*. In an interview in *Vogue*, Jane Bowles, disappointed by the play's reception, said, "There's no point in writing a play for your five hundred goony friends. You have to reach more people" ("Candidates" 137).

6

Sister Act

A Reading of Jane Bowles's Puppet Play

Regina Weinreich

A QUARRELING PAIR, a play first performed in 1945 with puppets by Kurt Seligmann and music by Paul Bowles, is a two-character sister act—on the surface, a mannered domestic take on sibling rivalries. Less a conversation, or a fight really, the drama between Harriet and Rhoda is a *tour de force* so private, context seems beside the point; observing them has great surreal effect. We've encountered this kind of *non sequitur* interaction before in the Jane Bowles *oeuvre*, in the various pairings of *Two Serious Ladies* and in some of the short stories, such as "The Iron Table." Here in the posturing of puppets is a pithy variation on the Bowles preoccupation with societal conformity and torturous familial intimacy.

What is a puppet play anyway? is there anything to which we can liken it? What exactly might Jane Bowles have been trying to accomplish in this rare genre?

At the time that Jane Bowles created *A Quarreling Pair*, both of the Bowleses were part of an artistic milieu in New York City that included several Surrealists who had emigrated from Europe to escape the war and American artists who were influenced by Surrealism—most notably members of the Kirk and Constance Askew salon, which both Bowleses frequented, and the literary duo, Charles Henri Ford and Parker Tyler, who were the founders of *View*, a Surrealist magazine that published art and literature by Man Ray, Max Ernst, André Breton, Yves Tanguy, Leonora Carrington, and Salvador Dali, among others. (See Caponi, *Paul Bowles* 103, 115; Dillon, *Life* 92–93; Sawyer-Lauçanno 22, 206, 242–43.) In the same year that Jane Bowles's puppet play was written and produced, Paul Bowles published his first short story, "The Scorpion" in *View*, and he was also invited to edit the South American issue. Jane Bowles, on the other hand, having received mediocre reviews of her novel, *Two Serious Ladies* (published in 1943), was turning her attention from fiction to drama, with the encouragement of her friends in the theater, such as Oliver Smith and John Latouche. She had begun writing her full-length play, *In the Summer House*, in 1945, and *A Quarreling Pair* was no doubt a part of her new experimentation with dramatic form. Although Jane had expressed a dislike of Surrealism (see Sawyer-Lauçanno 199 and Dillon, *Life* 93), primarily because of its theoretical bent, the Surrealist art world provided the opportunity to create a drama in an unusual genre suited to her offbeat sensibility.

A *Quarreling Pair* was written for John Myers, managing editor of *View*. As a young man of nineteen, Myers, from Buffalo, New York, had written in his diary, "I have three passions: poetry and puppets and paintings" (Young-Mallin n.p.). When he came to New York in 1944, he decided to make money by returning to his childhood love of puppeteering. Because his job at *View* put him in touch with the leading figures among European artists in exile and repatriated American writers, he was able to assemble a professional puppet troupe to produce what he called his "bizarreries" (Sawyer-Lauçanno 250).

When Myers first met émigré Surrealists Kurt Seligmann and his wife Arlette, he told them about his life-long fascination with puppets. Seligmann then contributed to their dramatic enterprise his knowledge of the relationship between puppets and magic in primitive rituals in which priests controlled the movements of wooden figures and snake puppets. The Seligmanns made five unusual hand puppets, several with two faces, and decorated with mirror shards, bright green feathers, and blue heads. For one of Jane Bowles's quarreling sisters, they created "a skyscraper" wig that could be tossed around in all directions (Young-Mallin n.p.).

The first plays opened at a popular, chic cabaret, Spivy's Roof, housed in a penthouse at Fifty-seventh Street and Lexington Avenue, where sophisticated patrons loved to hear Miss Spivy, "a lesbian, intellectual, hard-drinking and not very charming person," according to Ned Rorem.[1] Miss Spivy would sing ballads like John Latouche's "Existential Blues" and "The Ballad of the Tattooed Lady and the Surrealist." Spivy's nightclub had been one of Jane Bowles's favorite haunts since the late 1930s, and the owner was a friend. Well attended, the audience for the puppet premier included Charles Henri Ford, John Latouche, Morris Golde, the Bowleses, the Seligmanns, and Mary McCarthy (Young-Mallin n.p.). The first two plays presented were Charles Henri Ford's *A Sentimental Playlet* and Jane Bowles's work—each about ten minutes in length.

The composer Ned Rorem has no recollection of attending such a formal, public performance of Jane Bowles's puppet play even though Myers claimed Rorem was also at the premier (Young-Mallin n.p.). Rorem does recall in his memoir of the period providing the incidental music for Ford's "strange little puppet drama, *At Noon Upon Two*, in which two people take turns looking through a keyhole and asking one another vicariously: What's she doing now? What's he doing now? while those being spied upon dance, copulate, writhe, burn and perhaps die" (255).

Rorem says he saw *A Quarreling Pair* privately at a Halloween party given by Jane Bowles in 1952.[2]

A Quarreling Pair is a conversation between Harriet, the older, stronger-looking puppet, more concerned with propriety and pretension, the outgoing self, and Rhoda, the more tortured, inner, less able to conform sister; the dialogue is "biting, obsessional, absurd in a Beckettian way" (Sawyer-Lauçanno 250). Here is how they talk:

> HARRIET. Just mind your business. I mind mine and I am thinking about our milk.
> RHODA. I'm so tired of being sad. I'd like to change.
> HARRIET. You don't get enough enjoyment out of your room. Why don't you?
> (Bowles, *Works* [1978] 415)

So much for contiguous speech! Rather, the dialogue spirals around and makes unexpected sense with no topic left incomplete; each is enlarged by unlikely juxtapositions:

> RHODA. Oh because the world and its sufferers are always on my mind.
> HARRIET. That's not normal. You're not smart enough to be of any use to the outside, anyway.
> RHODA. If I were young I'd succor the sick. I wouldn't care about culture, even, if I were young.
> HARRIET. You don't have any knack for making a home. There's blessed satisfaction in that, at any rate.
> RI IODA. My heart's too big to make a home. (415)

No matter how much the dialogue seems dislocated and jarringly not a conversation, there is closure to the piece as a whole. The domestic scene comes full circle with each sister providing the other a nurturing/strangling milk, a discourse on the size of hearts, a tradeoff of slaps and songs; in short, having suggested the issues at stake in their lives, the plot goes nowhere in much the manner of those who wait in *Waiting for Godot*.

The play's discontinuities and resulting humor, although typical of Jane Bowles's comic style, are not so eccentric when seen as similar to the Surrealists' exploration of the world of dreams, the unconscious, and childhood. Both Jane Bowles's and Paul Bowles's works, in fact, can be seen in the tradition of the Franco-American Surrealist nostalgia for childhood. The quest for a childhood denied could be seen as a primary motivation behind Surrealism. A number of Surrealism's activities whether games, automatic writing, or political revolution—were on one level a way of trying to recapture childhood's "absence of any known restrictions," to satisfy a "hunger for the marvelous" (Polizzotti 8).

The marvelous in Jane Bowles's work has been noted by admirers like Tennessee Williams who have pointed out the magic, the almost indescribable artfulness that emerges ironically from her self-sense of artlessness. Her extreme insecurities made her doubt her talent and led to painful comparisons to Paul in which her own work is assessed as wanting: "When you are capable only of a serious and ponderous approach to writing—I should say solemn perhaps—it is almost more than one can bear to be continually doubting one's sincerity which is tantamount to doubting one's product" (Dillon, *Letters* 33). Despite her own doubts about her "experience," the reader is treated to a fresh, innocent, childlike glimpse of human nature and idiosyncrasy, apparent in all her work.

Jane Bowles's collected works takes its title, *My Sister's Hand in Mine*, from a song in *A Quarreling Pair*. Truman Capote's introduction to the *Collected Works* calls her "the eternal urchin," and "the most appealing of non-adults" (Bowles, *Works* [1978] v), and the composer Ned Rorem has noted her "childlike" quality "without being childish" (Interview in *Paul Bowles*). So it would not have been difficult for Bowles to recapture that childish banter, childish violence, childish fear of the outside world and put them in her puppets even though the puppets represent women who are, after all, in their fifties. The genre of the puppet play also allows for the on-stage violence in which the sisters clobber one another and which is unlike anything else in Bowles's work.

The discussion of the size of hearts is particularly curious. What is meant by a big heart? The capacity to be loved? To love others? Real love rather than formalities of what is expected in conventional domesticity? This idea has a poignant edge in terms of woman-to-woman relationships—indeed in all unconventional liaisons.

The biographical context for the two women in *A Quarreling Pair* is Bowles's relationship with her lover Helvetia Perkins, who was considerably older. (Interestingly, Puppet was the name of Helvetia's Pekinese [Dillon, *Letters* 41]—a possible allusion that is consistent with Bowles's sense of humor.) In contemporary parlance, women together in relationships are "sisters," especially emphasizing a kindred spirit, a oneness. Harriet sings of a dream, a vision of a girl running down the mountainside: "But wakened not yet knowing / If the name she bore was my sister's name / Or if it was my own" (418).

Sisterly alter egos? Perhaps. Where have we seen that before? If one of the early forerunners of the Surrealists were the Pre-Raphaelites, these siblings are rather like the sisters in Christina Rossetti's "Goblin Market"; Bowles's sisters could be contrasting aspects of the same personality. In Rossetti's poem, facing the lurid temptations of the goblins, one sister is reason and restraint, and the other is the more libidinous aspect of the Victorian sensibility. For Bowles, the duality is the self in the world, inner and outer, private versus posturing. The self in society is fragile, childlike, vulnerable. Fear overall predominates, fear especially of the outside.

But the inner world is also fraught with fears. One is fear of dependency (see D'Erasmo), as well as its flip side, fear of isolation. A letter to Paul dated 1947 connects isolation to the processes of writing: comparing herself to Paul she writes, "when you do write from it [isolation] . . . what you write is in true relation to your-self which is recognizable to the world outside. With me who knows?" (Dillon, *Let-ters* 33). Clearly she believes isolation a positive quality for writers, one that she lacks because hers is an "accident." The isolation may not have been her choice. Paul does say that choice itself terrified Jane, and so following Paul may have driven her to this state of isolation, emulating what for her was a way to be in the world.

In the sense that all couplings are marriages, the play can also be seen as a portrait of marriage with the Bowleses' marriage providing another biographical context for the play's embattled pair. The role of women in general at the time was widening out of the domestic scene. Furthermore, Jane's marriage, like that of many others in her circle, was between homosexual partners with extramarital liaisons. But even that freedom provided conflict for Jane Bowles, both in her work and in life. Marriage is depicted frequently in Bowles's work, and the partners are por-trayed as occupying separate and often noninterpenetrable realms. Except for occa-sional and intuitive glimpses into one another's psyches, true and sustained har-mony seems impossible. In her life, there was conflict as well. As Caponi has pointed out, the Bowleses' marriage was one of opposing temperaments and social needs (*Paul Bowles* 112–14), which led to both complementary pleasures and pain-ful conflicts. Jane asserted her independence but also committed herself to stay in the marriage. She was to follow her husband to places which were, in fact, danger-ous for her. For example, when Tangier proved to be "good for Paul but not for me [Jane]" (Dillon, *Life* 397), she stayed anyway—and drank.

If the relationship in *A Quarreling Pair* is seen as a marriage, Jane Bowles de-scribes a co-dependency that seems akin to the Surrealist concept of *femme-enfant*. As defined by Whitney Chadwick, this image was literally a woman-child, who "through her youth, naiveté, and purity possesses the more direct and pure connec-tion with her own unconscious that allows her to serve as a guide for man" (33); young, beautiful, talented, a female counterpoint to the male artistic spirit, a source of devotion to the man, she was also a repressed self that had a tinge of instability and madness. The artist Meret Oppenheim seemed to embody the *femme-enfant* attributes: a creature of grace and promise, "intuitively close to the worlds of the unconscious, the imagination and the irrational, capable of bewitching the male artist and leading him away from the confining world of the real" (Chadwick 49). But she was also a liability to herself. Most important to a reading of Jane Bowles, the *femme enfant* image provided a struggle: "the needs of the *femme-enfant* and those of the mature artist are incompatible" (Chadwick 237). This idea may go far to explain the peculiarities of the Bowleses' marriage and dependency. Rhoda's statement to Harriet, "You do live in the right, sweetie, so don't think about it" (419), suggests in tone and sentiment Jane's comparisons of herself to Paul in her letters. The Rhoda puppet also suggests that the possibility that this is the Jane character to

Paul's more stable self, the *femme-enfant* to her male muse. And there lies the contradiction—in playing muse, she is in conflict with herself as an artist and her own desire for independence. When Jane first met Paul, she declared, "He is my enemy" (Dillon, *Life* 41), yet they remained devoted to each other until her death. This puzzling statement may have been Jane's intuitive realization that the muse/wife and the artist were incompatible.

When Jane Bowles looked inside to innermost places, it terrified her. Like the heroines of Tennessee Williams's plays, she often relied on the kindnesses of others. In society, conformity and familial relationships, however untoward, however suffocating, are almost always guarantees to comfort. But the sisters are sealed in their hermetic world, stripped of pretense:

> HARRIET. You love to pretend that everything is a riddle. You think that's the way to be intellectual. There is no riddle. I am simply keeping up my end of the bargain.
> RHODA. Oh, bargains, bargains, bargains!
> HARRIET. Will you let me finish, you excitable thing? I am trying to explain that I am behaving the way I was molded to behave. I happen to be appreciative of the mold I was cast in, and neither heaven, nor earth is going to damage it. Your high-strung emotions are not going to affect me. Here's your milk. (418)

After Rhoda violently rejects Harriet's offered glass of milk, Harriet tells her, "Go away if you like." So perhaps the puppet play doesn't quite go nowhere, but somewhere. Rhoda is permitted to leave if she likes. The freedom is there for the taking. But words may permit what emotion will not. Instead of leaving, she procrastinates in a Beckettian stasis: "The moment hasn't come yet, and it won't come today because the day is finished and the evening is here. Thank God!" (419) And then, of course, Rhoda offers milk. Perhaps in milk's metaphor there lies a dubious affirmation: just enough bigheartedness, enough succor and solace to rein in the most terrifying emotions—for the moment.

Notes

1. Interview with the author, 29 January 1996.
2. Interview with the author, 29 January 1996.

7

Jane Bowles and the
Semi-Oriental Woman

John Maier

IN JULY 1948, while Jane Bowles was staying in Tangier at the Hotel Villa de France, she wrote to Paul Bowles of the "endless pleasure" she felt in looking over the Arab city: "I cannot stop looking" (*Letters* 81). For Jane it was a rare joy in "a purely visual experience." At the same time she tells Paul about the Moroccan women she has met, especially Cherifa, and notes the difficulty she had uttering her first words in Arabic: "I am slow and stupid but determined. I shall never of course be as clever as you are" (82). She was still very much the outsider when, three months later (writing from another hotel in Tangier), she explained to Paul that she finds herself "in a constant state of inferiority vis-à-vis these women" (*Letters* 108). The enormous rooms the women lived in, with "wonderful long high" walls, massive beds and printed spreads ("very Matisse") were disorienting (*Letters* 108). She worries about losing "face." The difficulty she has in placing herself finds expression in the joy of seeing things, in describing the town and the very un-Western rooms she has entered. She "cannot stop looking."

We have in English a powerful trope for this kind of displacement and the giddiness it causes. Eric Partridge reminds us of the rich associations that have developed from the Latin *oriens* (itself clipped from *sol oriens*, the sunrising), the East. Disoriented, we look east to orient ourselves. In this we are always necessarily west of the sunrising, the place of "origin" and of "aboriginal" peoples (457). Our orientation, social and sexual, requires in some way a positioning in space.

The fragmentation and repetition Millicent Dillon has found in Jane Bowles's fiction, the sudden shifts of plot, the unstable rhythms and uncertain authorial voices that mark her work ("Experiment as Character" 13–14) are evidence of a pro-

This essay is reprinted by permission of the publisher from *Desert Songs: Western Images of Morocco and Moroccan Images of the West*, by John Maier, © 1996 by State University of New York Press.

found disorientation. Like Dillon, I do not see this as Bowles herself seemed to consider it, signs of failure. Rather, that "oddity" Bowles accused herself of produced a
most compelling experimental fiction. The purpose of this essay is to examine three
stories that reflect Jane Bowles's experience in the East, in Morocco, by focusing on
the cultural construction of gender and sexual relations evident especially in spatial
imagery. Those spatial orientations indicate a wide gap between the sense of space
and gender in Moroccan and in American cultures.

It is important that Jane Bowles found herself disoriented in another culture,
an Eastern culture. That she found herself odd anywhere made it possible to see
more than other Western writers have—she could not stop looking, as mentioned
above—in the East. In the three stories considered here, "Everything Is Nice," "The
Iron Table," and "Emmy Moore's Journal," cultural constructs of gender and sexual
relations are deconstructed. Things most obvious and taken for granted turn odd in
these stories.

The disorientation that marks the protagonist in these three stories has a historical character to it as well. As Emmy Moore's wandering analysis of the self in relation to a scheme of geocultural types shows, Jane Bowles was aware of what is now
called Orientalism. For the West as a historical construct, the East provided *the* significant Other. It may have been partly by accident that Jane Bowles landed in Tangier, the gateway to the East. When she arrived, though, she already possessed a cultural map that was centuries old.

Linguists like Edward T. Hall have tried to characterize social and personal
space. Often Hall uses cross-cultural examples to bring the topic into view. Since
the Arab-Muslim world presents such a contrast to America in the way people behave in public, in their concepts of privacy, in their perceptions of personal distance
and boundaries, in matters of "face" and involvement with others, Hall devoted a
chapter in *The Hidden Dimension* to the Arab world. In *Beyond Culture*, he distinguishes between American and Arab societies as low context and high context cultures.

Jennifer Coates uses the notion of social networks in a similar way to differen-
tiate male and female language. Where she finds closed networks, with high density
and multiplex relations, Coates finds a certain kind of (nonstandard) language used
as a sign of communal identity. In contrast, where the network is open, low density,
and uniplex—where, for example, women are linked in only one way, Coates
notices a very different use of language, tending toward standard usage (78–91).
William Labov had introduced the concept of "lame" to indicate "isolated individuals on the fringes of vernacular culture." Coates asks if women, then, are "lames."
In the studies she reported on, Coates noted "that female speakers are less closely
integrated into vernacular culture, that female speakers use vernacular norms less

consistently than male speakers, and that these two findings are interrelated" (93). The feature may be related, in the case of Jane Bowles, to her odd, idiosyncratic language, doubly removed from the vernacular norms of male, buddy speech, which would have been seen as low and common, and from Standard English, the mark of educated and socially "better" speakers in the United States of her time.

Drawing on the work of Hall, Labov, and Coates, Deborah Tannen, increasingly well known for her distinction between "rapport-talk," used by women in American society, and "report-talk," more typical of men (76–77), crosses this distinction with another, less often noticed, between cultural conversation styles. In *You Just Don't Understand* she points out that a "high-involvement" style she notices among East Europeans, Italians, some Jewish groups, Africans—and Arabs—contrasts sharply with mainstream Anglo "low-involvement" style (207–9).

The advantage here is that, even when these sociolinguists cross cultures, they usually begin with an analysis of linguistic performance by white, middle-class, Anglo-American speakers. Hall, for example, makes explicit comparison with non-Indo-European speakers, while Labov examines the speech of minorities in the United States. The contrasts they note are useful in pursuing conversational styles, self-other relationships, and the handling of space as these are represented in Jane Bowles's fiction. Translated into the conceptual framework of the sociolinguists, Jane Bowles's encounter with the cultural other, Arab-Muslim "Orientals," highlights differences: her heterosocial, low-involvement, uniplex/low-density/open Anglo-American social networks with their characteristic monochronic, low-context speakers against the "Oriental" homosocial, high-involvement, multiplex/high-density/closed social networks, characteristically polychronic and high-context. In "Everything Is Nice," an American woman in a strange and fascinating locale is introduced to other women. In "The Iron Table," an American woman speaks with her husband about the East and West, about modern and primitive peoples, about alienation—while the conversation is a contest between the two of them. "Emmy Moore's Journal" makes explicit the strange fascination and dread of the cultural other when the middle-aged American writer names herself a "semi-Oriental" woman.

"Everything Is Nice"

Edward Hall coined the term "proxemics" to investigate what readers of modern, Western "realistic" fiction have long come to appreciate: the human use of space as a specialized elaboration of culture. According to Hall, the human sense of space is intimately related to a "sense of self, which is in an intimate transaction" with the environment. Humans "can be viewed as having visual, kinesthetic, tactile, and thermal aspects of [the] self which may be either inhibited or encouraged to develop by [the] environment" (155). Storytelling that takes into account the kinesthetic, tactile, and even thermal aspects of proxemics—in addition to the visual, which is markedly a characteristic of Western "modernity"[1]—can present the problematics of a "self" in a time when the existence of a stable "self" is called into question. Sometimes proxemics moves to the foreground of a story and reveals very different cultural constructs of the self.

"Everything Is Nice" has an unusual publication history. Jane Bowles first wrote it as a nonfiction essay, which appeared as "East Side: North Africa" in *Mademoiselle* in 1951. Later Paul Bowles transposed it to fiction by changing the first-person narrator to third-person and by removing certain comments about women and society (Dillon, *Life* 210). The edited short story is included in the *Collected Works* (1978), and recently the original piece was published in *The Portable Paul and Jane Bowles*, edited by Millicent Dillon. A comparison of the two endings of the story points out certain subtleties at work in the two versions.

Not much appears to happen. Jeanie, a Western woman—a "Nazarene," the catch-all Moroccan term for Western foreigners, as if they were all Christian—in an otherwise unidentified "blue Moslem town" meets a "Moslem woman." The woman identifies herself as Zodelia, and she takes the Westerner through a narrow alley and into a dark house, where a number of women and their babies are gathered. They talk. An old woman named Tetum puts questions to the Western woman in a brusque manner. Jeanie is offered tea and cakes (which she has purchased herself along the way), but refuses, giving the preposterous excuse that the other Nazarenes at her hotel will be angry if she is late for an appointment there. "They will hit me!" she cries, trying to look "wild and frightened" (Bowles, *Collected Works* [1978] 319).[2] The ploy does not work, and she is offered food again. She backs out of the room, but not before Zodelia has made her promise that she will return at four o'clock the next day. Jeanie returns to the spot where the story opened.

The original ended in this way:

> When I reached the place where I had met Zodelia I went over to the wall and leaned on it. Although the sun had sunk behind the houses in back of me, the sky was still luminous and the color of the blue wall had deepened. I rubbed my fingers along it; the wash was fresh and a little of the powdery stuff came off; but no matter how often I walked through these streets reaching out to touch the chalky blue wash on the houses . . . on the walls, I could never satisfy my longing for the town.
>
> I remember that once I reached out to touch the beautiful and powdery face of a clown because his face had awakened some longing; it happened at a little circus but not when I was a child. (Bowles, *Portable* 287)

Note the changes made for its publication as a short story:

> When she reached the place where she had met Zodelia she went over to the wall and leaned on it. Although the sun had sunk behind the houses, the sky was still luminous and the blue of the wall had deepened. She rubbed her fingers along it: the wash was fresh and a little of the powdery stuff came off. And she remembered how once she had reached out to touch the face of a clown because it had awakened some longing. It had happened at a little circus, but not when she was a child. (320)

Besides the change from "I" to "she," the wording has been changed slightly, mainly for the sake of economy: the sun "behind the houses in back of me" is reduced to "behind the houses"; and "the color of the blue wall had deepened" is shortened to "the blue of the wall had deepened"; "the beautiful and powdery face of a clown" becomes simply "the face of a clown." The changes shift emphasis: from the way the woman is situated in reference to the sun; from the blue of the wall, perhaps; from the "powdery" face of the clown, which is both "beautiful" and somehow explicitly like the powder on the walls of the town.

More significant is the decision to drop the comment about the woman's walking often through the streets and her inability to satisfy her "longing for the town." Instead of "longing" then echoing this "longing for the town," the "some longing" at the end stands alone in the revision. Everywhere the changes make for a neater, tighter presentation. The appearance of the strange clown and the little circus, "but not when she was a child" remains as striking as before. What is lost in the transformation is a certain rootedness to place, to the longing for "the town" and not just what would appear as a personal reminiscence. Dillon calls the original ending "one of Jane's most moving disclosures of her own puzzlement at what the town— the medina of Tangier—and its women actually meant to her" (*Life* 210).

That the unnamed "blue Moslem town" is Tangier, as Dillon suspects, is shown by the details early in the story. The scene opens on the highest street of the town, with a thick wall at the edge of a steep cliff. The Western woman looks down over the wall at the skinny boys, a dog, a woman washing her legs all far below where the sea meets "flat dirty rocks" while the tide is out. The streets of the town lead down steeply to the place where Zodelia takes the woman. The houses of the medina—the Moroccan native quarter—in the crooked streets are "so close that she could smell the dampness of the walls and feel it on her cheeks like a thicker air" (320). The scene is quite like the area in which Jane Bowles chose to live in Tangier.

The story is about spatial boundaries. It is true that Bowles (or, properly, the Bowleses) preserved in the fictional account names of people Jane knew in Tangier. Jeanie is a thinly enough disguised "Janie" Bowles. Zodelia knows who the Nazarene is because Jeanie is "Betsoul's friend" (314). (Betsoul herself does not figure in the story.) The old woman in the house is named Tetum, and she is described in a peculiar way: "Only a few feet away, in the middle of the carpet, sat an old lady in a dress made of green and purple curtain fabric. Through the many rents in the material she could see the printed cotton dress and the tan sweater underneath" (317). The old woman, in the middle of the carpet (in the deep interior of the house), has "tiny blue crosses" tattooed on her "bony cheeks," and her knuckles are tattooed with the same design. Jane had written about one Tetum to Paul, the "yellow ugly one," also described as "the Mountain Dyke" (Dillon, *Letters* 85). In other words, the fictional version retains the real names of Moroccan women, but disguises, if only barely, the protagonist's name.

Moroccan sociologist Fatima Mernissi devoted a chapter in the important *Beyond the Veil: Male-Female Dynamics in Modern Muslim Society* to "The Meaning of Spatial Boundaries." Traditionally, the seclusion of women basic to the social system of Morocco, as in other Arab-Muslim societies, meant that women using public spaces were highly restricted:

> Traditionally, only necessity could justify a woman's presence outside the home, and no respect was ever attached to poverty and necessity. Respectable women were not seen on the street. . . . Only prostitutes and insane women wandered freely in the streets. (143)

From Edward Hall, Mernissi noted two tendencies in her own culture. On the one hand, "it is not possible for an individual to claim a private zone in a public space." On the other hand, "space has a primarily social rather than physical quality" (143). Trespassing, for example, would mean something different in Morocco than it would in, say, the United States. "A friend, for example, never trespasses, while a foe always does," according to Mernissi.

Mernissi has attempted to explain a phenomenon observed by many people inside and outside Arab-Muslim society, among the latter, Jane Bowles, that the spatial boundaries reflect a deep division between men and women in that society:

> A society that opts for sexual segregation, and therefore for impoverishment of heterosexual relations, is a society that fosters "homosocial" relations on the one hand and seduction as a means of communication on the other. Seduction is a conflict strategy, a way of seeming to give of yourself and of procuring great pleasure without actually giving anything. It is the art of abstaining from everything while playing on the promise of giving. (140)

"Everything Is Nice" is about the handling of space in a setting that pits two different kinds of societies against each other. The Moroccan women in the story constitute a homosocial group, and Jane Bowles is carefully attentive to the nuances of cross-cultural misunderstanding. Alice Toklas was no admirer of Jane, but she made the shrewd observation that "Jane is strange as an American but not as an Oriental. . . . If accepting this makes her more foreign it at least relieves the strain—that morbidity—she originally seemed at first to be consumed by" (Qtd. in Dillon, *Life* 211).

The great wall along the highest street of the "blue Moslem town," where Jeanie walks freely, alone, is a protective wall, but it cuts the wanderer off from the scene below even as it allows her to see it. The rocks, the dog slipping into the sea, the skinny boys, the woman washing her legs—the people in immediate, if dangerous, contact with the natural world—are observed with a clarity that dissipates once Jeanie crosses over into the life-world of Moroccan women. The crossing-over is most obvious when she is taken through a narrow alley and a door is opened to her and Zodelia, a door marked by a "heavy brass knocker in the form of a fist" (316). In the presence of the women sitting in a dark room Jeanie is an intruder, and the conflict in the story rests entirely on the cultural distance between her and the women. The visit to the women's home is framed by Jeanie alone on the high street.

The conflict is already, though, a matter of struggling for space and power. Jeanie is drawn into the women's world by Zodelia. The Moslem woman leads her, and Jeanie seems almost helpless to resist. Hall first noticed the conflict between Americans' and Arabs' sense of privacy when, in a hotel in Washington, a man violated "the small sphere of privacy" which balloons around an American in a public place:

> As I waited in the deserted lobby, a stranger walked up to where I was sitting and stood close enough so that not only could I easily touch him but I could even hear him breathing. In addition, the dark mass of his body filled the peripheral field of vision on my left side. If the lobby had been crowded with people, I would have understood his behavior, but in an empty lobby his presence made me exceedingly uncomfortable. (*Hidden Dimensions* 155)

The fellow seemed to want to drive Hall out of his position. Later, an Arab colleague thought Hall's response puzzling: "After all, it's a public space, isn't it?" Hall found that "in Arab thought I had no rights whatsoever by virtue of occupying a given spot; neither my place nor my body was inviolate. For the Arab, there is no such thing as an intrusion in public. Public means public" (156).

While the anthropologist attempts to explain the proxemic phenomenon, the writer of fiction displays it. Choosing as a setting the special place that was Tangier, an "international city"—really a border town, a refuge for tax-dodgers during the years Paul and Jane Bowles were living there (see Landau 174–83), made it a particularly good showplace for the stresses Mernissi found in modernizing Arab-Muslim society, since it preserved a large Moroccan population in a very heterogeneous

European community. The women in Jane Bowles's story have only been super-ficially changed by Westerners in their midst, while many other Moroccans were struggling to become Westernized.

Into the scene with Jeanie on the highest street of the town comes one of the Moslem women who have maintained their traditional ways. The woman stands next to Jeanie, "grazing her hip with the basket she was carrying." Jeanie pretends "not to notice her" and gazes intently, instead, on the scene far below them. "Then the woman jabbed the basket firmly into her ribs," and Jeanie is forced to notice her (313).

It is Zodelia, then, who pushes herself onto Jeanie; Zodelia who introduces her-self (and explains who Jeanie is: "Your name is Jeanie and you live in a hotel with other Nazarenes"); Zodelia who asks immediately what Jeanie pays for her hotel room, breaking an American taboo; Zodelia who, unasked, puts on a skit mimicking the people at the hotel; Zodelia who invites Jeanie to attend a wedding, but takes her instead to a shop, where Jeanie buys sweets, and to the house, where Jeanie has the encounter with old Tetum. Indeed, so much is Jeanie drawn along by Zodelia, who pries into matters that Americans are trained to think strictly private, that the American woman has only one free act of will. When the women offer her tea and the cakes she had just bought, Jeanie refuses:

> "Eat!" the women called out from their mattress. "Eat the cakes."
> The child pushed the glass dish forward.
> "The dinner at the hotel is ready," she said, standing up.
> "Drink tea," said the old woman scornfully. "Later you will sit with the other Nazarenes and eat their food."
> "The Nazarenes will be angry if I'm late." She realized that she was lying stu-pidly, but she could not stop. "They will hit me!" She tried to look wild and frightened.
> "Drink tea. They will not hit you," the old woman told her. (319)

In this test of wills, Jeanie holds out—although she ends up backing away out of the room.

The story is filled with puzzling and odd details that are never clarified. Zodelia carries a basket with a "large dead porcupine" in it, "a pair of new yellow socks folded on top of it" (313). Talk of this porcupine leads the two around. At one point the porcupine seems to be on its way to Zodelia's aunt. But when Jeanie asks about it later, Zodelia tells her, "The porcupine sits here . . . in my own house" (319).

More obviously of cultural importance is the talk about family. Old Tetum wants to know where Jeanie's husband is. Zodelia adds to Jeanie's answer—that her husband is "traveling in the desert"—an explanation that, though false, seemed reasonable enough to the group. Jeanie's husband is "selling things." More puzzling to the group is the absence of Jeanie's mother.

> "Where is your mother?" the old lady asked.
> "My mother is in our country in her own house."
> "Why don't you go and sit with your mother in her own house?" she scolded.
> "The hotel costs a lot of money." (318)

Whatever this may have meant for Jane Bowles and the relationship she had with her own mother, the dialogue points out one of the major differences between traditional Arab-Muslim society and modern American society. That a woman would be on her own—would *want* to be on her own—when she has a mother in whose home she could be "sitting" is incomprehensible, as a number of Western writers have observed.[3]

There is no ban on Muslims associating with or eating with "Nazarenes," but it is considered a privilege for an outsider to be treated the way Jeanie is treated by the women. The very familiarity the women seem to demand of her and the very direct way they talk to her indicate the way she has been accepted. Hospitality, that ancient and fundamental principle of Arab-Muslim society, is offered her (even though she is offered the cakes she herself had bought). When Jeanie refuses to eat with them, she violates, it appears unwittingly, their hospitality.

Still, the women urge her to return to the room, and Zodelia extracts a promise from Jeanie to return the next day. Jeanie may be led around easily, but she learns quickly. As the door of the house "opened . . . just enough to let her through" (320), Jeanie tries waffling about her return to the place. The two women change roles momentarily. Jeanie speaks in the language of the Arab-Muslim world: "I shall see you tomorrow, if Allah wills it" (a translation of *ghedda, enshallah,* where "tomorrow" has much the same force as Spanish *mañana,* and the pious submission to Allah's will is another way to get out of a promise without appearing to offend). Zodelia is not fooled. She demands an answer in "American time" (or what Hall elsewhere calls M-time or monochronic time), a precise four o'clock, rather than in P-time or polychronic time.[4]

As Jeanie is leaving Zodelia's house, Zodelia presses two of the cakes into Jeanie's hand and tells her, "graciously," to eat them "at the hotel with the other Nazarenes" (320). Jeanie returns through the narrow alley to the place where she had met Zodelia. The walls, at first a barrier between Jeanie and the people below, now are seen—or rather felt (with more immediacy, though with less clarity than sight)—from within, and the blue wash of the wall becomes the major symbol of Jeanie's encounter with the cultural other.

The reader is led back to images that connect with the powdery blue on the wall and Jeanie's attempt to touch the powdery face of the clown: to images of masks and costumes. Before her name is revealed to Jeanie, Zodelia is a woman "dressed in a haik" (an all-enveloping length of material worn in public), her "white cloth covering the lower half of her face" loose (313–14); her "henna-stained finger" indicates she has decorated her hands. The woman on the rocks far below them has taken off her haik in order to wash in the sea water.

Tetum reveals layers of garments and is decorated with tiny blue crosses. Zodelia reappears inside the house without her haik—in a "black crepe European dress" that hung down to her ankles. Access to the house, down the steep street, in a narrow alley—far from public gaze—is guarded. A child opens the door and "quickly hid behind it, covering her face" (316). When she leaves, Zodelia opens the door "just enough to let her through" (320).

In contrast to the sunlight on the high street, there is little light inside the house: "Because her eyes had not grown used to the dimness, she had the impression of a figure disappearing down a long corridor. Then she began to see the brass bars of a bed, glowing weakly in the darkness" (316). It is difficult to know these women— difficult to see them—sitting in the darkness, decorated, wearing one garment in public, another in the privacy of the home. The expression Bowles uses to capture the Moghrebi Arabic, the local dialect, used by the women reinforces this contrast between inside and outside. "Why don't you go and sit with your mother in her own house?" Jeanie is asked. In a society where interaction with strangers is restricted and where, on the other hand, "sitting" is not devalued, as it is in the American work ethic, sitting with the mother in her house is the mark of ordered social life.

The American, alone, on the public street, or with the "other Nazarenes" (neither kin nor designated as friends) in the hotel becomes, as the story progresses, as odd a figure as the Moroccan women in their private dwelling. Jeanie has more than a little difficulty penetrating their masks. The ending of the story indicates, though, that something deeply moving has occurred in the encounter with the women. The wall between the two cultures is never removed, but Jeanie feels an intimacy, a longing, in touching the wall with its powdery blue decoration.

The language Bowles gives to the Moroccan women reinforces the bind, and Zodelia's "skit"—playful, a play, a representation—gives the best account of it. The skit is successful, "since all the people of the town spoke and gesticulated as though they had studied at the *Comédie Française*" (314). As she plays the people in the hotel, though, Zodelia betrays a cultural style very different from Jeanie's. Known as the "wa-wa" style (after the Arabic *wa* or "and" coordinator used to string phrases and clauses together like beads on a necklace), the style is a marked characteristic of traditional Arabic writing and, as Zodelia's speech shows, ordinary speech.[5] It contrasts sharply with the tendency in Western writings—fiction as well as nonfiction prose—to use subordination and, through it, a hierarchical organization of thought. Zodelia mimics the people at the hotel:

"Good-bye, Jeanie, good-bye. Where are you going?"

"I am going to a Moslem home to visit my Moslem friends, Betsoul and her family. I will sit in a Moslem room and eat Moslem food and sleep on a Moslem bed."

"Jeanie, Jeanie, when will you come back to us in the hotel and sleep in your own room?"

"I will come back to you in three days. I will come back and sit in a Nazarene room and eat Nazarene food and sleep on a Nazarene bed. I will spend half the week with Moslem friends and half with Nazarenes." (314)

Conversation between Jeanie and the Moroccan women quickly becomes futile. Misunderstandings abound, partly because of a language barrier, and partly because certain features of one culture are not understood in the other. Why the porcupine? Is it large or small? Why does Jeanie, when asked about her mother, avoid the question and talk instead about the many automobiles and trucks in the city where she was born? Tetum, in particular, cannot understand why Jeanie would want to spend half her time with Moslem friends and the other half with Nazarenes. In many cases the exchanges end with an exhaustion of language—with the women using that most empty of American words, "nice." While the "nice" of the title is, in one sense, a translation of the ubiquitous *mlih* of Moroccan Arabic, Bowles's use of the term betrays the characters' inability to make the kind of subtle distinctions that come from genuine familiarity. Zodelia asks Jeanie if the Spanish cakes are "Nice?" or "Not nice?" (316). Jeanie thinks them disgusting, but buys a dozen of them. "They are very nice," Jeanie replies. Later Zodelia asks twice if the "dimly lit room" Jeanie is taken to is "nice?" Jeanie does not respond to either question (317). When the women hear that Jeanie spends half her time with Muslims, half with Nazarenes, the women—except for Tetum—say, "That's nice." Trucks are nice, even "very nice" (318).

By the time the conversation has degenerated to an exchange about trucks, Jeanie seems "lost in meditation" for a moment but then announces, "with a look of triumph"—"Everything is nice." The women around her agree: "Everything is nice" (318).

What follows is the offer of food and drink—and Jeanie's awkward refusal of the women's hospitality. She did not want to eat the cakes. It is at this moment that Jeanie wanted "to go home" (319). The expression marks the rift between the women and the two cultures. Significantly, the term "home" is avoided by the Moroccans when they talk of what Americans mean by "home." Bowles has them using "house" instead.[6] Both Jeanie and Tetum speak of Jeanie's mother "in her own house" (318). Zodelia says her aunt is "in her own house" (319), and, more revealing, tells Jeanie, "The porcupine sits here . . . in my own house" (319).

Jeanie, like the expatriate Jane Bowles, who lived much of her life in hotels,[7] wants to go home, but the rhetoric of the story denies her any such place. The displacement of Jeanie is most evident in the split between the public space of the high street, where she is free to look at the scene around her and lives in the private bubble Americans create around themselves, and the hotel, where she lives with the other Nazarenes. Neither place is a home in the sense Americans use the term. Ironically, the Moroccan women live privately in the home the story calls a "house." The self is almost entirely hidden from public view behind haiks, veils, hennaed hands, walls, doors, and is disclosed, if only dimly at first, in a windowless room with women "sitting" together on mattresses, children and babies around them. The final passage of the story, with Jeanie rubbing her fingers along the blue of the wall and awakening some kind of fantasy about the face of a clown in a "little circus," marks the intimacy of barriers.

The reader of "Everything Is Nice" is as disoriented as the main character. The locale is most likely unfamiliar; customs and cultural expectations of the Oriental women in the story are puzzling. Conflict and resolution (if the ending can in any way be seen as a resolution) are decentered. As usual, Jane Bowles does not provide explicit authorial comment to dispel questions the reader might have. Still, "Everything Is Nice" is a brilliant depiction of an exotic cityscape and a thoroughly honest presentation of a woman among women in a homosocial community. Led ever more deeply into the Orient, Jeanie remains disoriented. Conversations do not work. But far from adopting a superior attitude, the main character and the work as a whole establish a rapport with the cultural Other that is indeed rare in Western literature. A second story, "The Iron Table," isolates a woman with her husband, and the rapport so evident in "Everything Is Nice" quickly falls away.

"The Iron Table"

Jennifer Coates and Deborah Tannen make much of the shift women's conversation takes when they talk with men. Such a shift, and the tension that develops across the space of a table when the woman talks to her husband are exhibited in this minimalist story.

"The Iron Table," written in 1950, in the same period Bowles had been working on "Everything Is Nice," is a very different kind of story, a brief exchange between a wife and husband, both unnamed. The story contains a very brief setting, a very restrained but intense argument between the two people, and a tiny summary. "The Iron Table" is, in fact, a fragment from Jane Bowles's notebooks that was prepared for publication by Paul Bowles. The edited version was published in the *Collected Works* (in both 1966 and 1978), while the original version in the notebooks was published by Millicent Dillon in her biography of Bowles. As with "Everything Is Nice," the two versions differ in a number of subtle ways. The differences between the notebooks and the published story bring the major themes of the work into high relief.

It is a story about moving and not moving. In sharp contrast with "Everything Is Nice," where moving about, walking up and down, even walking backwards, is opposed to sitting at the center, "The Iron Table" includes no movement at all. The unidentified couple sit at a table that has been dragged out for their use:

> They sat in the sun, looking out over a big new boulevard. The waiter had dragged an old iron table around from the other side of the hotel and set it down on the cement near a half-empty flower bed. A string stretched between stakes separated the hotel grounds from the sidewalk. Few of the guests staying at the hotel sat in the sun. The town was not a tourist center, and not many Anglo-Saxons came. Most of the guests were Spanish. (Bowles, *Works* [1978] 465)

The scene immediately suggests torpor and separation. The "old iron" table has been "dragged around." It has been set down in a bleak scene, on cement "near a half-empty flower bed." The string marks off the public domain from one less public but hardly private or personal. The two are odd ones in the town, which receives few of their sort: Anglo-Saxons in a world inhabited mainly by Spaniards.

The reader discovers, in small hints, that these are Americans not in Spain but in a Moroccan town from which they are doubly estranged. Millicent Dillon provides a context for the scene (from the notebooks), but the context is never explained in the published piece: a Mr. Copperfield and his wife have been prevented from continuing on a journey that will take them into the desert because of a washout in the mountains. The husband is angry. The trip will cost them more than they had expected; and the villagers are wearing, not traditional garb, but a "jumble of Oriental and Western costume" (*Life* 256).

The ostensible subject of their discussion is the decline of Western civilization and the way in which the West is corrupting North Africa, a favorite topic of Paul Bowles. (It is a preoccupation in his short stories and novels, and, in the Foreword to *Their Heads are Green*, he remarks, "My own belief is that the people of the alien cultures are being ravaged not so much by the by-products of our civilization, as by the irrational longing on the part of members of their own educated minorities to cease being themselves and become Westerners" viii.) What makes "The Iron Table" such an intense piece is that the ostensible subject is not just annulled by a different subtext. A subtext there is—the relationship between the woman and the man—but it stands in a particular tension with the topic they discuss: East/West is to wife/ husband as inside/outside is to woman/man.

There is no stable center. An image of loss repeats itself in the short piece. Talk itself is difficult, strained, clipped, elliptical, and the piece ends with the woman's fear of silence:

> She was as bitter as he about the changes, but she felt it would be indelicate for them both to reflect the same sorrow. It would happen some day, surely. A serious grief would silence their argument. They would share it and not be able to look into each other's eyes. But as long as she could she would hold off that moment. (467)

In the time taken up by their conversation, they tear at each other and maintain a kind of relationship. His weapon is anger, hers sorrow. She takes a "sorrowful" tone when she acknowledges to him that "the whole civilization is going to pieces" (465). Her tone is "sepulchral" when she adds that it is going to pieces "so quickly, too" (465).

For some reason, the two versions differ when they begin to talk about the desert. For him, the desert is an escape from the disintegrating civilization, a place "where the culture has remained untouched" (466). She wants nothing of it—at least while she is sober. In the notebooks Jane writes: "He was getting back at her for mourning with him over his remark" (*Life* 256). In the published version, she writes instead: "He was punishing her for her swift agreement with him a moment earlier" (*Works* [1978] 466). The notebook states that the woman would never say she would go into the desert "unless she was drunk" (*Life* 257), versus the published version: "But she never did this if she was sober" (*Works* [1978] 466).
Many small changes like these have been made in the text. In one of the more powerful images, the language is changed from:

> The sun was beating down on her chest making it flame: Inside her heart felt colder. It was hard to believe that deep inside her breast there was always a cold current that seemed to run near her heart. (*Life* 256)

to:

> Although the sun was beating down on her chest, making it feel on fire, deep inside she could still feel the cold current that seemed to run near the heart. (*Works* [1978] 466)

Occasionally a comment is deleted. When she wants to know if he would really be happy in an oasis—and she thinks perhaps she could be happy for his sake, the conversation breaks down. The notebooks include the comment, "He was pretending not to have heard, more for his own benefit than for hers. He was not a faker" (*Life* 257).

The comment disappears in the published version. Sometimes the changes, like the one above, suggest economy. But after the two debate about their "friends," the notebook contains the utterly simple, "They both secretly rejoiced that they were not going to feel tenderhearted after all" (*Life* 257), while the published version expands it: "The moment when they might have felt tenderness had passed, and secretly they both rejoiced" (*Works* [1978] 467). He wants desperately to escape, to keep moving. She wants to stop the "ceaseless whining over the piecemeal disintegration of Moslem culture" (*Life* 256); as the notebooks have it: "I'm tired of hearing the word 'civilization.' It has no meaning or I've forgotten what is meant anyway" (*Life* 257).

The story is seen from the woman's point of view. It may well reflect a long-standing argument between Jane and Paul Bowles. (Dillon thinks it is "the most directly autobiographical rendering of a conversation between herself and Paul that she was ever to write" *Life* 256.) Still, it remains a piece about the way things hang together—civilization, a marriage, the cultural construction of gender—and the way they are tested. She gives him the last word:

> "I think it's uninteresting. To sit and watch costumes disappear, one by one. It's uninteresting even to mention it."
> "They are not costumes," he said distinctly. "They're simply the clothes people wear." (467)

At this she keeps silent, not to indicate that she has been defeated but to keep the awful game of language alive. In fact, at this moment she agrees with him. She would "hold off that moment" when it must happen that "a serious grief would silence" not one or the other but "their argument" (467). In "The Iron Table" the dialogue reveals, as Dillon puts it, "a searching for what went on between herself and Paul in the spaces between the words" (*Life* 256). But the agreement about the two cultures, where the woman and the man are closest, cannot be spoken.

Separated by an iron table, situated between the hotel and the Oriental town, the characters—especially the woman who tries to resist being carried further away from a "home" that hardly seems to exist—do not fit together, cannot find a place of origin, cannot reorient their selves (themselves constructed by history and culture). The possibility, explored in "Emmy Moore's Journal," remains that a social/sexual orientation may come if the woman can only get away, to a place where she can be comfortable and speak with her husband in another way, through her writing.

"Emmy Moore's Journal"

One of the most telling blows in "The Iron Table" is the moment when the woman talks about her "friends." "My friends and I don't feel there's any *way* of

escaping [Western Civilization]. It's not interesting to sit around talking about indus-
trialization" (467). His retort is to attack, "What friends?" She is forced to think that
she had not seen "most of them" in many years, and she "turned to him with a
certain violence." Friendship is a code word in "Everything is Nice" and in "The
Iron Table" as well. She adds the comment, preserved in both versions of "The Iron
Table," that "He liked her to feel isolated."

The isolation of the woman is most painfully revealed in "Emmy Moore's Journal." Unlike "Everything is Nice" (set in Morocco and introducing Moroccan characters), and unlike "The Iron Table" (set in Morocco but with no Moroccan characters), "Emmy Moore's Journal" is basically a monologue that is neither set in the East
nor concerned with any individuals in the East. But the conflict between East and
West figures centrally in this story as well.

"Emmy Moore's Journal" is another fragment, written in 1949–50, a piece that
was to be part of a novel called *Out in the World.* Still, like "The Iron Table," the
piece possesses a unity that does not depend on a larger context. In it the character,
Emmy Moore, constructs a crude theory of cultural types and tries to situate herself
in it. Since the types are "American," "Turkish," and "Oriental," the story has a bearing on Jane Bowles's image of Moroccan women—and of herself. In the work, she
names the "semi-Oriental" woman, located between the extremes of America and
the Far East.

In the self-conscious authorship (a journal intended to be published) and in the
shifting point of view (from first person to second person to third person), "Emmy
Moore's Journal" takes a turn that today would be considered postmodern. Emmy
Moore, forty-seven and fat, is alone in a place, Hotel Henry, that is the very figure
of isolation. To talk of the place required a change in point of view. Emmy Moore
opens her journal in the first person, includes a letter she has written to her husband
(second person), and disappears into a third-person limited narration at the end—
when the place is briefly described. It is an overheated room, with a wicker chair
and a bottle of whiskey (Bowles, *Works* [1978] 449).

"Everything Is Nice" refers to the hotel where the Nazarenes spend their time,
but does not describe it. In "The Iron Table," the woman is with her husband at the
boundary of the hotel and the public space around it. In "Emmy Moore's Journal,"
the woman is alone, and the description of her room in the Hotel Henry brings the
story to its despairing close:

> She could not stand the overheated room a second longer. With some diffi-
> culty she raised the window, and the cold wind blew in. Some loose sheets of
> paper went skimming off the top of the desk and flattened themselves against
> the bookcase. She shut the window and they fell to the floor. The cold air had
> changed her mood. (449)

Only at this moment does the world outside impinge on the space that encloses her. Overheating—the sign of imbalance—brings Emmy to act, and what she does further throws off any chance of balance. She picks up what she had written and, finding it inadequate, abandons herself to her whiskey and her favorite chair: " 'I have said nothing,' she muttered to herself in alarm. 'I have said nothing at all. I have not clarified my reasons for being at the Hotel Henry. I have not justified myself' " (449).

The notebook includes an additional, short passage that was deleted in the published version but reprinted by Dillon in the biography. Emmy sees what Dillon interprets as "a representation of power made impotent" (*Life* 196): "the distinct image of a giant steamship lying on its side. She turned her head slightly to the left as she had done in actuality to avoid the sight when the Hewitt Moores had taken her to see the boat dragged up from its ocean bed several years ago" (*Life* 196). More disturbing is a line Jane Bowles wrote, crossed out, wrote again, then finally canceled: Emmy was "very nearly throwing everything into the fire (mentally)" (*Life* 197).

"Emmy Moore's Journal" opens with a monologue in the form of a journal that is very personal but "is intended for publication." In order to explain why she is living alone in the Hotel Henry, she copies into the journal a letter to her husband, Paul Moore, a lawyer. Even more than in the other stories, Jane Bowles emphasizes not the statement but the process of thinking and writing. In Emmy's case, the process is slow and difficult, with ironic turns, contradictions, erasures, and spiraling back to the themes of Emmy's obsessions: her attempts at independence and change, her inability to justify herself.

She constructs her theory of three cultural types of gender in order to justify herself. She is not like "Americans"—independent and masculine—though she would like to be: "I am unusually feminine for an American of Anglo stock. (Born in Boston.)" (444). The women of the Far East, she thinks, may be just as independent and masculine as the "Americans," although she is not sure. "I am almost a 'Turkish' type," Emmy writes, what she will come to call the "semi-Oriental":

> But sometimes I feel certain that I exude an atmosphere very similar to theirs (the Turkish women's) and then I despise myself. I find the women in my country so extraordinarily manly and independent, capable of leading regiments, or of fending for themselves on desert islands if necessary. (These are poor examples, but I am getting my point across.) For me it is an experience simply to have come here alone to the Hotel Henry and to eat my dinner and lunch by myself. If possible before I die, I should like to become a little less Turkish than I am now. (444)

Even in her theory, Emmy is uncertain, and she apologizes to the "Turkish" women she wonders about. Have they discarded their veils? An "American" woman would be sure. The "Turkish" women, it should be clear by now, located between America and the Far East in a cultural map, are a generalization of the secluded Muslim women she was getting to know in Morocco, "semi-Oriental."

The disorientation in "Emmy Moore's Journal" appears in the repetitions and wanderings of Emmy's thought. The brutally honest close, with the protagonist at home as much as she may ever be with her bottle in the profoundly alienated and overheated hotel room, denies consolation that might come from conversation, from relationships with the other, or from a space that can be shared by the other. As in the other stories, the fiction is disorienting. The fragmentariness and oddity of Jane Bowles's fiction that Millicent Dillon had come to value in "Jane Bowles: Experiment as Character" are much in evidence in these three stories. There is neither a place of origin, a home, nor an Orient to which one can escape to find an authentic self. Endings of stories are in some ways necessarily reorientations. But though two of the stories, "Everything Is Nice" and "Emmy Moore's Journal," have very striking endings, they do not return to the beginnings, and even these stories remain open, dislodged. At their most comforting, when the woman meets the Oriental women of Tangier, the stories preserve the fascination with the Orient and the possibility of rapport.

Recent work by linguists, anthropologists and the sociologists of knowledge has explored systematically many of the areas Jane Bowles, by reason of her own peculiar development and the socio-historical situation she found herself in, had already explored in her fiction. We now possess ethnological studies and even some empirical research that can "place" Jane Bowles in a white, middle-class Anglo-American culture, variously heterosocial (and thus dominated by "report-talk"), and disconnected (with a "low-involvement" conversation style and social networks that tend to be uniplex and low-density, low-context M-time alienated). Jane Bowles was odd in that place, disoriented I claim here, a "lame" in more than just the way William Labov meant when he used that term. When she had occasion, not entirely of her own making, to meet a group of Arab-Muslim women in Morocco, she was prepared to see them as equals, if different. They were different in precisely the way the social scientists have come to describe. The Orient Jane Bowles found retained the otherness the West has inscribed on it since the Greeks, and that difference appeared to liberate something in the American. At least "Jeanie" in "Everything Is Nice," though still disoriented at the end of that story, had found a place that opened her to others and to her own past. The handling of space, always important in narrative, is the clue used in this essay to follow the orienteering that goes on in the three stories.

The three stories are not connected in any obvious way. Jane Bowles worked on them at roughly the same time, after her initial encounter with North African culture. The temptation to read Jane Bowles directly into Jeanie, Mrs. Copperfield, and Emmy Moore is difficult to resist; but the point of this essay is not to pursue that route. Rather, it is to suggest that an encounter with a very different way of drawing gender and sexual boundaries brought Bowles not just to fiction about the "other" but also to a reconsideration of an "American" social identity.

When the protagonist is situated inside her hotel room, she is, "alone and disconnected," finding it difficult (if necessary) to justify herself, difficult to keep writing. When the protagonist sits at the "iron table," immobile, playing language games with her husband, she has only a temporary place. (Perhaps she will be pressured into following her husband's dream of the desert.) When she leaves the hotel that allows Westerners free travel, the woman is displaced, still, but she senses in Zodelia's house the home lost to the freely-moving American.

Notes

1. Palmer, "Hermeneutics and the Postmodern" 7: "Modern man begins to dream of reducing everything to measurable terms, of making everything visualizable, i.e., spatial. And the mind, with its armory of mathematical symbols—better and more reliable than any ordinary languages, nominates man as the absolute monarch of the world."

2. All page references are to the 1978 *Collected Works* except where comparisons are made to other versions of the texts under discussion.

3. Elizabeth Warnock Fernea ran into this question both in Iraq and in Morocco. The reaction was always the same, "Poor girl." Fernea remarks, "To be alone without any of one's womenfolk was clearly the greatest disaster which could befall any girl" (*Guests of the Sheik* 36).

4. The concepts of cultural differences in the handling of time are developed by Hall in *The Silent Language*, where he distinguishes American time and Arabic time (19–21, 134–39), and in *Beyond Culture* where he calls them M-time and P-time (17).

5. On the "wa-wa" style, see Kaplan 6–10, and Yorkey 68–69, 80–82.

6. Moroccan Arabic, like English, distinguishes among several words for home and house (*'a'ila, dar, mahell*), such that different terms can be used for "My home is in Casablanca," "I have to go home," and "There's no place like home." See Harrell and Sobleman, *Dictionary*, 100.

7. Dillon's biography lists no fewer than fourteen hotels by name, at least four of which are in Tangier (457). Following the moves of the Bowleses through their houses and hotels in Tangier is a bewildering task for the reader.

8

Jane Bowles in Uninhabitable Places

Writing on Cultural Boundaries

Carol Shloss

1

Strangely, the foreigner lives within us; he is the hidden face of our identity, the space
that wrecks our abode, the time in which understanding and affinity founder.
—Julia Kristeva, *Strangers to Ourselves*

J ANE BOWLES WAS one of the most displaced writers of her generation, a woman whose
transient, makeshift life lends poignancy to Heidegger's observation that "[h]ome-
lessness is coming to be the destiny of the world" (qtd. in Vidler 8). Not belonging to
any place, to any time, to any abiding love, she struggled to understand her lost origins
and to encode the meaning of such rootlessness in her writing. Meeting, perching,
wandering, going toward others and then retreating from them, the figures of her
imagination enacted an interior drama whose enunciation suggests how structures of
consciousness can rely on and be expressed by the very structures of human habitation
that they seem initially to resist.

Like the American writer Henry David Thoreau, Jane Bowles reminds us of the
power and appropriateness of thinking of the ideological dimensions of habitation.
"What is a House?" Thoreau had asked about his experiment in living at Walden
Pond in the 1850s, and immediately established the symbolic and political terms for
answering his own question by creating an analogy among books, houses, and nar-
rators: "When I wrote the following pages, or rather the bulk of them," he tells us,
"I lived alone, in the woods, a mile from any neighbor, in a house which I had built
myself, on the shore of Walden Pond, in Concord, Massachusetts, and earned my
living by the labor of my hands only" (*Walden* 45). For him, building the house,

writing the book, and defining himself within his own historical situation were inseparable activities: the material structure of his cabin served to identify events happening in the interior of his body, in the invisible geography of his psyche, and to tie these to the exterior world of human endeavor.

Both Freud and Marx, the two great cultural philosophers of the modern world, have devoted their work to explaining, in a more general way, how the material structures of civilization, like Thoreau's house, can act as referents for what is originally interior and private. This projection into the material world offers us the means of a reversal, a turning of the inside surface out so that it can be expressed and shared. In this way, a house can become a text, a materialized objectification of shelter, of the skeleton, of the very bones of existence (see Scarry 281).

If we use these general comments about made objects as the site of projection, both for whole cultures and for individuals, we can begin to discern the parameters of Jane Bowles's fictional universe where the very nature and possibility of habitation become some of the most pressing problems addressed by the narrative. Where Thoreau had understood his house and his writing to express a being-at-home-in-the-world that had its origins in psychic integration, Bowles comes to see the activity of writing as a home whose material absence is articulated in the work. For Thoreau, to represent a house in narrative was to represent the psyche and to make manifest the shelter achieved by writing-about-the-psyche. For Bowles, no such formula works; for in her world, a house never offers the protection that the activity of writing can potentially provide. One does not serve as the material projection of the other. Her writing thus expresses and mediates against the discomfort, the transience, the shelterlessness of sentient life. It repeatedly encodes the experience of literal dislocation and psychic displacement, where houses offer neither a sense of possession nor of self-possession. They are places that one goes out from, that one has to leave for the sake of survival, and that remain as a reminder of the entrapment that had originally propelled one out into a hostile exterior. Rarely do they serve even the most rudimentary function of shelter: to protect and to form a clear boundary between inside and outside. In "Emmy Moore's Journal," Bowles's protagonist writes to her husband about her attempted solution to the problem of being-at-home. "I cannot simply live out my experiment here at the Hotel Henry without trying to justify or at least explain in letters my reasons for being here," she says, "I am certain that until the prayed-for metamorphosis has occurred I shall go on feeling just this need [to justify my actions]" (Bowles, *Works* [1978] 445).

In some ways, we can understand Bowles's entire writing career as a similarly prolonged effort to justify or at least to explain an anxiety about displacement that could not otherwise be put to rest. In her work, the urge to leave is commensurate with the fear of leaving; the impulse that compels one out into the world coexists with the anxiety of going away, and this indeterminacy is enacted in the various texts through a series of intermediate images of shelter that are built on the premise of transience. Repeatedly Bowles resorts to the image of the re-sort, of the way station, the pension, the hotel, the bar, the garage, to perches which imply further travel as a way to ameliorate distress and to effect trans-formation. Shelter becomes important only insofar as it plays a part in a self-desired metamorphosis, or as Elaine Scarry writes in *The Body in Pain*, "[e]ach stage of transformation sustains and amplifies the artifact that was present in the beginning. Even in the interior of consciousness, pain is 'remade' by being wished away in the external action, the private wish is made sharable finally in the artifact" (291). Because of the primacy of this desire to re-make, Bowles's fictional habitations are rarely permanent or whole or even the site of domestic activity but function instead as indicators of the need to re-move pain and to transform the self and the world into something other. The form of each habitation is established and then abandoned; the act of leaving becomes the outward embodiment of the wish to leave, to move outside the confines of what is toward something else. No interior is habitable even while the exterior world is hostile and full of threat. One might say that in acting out this drama of being-not-at-home, Bowles's characters let us see the nature of what is foreign in culture, for they live uncomfortably on borders or as perpetual outsiders. Julia Kristeva might have been thinking about the issues that propel Bowles's creativity when she wrote in *Strangers to Ourselves* that "to live in a foreign country . . . herald[s] the art of living of a modern era, the cosmopolitanism of those who have been flayed" (3).

2

. . . a strange land of borders and otherness ceaselessly constructed and deconstructed
—Julia Kristeva, *Strangers to Ourselves*

"Camp Cataract," completed in 1948, is one of Bowles's finest attempts to represent the impossibility of being at home in the world. Here that conflict is played out within a single family whose customary domestic arrangements are challenged by one of two unmarried sisters. While one sister flourishes at an adult nature camp, the other languishes at home in their urban apartment, torn between her pleasure in domesticity and the anxiety occasioned by Harriet's absence. Sadie attempts to ameliorate her pain by writing frequent letters that ostensibly wish her sister well—"have a nice time, dear" (Bowles, *Works* [1978] 360)—but that serve equally to express her own need for security. "I fear nomads. I am afraid of them and afraid for them too. I don't know what I would do if any of my dear ones were seized with the wanderlust" (360). She ends her letter by making explicit the connection she draws between dwelling places and the interior states that they protect and express: "Remember, the apartment is not just a row of rooms. It is the material proof that our spirits are so wedded that we have but one blessed roof over our heads" (361).

The delusion of this sentiment is announced by the very envelope that encloses it, for a letter is "material proof" of absence and of the need to speak across distance. In this case, it also expresses Sadie's misplaced faith that her sister supports their "marriage"; but we learn, to the contrary, that Harriet's journey is calculated to transgress the boundaries of the familiar. What for Sadie is "blessed" security is for her sister a form of psychic imprisonment, a situation Sadie bizarrely admits when she writes "we've stayed together, just the two of us, with the door safely locked so you wouldn't in your excitement run to a neighbor's house at all hours of the morning" (361)—one that is even marked by a barricade. Bowles further represents the constriction of urban domestic life by the uncanny image of a dining room that is too small to contain a table with people sitting around it and that must be shifted from wall to wall, giving the people assembled the choice of either eating or breathing. Like the table of Kafka's imagination in *The Metamorphosis*, this dining room expresses a world in which nourishment actively prohibits the life it is supposed to sustain.

With such a home behind her, Harriet needs Camp Cataract quite badly. For her, it embodies the very possibility of survival, assuring her of air to breath as well as providing the shelter that any emergent life requires. Neither wilderness nor permanent settlement, it gives her an edge as if it were an outpost of the possible: to approach that border, Harriet must be a boarder. She regards it as a "tree house" of the kind that children build: "You climb into them when you're a child and plan to run away from home once you are safely hidden among the leaves" (362).

She will take her own "leave" gradually, for though she claims to admire nomads, "vagabonds, gypsies [and] seafaring men" (361), setting herself up as her sister's opposite, she also despises "anything that smacks of a bohemian dash for freedom" (362). Her ambivalence is as deep as her roots, as Sadie discovers when she boards a bus to retrieve the promise of her own broken life. Expecting reunion with Harriet, she finds isolation. Extending herself in friendship, she meets both avoidance and hostility. Her sister will neither share her bungalow nor her time, for Sadie's visit violates her own life's project: as Harriet explains to Beryl, a camp waitress:

> My plan is extremely complicated and from my point of view rather brilliant. First I will come here for several years . . . I don't know yet exactly how many, but long enough to imitate roots . . . I mean to imitate the natural family roots of childhood . . . long enough so that I myself will feel: "Camp Cataract is *habit*, Camp Cataract is life, Camp Cataract is not escape." Escape is unladylike, habit isn't. As I remove myself gradually from within my family circle and establish

myself more and more solidly into Camp Cataract, then from here at some later date I can start making my sallies into the outside world almost unnoticed. (363)

Sadie's unexpected appearance at the camp reinserts the family within the place of Harriet's escape from the family and reactivates her sense of suffocation. It is as if the boundary between the self and its unwanted origin had suddenly burst, bringing with it a kind of psychic catastrophe. The camp's function as a "re-habit-ation"—a place for relearning the interior modes of self-reliance—falters, even though Harriet tries to distance her sister in space, giving her sleeping quarters in a "grotto," and refusing to cancel her wilderness expedition in a canoe.

These behaviors permit us to see more clearly the private ideology that Harriet has invested in her summer residence: the camp, even with its ugly primitive furnishings, tourist attractions, and souvenir booths, has allowed her to "play," that is, to try out a symbolic system that is remote from her emotional heritage and to explore the nature of her own desire "by means of a detour through otherness" (Porter 288). It is her means of re-formation.

For Sadie the camp offers no such promise. Far from liberating her, it destabilizes the world beyond recovery. With the structures of habit (including habitual dependence) broken, she faces Harriet's detestation and through it, her own identity as an irritating intruder and a stranger to her own motivations. Waiting for Harriet to come to lunch, she makes her own journey to the interior and finds the world inside herself to be raw, brutal, and full of portents: She imagines, quite literally, her own unrootedness, "step[ping] over to a felled tree whose length blocked the clearing. Its torn roots were shockingly exposed . . . she noticed a dense swarm of flies near the roots. Automatically she stepped toward them. 'Why are they here?' she asked herself" (395), as if the ground could show her the figure of her own unmoored psyche.

Bowles's narrative places these two sisters in opposition to one another, and it lets only one of them survive. But if we were to translate this drama into its internal dimensions, understanding it to be the representation of the interior of a single consciousness, we could see that each character—whether she is the predator or the prey—plays a role in sorting out a boundary dispute. In this respect, even the landscape serves as an externalization of interior events. Chasms, precipices, waterfalls, precarious bridges all identify Bowles's story as an exploration of liminality, of transience as a willed mode of being, the prelude to transformation.

Seen in this light, her fiction serves to express an anxiety and at the same time to ameliorate it: psychoanalysis might recognize these representations of ambivalence as characteristics central to understanding a "borderline personality disorder," noticing that the dynamic expressed by Sadie/Harriet is more commonly the dynamic of certain mothers and children when mothers require their children's compliance in order to defend themselves against their own separation anxieties (see Masterson). Sadie eventually recognizes that her stalking of Harriet grows out of an anterior depression or emptiness and that she demands Harriet's allegiance even though she refuses to be emotionally available herself: "It did not occur to her that a connection might exist between her present dismal state and the mission she had come to fulfill at Camp Cataract" (384). When she looks up out of her discomfort, she does not see Harriet as a separate person but as a "woman who stood on the threshold" (384); that is, as an indistinct extension of her own troubled sense of self.

From the child's (Harriet's) perspective, this looming mother figure creates an insoluble dilemma; for its efforts to grow and to become independent—efforts that require the support of the mother—instead induce the withdrawal of her love (Masterson 33). To remain with the mother is to be overwhelmed; to leave the mother is to evoke her wrath; thus no behavior—going forth or staying with—promotes well-being. To move toward individuation is to open an interior chasm; to remain is to remain in bondage. With no healthy alternatives, the borderline becomes the site of psychological possibility (if one could leave one could live) and of devastation (if one could leave, one would "kill" the love of the mother). Since these are impossible choices, ambivalence often remains the predominant mode of existence for such people, and we can follow the alternation between dependence and independence in the unresolved ending of the story. Although Sadie dies, the guilt for her death will remain with Harriet, ensuring that she will maintain a conflictual bond with her own past. Using Camp Cataract as a purposeful dislocation where she can hold the unthinkable and the possible in the same frame of reference, she will continue living on at the bo[a]rder where her one friend, the waitress Beryl, will also wait on.

3

Estrangement from the world is a moment of art.
—Theodor Adorno, *Minima Moralia*

Although many of Bowles's narratives can be seen in light of similar unresolved internal conflicts, the distress recorded in her fiction does not remain private. In fact, it is important to see how Bowles transforms foreignness or estrangement within the self into a means of identifying with foreigners in more widespread, geopolitical situations. If one is "not at home" spiritually, one has a powerful resource for exploring the logic of exclusion even when the dividing lines cease to define the margins of the psyche and become, instead, markers of ethnic or national antagonisms.

In this respect, Bowles's writing contributes to a growing body of work that takes as its subject the positioning of individual subjectivity within collective experience, especially when that individual speaks from the margins of a dominant group, giving voice to the experiences of those who are part of a minority or who are living in exile. We could say that in Bowles's work, there is a moment when the stranger invading the old, familiar world of personal habit becomes the vehicle for deconstructing the barriers between the increasing number of transient people on the earth and those who would disown them.

In our time, Theodor Adorno and Julia Kristeva are two writers who have turned their attention to this process of transformation and to understanding the dynamics between deeply private inclinations and their political analogues. One way to recognize the distinctively modern cast of their thinking is to place it in the context of the work of Gaston Bachelard whose book, *The Poetics of Space*, expresses what we might call a traditionally high bourgeois understanding of the meaning of habitation. "Not only our memories, but the things we have forgotten are 'housed,' " Bachelard claims. "Our soul is an abode. And by remembering 'houses' and 'rooms' we learn to abide within ourselves" (xxxiii).

The premises underlying Bachelard's book are ones that both Adorno and Kristeva could easily share: that there is a "metaphysics of consciousness" and that "all great, simple images reveal a psychic state" (72). If we follow Bachelard through all the permutations of his imagination, we learn that he meditates upon the meaning of drawers, wardrobes, nests and shells; but his inquiry begins with "the passionate liaison of our bodies . . . with an unforgettable house" (7), and with the "dynamic rivalry between house and universe" (47). Aligning all the threatening aspects of life with exterior "storms," Bachelard makes the house into a refuge against danger, a "haven that ensures immobility" (132) as well as a space that protects and sustains intimacy. It is a place of seclusion, of hiding, of withdrawing into oneself, and by extension, it provides the ground of any human creativity, since it "allows one to dream in peace" (6). From these characteristics, he extrapolates, claiming that "being reigns in a sort of earthly paradise of matter. . . . It is as though in this material paradise, the human being were bathed in nourishment, as though he were gratified with all the essential benefits" (7).

Listening to Bachelard, one thinks immediately of the European middle and upper-middle classes of the nineteenth century with their well pressed linens and carefully polished furniture; and one remembers that the well-being that suffuses his imagination has been bought by the efforts of innumerable wives and servants who might think differently about this domestic order. Ultimately it is the idea of domestic work that destabilizes the neatness of the figure, for Bachelard is blind to the origin of comfort in human effort and cannot see the potential for strife that exists within seemingly secure walls. Although he can assert that "the gestures that make us conscious of security or freedom are rooted in a profound depth of being" (224), he does not seem to consider that the roots of insecurity and servitude can be equally profound and that the creativity which he so values is often buttressed by the labor of those whose efforts may never result in a similar repose. We can see that what he excludes from his architectural metaphor has the potential for being included and that its presence within might be dangerous. And I will note, here, that Bowles confronts such a possibility when, in *Two Serious Ladies*, she writes that "Mrs. Copperfield's eyes were glazed. She was becoming hysterical. 'No, no—I have always promised myself that I would open the door if someone was trying to break in. He will be less an enemy then. The longer he stays out there, the angrier he will get' " (Bowles, *Works* [1978] 51).

Bachelard wrote *The Poetics of Space* in 1958, but to a contemporary audience his work seems oddly anachronistic, as if it preceded modern history, with all of its ethical dilemmas about housing in a world of radical inequality and with all the problems of transience that result from economic disparities on both national and international levels.

Theodor Adorno was one of the most significant social theorists to address this issue of homelessness after World War II, and he began his work by challenging the myth of outside and inside that informs Bachelard's dream of houses as protected and protective spaces. "Dwelling," he claimed in *Minima Moralia* (1951), "is now impossible. The traditional residences we grew up in have grown intolerable: each trait of comfort in them is paid for with a betrayal of knowledge, each vestige of shelter with the musty pact of family interests" ("Refuge for the Homeless" 38). The dangers that threaten human peace and creativity are no longer located, as Bachelard would have it, outside the home. They have entered into internal space as if to undermine its security from within. In Adorno's eyes, "the bombings of European cities, as well as the labour and concentration camps, merely proceed as executioners with what the immanent development of technology had long decided was to be the fate of houses. These are now good only to be thrown away" (39).

Surveying Western history from the vantage of a German Jewish philosopher living in exile, he could see the civic destructiveness of Hitler and of the Allies' response to him as chapters in an economic narrative already long underway. In the context of a socialist rethinking of history, the private family house had become obsolete—both an ethically weighted sign of the persistence of private property relations and a throwback to a time before industrial technology had turned habitations into "living cases manufactured by experts for philistines" (38). To Adorno, Bachelard's thinking about the meaning of private space would have seemed dangerously nostalgic, and as he put it, a way of "embalming" oneself within a false system of signs: the individual life that private homes had been designed to symbolize and to sustain was past.

When trying to answer questions about what ethically responsible people should do about their living situations, Adorno arrived at tentative solutions designed to announce their tentativeness. "The best mode of conduct," he suggested, "still seems an uncommitted, suspended one: to lead a private life, as far as the social order and one's own needs will tolerate nothing else, but not to attach weight to it, as to something still socially substantial and individually appropriate" (39). Quoting Nietzsche, who considered it to be "good fortune" not to own a home, he added that today "it is part of morality not to be at home in one's home" (39).

As part of a history of the meaning of human habitation, one of Adorno's contributions was a tacit admission of the dangers lurking within the bourgeois home. Where Bachelard had imbued the house with every aspect of abundance, Adorno looked at such plenitude as a sign of greed that left unspoken the story of what had been sacrificed to create such comfort. Where Bachelard saw houses as images of psychic wholeness, Adorno recognized how social and economic relations were able to reach into the deepest recesses of private life and to corrupt the very possibility of harmony. His contribution was a negative one whose function, like so much of his negative, dialectical thinking, was to disrupt and to fragment in the anticipation of some future, more authentic wholeness.

Julia Kristeva could, in this one respect, be seen as his intellectual heir, for her discussion of "not-at-homeness" in *Strangers to Ourselves* carries forward Adorno's understanding of the purposes of negativity. Not only does she recognize the alarms and hesitations inherent in modern habitations but she also devises a connection between such discomfort and a new mode of civility in the political arena.

Like Adorno, Kristeva challenges Bachelard. Although she might agree that "our soul is an abode," she would scarcely support his assertion that "by remembering 'houses' and 'rooms' we learn to abide within ourselves" (xxxiii). To the contrary, she reminds us that postmodern culture rarely gives its participants any way to find such comfort and that anxiety can, if rightly understood, prove to be a valuable resource. In her judgment, the extent to which we do not abide within ourselves is the measure of our potential for peaceful coexistence with those who are different from us. "Henceforth," she declares, "we know we are foreigners to ourselves, and it is with the help of that sole support that we can attempt to live with others" (170).

Such statements help us to discern the particular way that Kristeva elides the boundaries of the real: following Adorno's example, she challenges Western culture's unthinking categories of inclusion and exclusion, showing us the ideological nature of an opposition that we find so familiar that it appears to be natural. Without a "social group structured about a power base and provided with legislation," she observes, "the externality represented by the foreigner and most often experienced as unfavorable . . . would simply not exist" (96).

Using the "uncanny" and "unhomeliness" as metaphors for both psychic and social constructions of reality, she indicates how individual consciousness can replicate political resistance to the outsider: both can be subject to the fearful invasion of an alien presence; both can experience a secret intrusion of terror; both can try to shut out what is fearful without even facing the nature of that which is rejected. Kristeva meets these others in several ways. She imagines them as fully as possible, asking questions about their origin, motivations, and cultural positioning:

> For it is on account of having no one at home against whom to vent their fury, their conflation of love and hatred, and of finding the strength not to give in to it, that they wander about the world, neutral, but solaced for having developed an interior distance from the fire and ice that seared them in the past. (9)

> As far back as his memory can reach, it is delightfully bruised; misunderstood by a loved and yet absent-minded, discrete, or worried mother, the exile is a stranger to his mother. (5)

> The foreign is rejected, detested, ready to flee because of insults suffered, staying only when intrusion is tolerated. "You do not count for anyone." (14)

In this contemplative mode, Kristeva weaves an image of the other of culture, separating herself from that culture by the steadfastness of her scrutiny and by her form of direct address. To speak to others as "you" is inclusive; it is a way to initiate dialogue. In a similar manner, she constructs a journey through the historical images of the foreigner, asking questions about how the West has construed difference and either extended or failed to extend hospitality to strangers: "From heart pangs to first jabs, the foreigner's face forces us to display the secret manner in which we face the world, stares into all our faces, even in the most familial, the most tightly knit communities" (34).

To another social philosopher, this staring back and forth that catches people in the dynamics of resentment and fear might be considered to continue indefinitely and might, in fact, be identified as the signature of modern life: once positioned in conflict, the rejected person "takes root" in his world of rejection while the "rooted one" (17) grows deaf to the speech of the other. But to Kristeva, this "seemingly peaceful coexistence . . . hides the abyss: an abysmal world, the end of the world" (17). The aporia, the break in the system, as she analyzes it, will come, if at all, from our recognition of similarity in difference: "The foreigner's friends . . . could only be those who feel foreign to themselves" (23). That is, it is by recognizing the exiled regions of our own hearts, by shattering repression, by acknowledging the divisions within ourselves that we are led to cross borders into new interpersonal and political territory: "There will be a 'we' thanks only to that splitting that all wanderers are urged to discover in themselves and in others" (82).

To be sure, Kristeva imagines this social realignment in a "beyond": there is no "housing" for such a project as the world exists today, but it is important to notice that her dream is grounded not on utopian longing but on the disease of the present and on brokenness that can be used without disdain.

4

> "You misunderstand," said Mrs. Copperfield in a trembling voice. She wanted very
> much to remind him gently that this was not a house but a room in a hotel.
>
> —Jane Bowles, *Two Serious Ladies*

If we return now to thinking about the nature of Jane Bowles's fiction, we can see how her work mirrors, with an almost uncanny exactness, the discomfort and estrangement that both Adorno and Kristeva posit as the prerequisite of human transformation. Indeed, they help us to identify her accomplishment as that of a cultural "vagabond," for, without family, regular work or customary residence, she writes always from an unhoused and transient position, confronting fixed contexts as an unfixed and roving subject. Toward the end of her writing career, Bowles seemed to be on the verge of making explicit the connection between her own marginality and the emergence of a new moral order. In "Emmy Moore's Journal," for example, Bowles's protagonist writes to her husband about her attempted solution to the problem of not-being-at-home: "I cannot simply live out my experiment here at the Henry Hotel without trying to justify or at least explain in letters my reasons for being here," she says, "I am certain that until the prayed-for metamorphosis has occurred I shall go on feeling just this need [to justify my actions]"(445). But we can see the seeds of this tendency in her earliest writing. It is the same ambivalence about shelter that had prompted Edgar in *Two Serious Ladies* to write to his wife, "I can only say that there is, in every man's life a strong urge to leave his life behind him for a while and seeks a new one. . . . Will you take me back?" (181); and, indeed, we can see that the entire structure of this novel is built on maintaining a similar tension between the familiar and the foreign, a tension which, once again, is expressed in images of houses and in a movement out of their protection or an unsatisfactory return. *En route*, Bowles's characters perch precariously in cafes, bars, restaurants, garages, hotels, and pensions—in places which imply further travel as a way to ameliorate distress and to effect transformation. If we look at the narrative in terms of its desire to remain unsettled, then we can find a satisfactory way of explaining its two seemingly unrelated plots: the story of Miss Goering's dismantling of her family home and the story of Mrs. Copperfield's "honeymoon" trip to Panama; for their contrary motions achieve similar, disquieting results: Miss Goering reestablishes a domestic situation, bringing foreign or discordant elements into it; and Mrs. Copperfield ventures out into the Latin world carrying with her the need to domesticate what is alien. Both emplotments turn on the paradox of the uncanny—the unhomely home—which provides stasis only at the moment when it will be destroyed.

The novel opens in a bourgeois setting that could serve as an emblem of Bachelard's earthly paradise. Christine Goering, a young, single woman, has inherited her family's home, which provides her with an easy, even luxurious lifestyle, and which she fills with beautiful objects. Into this bourgeois order, she invites a woman to act as a companion, a job Miss Gamelon is eager to fill since she loves beauty and ease but has the resources for neither. No sooner has she moved in than Miss Goering announces her plan to sell the house and to move to smaller, more primitive quarters. Like Harriet in "Camp Cataract," she needs to inch away from security in stages—once she has "mastered" the ungainly little island cottage, she will venture forth again.

To her companions, who now include a casual lover named Arnold, her plan is senseless, and in arguing against it, they recite what Bachelard would have regarded as the chief virtues of bourgeois habitation. Arnold tries to dissuade her by saying, "This is a really beautiful house. . . . It has a quality of past splendour about it which thrills me" (30). And he later reinforces his view by remarking that "[t]he house is done in exquisite taste . . . and it is filled with rest and peace" (31). Miss Goering admits that it gives her a "comfortable feeling of safety" (28), but her own goals have nothing to do with domesticity. In her view, to abide in physical comfort is to condone the complacency that such comfort supports. To change, to go into uncharted spiritual territory, she feels it necessary to challenge the barriers that promote the unthinking continuation of habit. It is almost as if she were living out Adorno's injunction "not to be at home in one's home" (39) or purposefully courting the *unheimlich*, as if one could invite the transformation of the homely into its dreaded opposite. With her freeloading about to be curtailed, Miss Gamelon becomes vitriolic: " 'There are certain people,' she says, 'who turn peace from the door as though it were a red dragon breathing fire out of its nostrils' " (31), not knowing that the "dragon" of insecurity is, in fact, an excellent way of describing the goal of Miss Goering's quest.

Other trials appear as soon as the three move and the entourage is joined by Arnold's father. The house, already ill-equipped and too small, becomes so cramped that every meal and every evening's sleep must be improvised in little corners of space. Like the apartment that served as the background to "Camp Cataract," this space becomes the material counterpart of anxiety, a place where friction increases until its inhabitants are literally bruised and wounded. Arnold eventually breaks a bottle on Miss Gamelon's head, cutting her and drawing blood. The experience is so disorienting for her that she feels herself to be sliding between coziness and

dread: "The world and the people in it had suddenly slipped beyond her compre-
hension and she felt in great danger of losing the whole world once and for all"
(116). All that she had once considered certain grows unfamiliar, and Bowles expresses her distress by investing buildings with human attributes: it is Miss Goering's
fault, for example, for not caring enough about "who gets under the same roof with
them" (116). Although Miss Gamelon eventually takes Arnold as a lover, betraying
her patron, and becoming herself one of the hostile elements she laments, she regards Miss Goering as sinister for opening the way for the invasion of the foreign.

As we have seen in Bowles's previous fiction, what is intolerable for one character proves to be intolerable for another, but for different reasons. When Miss
Gamelon's threshold for anxiety has been reached, Miss Goering's capacity for tension has just begun. Because her house had grown too familiar, she decides that it
is now necessary for her to take little trips to the tip of the island. Here Bowles
begins a new dialectic of estrangement, sending her character into more and more
bizarre situations, all of them marked as transient by the cafes, bars, cabarets, bowling alleys, and restaurants that so frequently inhabit her writing. And here, too, she
continues to elide psychic events and their material counterparts. Miss Goering's
second lover, Andy, explains how he betrayed his fiancée in terms of the very architecture of the world: "I didn't tell her because I wanted the buildings to stay in place
for her" (151). And he excuses his dishonesty by transcribing it into a prison: "I didn't
want her to have to lock something up inside her and look at the world through a
nailed window" (151).

Once again we are faced with an imaginary world of mutually futile alternatives, where public space can collapse even as internal space can hold one hostage.
Boundaries or thresholds come again into play as the narrative struggles to avoid
any committed extremes; willed instability replaces steadfastness of residence, passage becomes a permanent way of life; spaces are defined between other places,
other times, as if they were all cafes or bars that shelter those who have no home.

With Miss Goering this liminal space is created by purposeful estrangement;
with Mrs. Copperfield, the second of the "two serious ladies" in the novel, the voyage out is forced on her by marriage. The consequence of her insecurity is a contrary
need to allay her fear of unknown places. Bowles tells us that "Mrs. Copperfield
always hated to know what was around her, because it always turned out to be even
stranger than she had feared" (59), and that the foreign landscapes filled her with "a
rising feeling of dread" (59). Urged to the edges of jungles, the edges of oceans and
to the very limits of civilization, she draws back: " 'I think I've gone far enough,' she
said" (59). While her husband pursues his explorations, Mrs. Copperfield will try to
reestablish some recognizable mode of domestic life: "I must try to find a nest in
this outlandish place" (40). And, as we might by now expect, her solution is not a

full-scale retreat but the compromise offered by hotels: "She . . . closed her eyes, hoping that perhaps she might become exalted enough to run down and join her husband. But the wind did not blow quite hard enough and behind her closed eyes she saw Pacifica and Mrs. Quill standing in front of the Hotel de las Palmas" (60). She tells Mrs. Quill, "You sound so happy I have a feeling I'm going to nestle right here in this hotel" (56).

Eventually Mrs. Copperfield feels compelled to make clear the distinction between transient and permanent shelter: " 'You misunderstand,' said Mrs. Copperfield in a trembling voice. She wanted very much to remind him gently that this was not a house but a room in a hotel" (52). And having found a temporary respite from the fierce sway of more extreme opinions, she stops. Mr. Copperfield may have found her reprehensible ("I won't come back because I can't look at you. . . . You're a horror" [108]), counting her temerity as sufficient reason to abandon her; but Theodor Adorno would have understood the politics implicit in her stance: "The attempt to evade responsibility for one's residence by moving into a hotel or furnished rooms makes the enforced conditions of emigration a wisely-chosen norm" (38).

Beyond focusing attention on this hesitant choice about where and how to live, Bowles's novel does not make connections between Mrs. Copperfield's intensely private inclination and the social implications of her conduct. Bowles ends *Two Serious Ladies* with Miss Goering and Mrs. Copperfield meeting in a restaurant at a moment just before each will be betrayed; but she leaves them both feeling displaced and thus, according to either Adorno or Kristeva, vulnerable to the intrusions of the other, whether the other comes from a home down the street or off-island or outside the state. "The foreigner's friends," Kristeva reminds us, "could only be those who feel foreign to themselves" (23). She concludes that, "Henceforth the foreigner is neither a race nor a nation. The foreigner is neither glorified as a secret *Volksgeist* nor banished as disruptive of rationalist urbanity. Uncanny, foreignness is within us: we are our own foreigners" (181). And, indeed, when we look at the fiction in which Bowles does portray international confrontation, we find the not-at-home characters, those who have introjected the strange into their own psyches, to be responsive to the alternative values and perspectives espoused by strangers.

We see this in "Everything Is Nice," which begins in a street in "the blue Moslem town [that] skirted the edge of a cliff" (Bowles, *Works* [1978] 313). Here a Western woman meets a native who introduces herself as Zodelia and recognizes her interlocutor as "Betsoul's friend. . . . You sit in her house and you sleep in her house. . . . Your name is Jeanie and you live in a hotel" (314). Zodelia is wearing a haik and carrying a basket with a loaf of bread stuffed between the quills of a porcupine— even in foreign territory, Bowles does not find nourishment to be an uncomplicated issue. The distinctive tensions of this story comes from its dramatization of ambivalence and unmoored loyalties. The Moraccan woman, and indeed all of the native women Jeanie meets, cannot understand why she does not remain firmly within her ethnic group but longs, instead, to be invited into the interiors of Moslem houses. Zodelia even pantomimes the anomalous situation:

> "I am the people in the hotel," she said, "Watch me." . . . "Good-bye, Jeanie, good-bye. Where are you going?"
>
> "I am going to a Moslem house to visit my Moslem friends, Betsoul and her family. I will sit in a Moslem room and eat Moslem food and sleep on a Moslem bed."
>
> "Jeanie, Jeanie, when will you come back to us in the hotel and sleep in your own room?"
>
> "I will come to you in three days. . . . I will spend half the week with Moslem friends and half with Nazarenes." (314)

While Zodelia performs her little skit, Jeanie becomes aware once again of the cliff and its shadow. The location itself is menacing to her as is the difference of perception between the women. In the distance at the water's edge, they can see another woman wearing a haik. Zodelia announces that the distant woman is looking at the ocean, while Jeanie decides that she is looking down and washing her feet. Neither of them will change her view, and we can read this scene as a parable, writ small, about the internal coherence of ethnic groups and their customary differences of perspective.

Eventually the Moroccans invite her into their home, but they continue to maintain their worried scrutiny of her. "Where is your mother?" they ask (315), and "Where is your husband? . . . Where is your mother? . . . Why don't you go and sit with your mother in her own house?" (318), and they wonder "Is she crazy?" (317). Zodelia invites Jeanie to a wedding and then goes back on her promise; there will be no marriage, either between brides and bridegrooms, or between women of different ethnic groups. Jeanie is riveted in her unmet desire for inclusion and for a "we" of experience. Instead she is rejected, implicitly insulted, and left as hungry as Kafka's hunger artist who could find no earthly food that he liked. She is suspended in her awareness of difference, barely touched before she must move away, barely met before she must go further.

Among the varied and rich travel literatures of the Western tradition, few writers, if any, have written about the attempted meetings of strangers with such abjection. One is reminded of Jane Bowles's letters to Paul Bowles from the Hotel Villa de France in Tangier where she describes her own private search for a realignment of belonging:

> I continue loving Tangier—maybe because I have the feeling of being on the edge of something that I will someday enter. . . . Perhaps I shall be perpetually

on the edge of this civilization of theirs. When I am in Cherifa's house, I am still on the edge of it, and when I come out, I can't believe I was really in it. (*Letters* 85)

She also wrote him of her frustration: "I can't bear to be continuously hurled *out* of the Arab world. . . . Perhaps you have never been in this inferior position vis-à-vis the Arabs" (*Letters* 93).

Jane Bowles did not consider this international project, this going-out-into alien experience, to have value to anyone other than herself. For her it was an intensely private journey that was propelled by her need to establish and then transgress boundaries, as if living on the edges of new cultural situations could somehow enhance the life of the spirit. But if we listen to the comments of Gilles Deleuze and Felix Guattari, we are reminded that such confrontations of the alien can never remain totally private. According to them, "border writing," because it uses the language of a dominant culture in the service of challenging cultural hegemony, is always political (see *Kafka: Toward a Minor Literature*). Julia Kristeva would have also understood the political dimension of Bowles's imagination, for she would have seen that what divides people within themselves, making them anguished or frightened, can become the vehicle of a more encompassing social integration. She claims that:

> The foreigner is a "symptom": psychologically he signifies the difficulty we have of living as an other and with others; politically, he underscores the limits of nation-states and of the national political conscience that characterizes them and that we have all deeply interiorized to the point of considering it normal that there are foreigners, that is, people who do not have the same rights as we do. (103)

It is by recognizing the unhomely aspects of our psyche, by espousing our own interior distress, that we make symbolic integration possible; for the divisions of the social world will only disappear, Kristeva insists, when we acknowledge ourselves as foreign.

If we bear in mind Kristeva's comments about the political uses of being-not-at-home in ourselves while we reconsider all of the abject wanderers of Bowles's creative universe, we can think not just of their dis-ease but also of their promise: "No obstacle stops [them], and all suffering, all insults, all rejections are indifferent to [them] as [they] seek . . . that invisible and promised territory, that country that does not exist but that [they] bear . . . in [their] dreams, and that must indeed be called a beyond" (5). When Mr. Copperfield first takes his young wife to Panama, he asks, "Do you care whether or not you have a private bath?"; she replies, "No, no. I don't care about that. It's not a question of comfort at all. It's something much more than that" (39). Although others tell her repeatedly that her hotel is "a cheap place; awful place; it's filthy dirty besides" (101), she holds tenaciously to her project of refusing the formation of habit. Inexperienced as she is, she insists on constantly renegotiating the uncomfortable boundaries between flesh and spirit, social and solitary, one nation's customs and another's. Her goal is nothing less than the transformation of culture. Like so many of the characters of Bowles's imagination, she has learned that it is only through anguish that we come to inhabit the earth.

9

"Some Fun in the Mud"

Decrepitude and Salvation in the World of Jane Bowles

Robert E. Lougy

"You should come out, really. It's a madhouse. The streets are full of soldiers and sailors and whores. The women are all in long dresses . . . incredibly cheap dresses. They'll all talk to you. Come on out."

—Jane Bowles, *Two Serious Ladies*

THE WORLD OF Jane Bowles is inhabited by the lost and strayed, by derelicts, whores, misfits, wanderers, the homeless, and the frightened. They live, exposed and vulnerable, within a world that is in a state of decrepitude, having lost a wholeness for them that is probably never possessed. Yet it is within this world that salvation must be sought: "you've got to admit," says one of her characters in *Two Serious Ladies*, "we're living in the world, unless we want to behave like crazy kids or escaped lunatics or something like that" (Bowles, *Works* [1978] 172). On the one hand, then, there is the world; and, on the other, there is childhood, lunacy, eccentricity, and various forms of mysticism. And although happiness and salvation must be sought within it, Bowles's world stands forth as evidence of our fall from happiness, an outrageously real and undeniable contrast to those centers of value that exist only as pockets of memory incapable of being retrieved or lived in again.

In speaking at one point of a novel she was working on, Bowles spoke of how

The more I get into it [the novel in progress] . . . the more frightened I become at the isolated position I feel myself in *vis à vis* of all the serious writers whom I consider to be of any serious mind. . . . I am serious but I am isolated and my experience is probably of no interest at this point to anyone. (*Letters* 33)

Her art, though, does connect with our condition, but it establishes those connections in its own mysterious and ambiguous ways. Her characters, however, exist within an isolation that cannot be broken down, always wandering in search of that which eludes them. "It's all so strange and it has no connection with anything," says Mrs. Copperfield of *Two Serious Ladies* of her particular sense of dislocation (60). Isolation in Bowles's fiction is an existential condition, a metaphysical given for those who inhabit a world stripped of myth, deprived of God. "It is intolerable," Jane Bowles once wrote, "to be in this world without a myth" (qtd. in Dillon, *Life* 299), and most of Bowles's characters either seek to flee from such a recognition or attempt to endure the pain that such a condition creates. And for her central figures, this choice is never casual or to be taken lightly: young Christina Goering of *Two Serious Ladies* tells a girlfriend that "I'd rather have God and no sun than the sun and no God. Do you understand?"(5).

Bowles's characters are haunted by the lack of a sense of place or home. For a political radical in *Two Serious Ladies*, the bar that he and his girlfriend frequent is "just another shithouse where poor people imbibe spirits in order to forget the state of their income, which is non-existent," but for her, as she tells him, "we come here only because it is . . . becoming a home to us; a second home . . . I love it very much" (139). Molly of *In the Summer House* similarly regards the summer house as a sanctuary, a place of retreat and love, until she too, like so many of Bowles's characters, must enter the world, with all of the guilt, sin, and loss that it involves. But if Bowles's figures are haunted by a sense of place or home, either imagined or remembered, her landscapes and topographies are most often fairly vaguely drawn, more like those of medieval morality plays or like the landscapes of Beckett and Kafka, spatial enclosures within which salvation is sought amidst the experience of a sense of sin and guilt that most often has no specific or identifiable origin.

Exploring questions of sin and salvation, as they are variously and paradoxically manifested in a world from which God has withdrawn, Jane Bowles explores, with at times painful intensity and beauty, the essential loneliness of all human beings, that darkness and terror that linger around even the happiest and most intimate of moments. But it is a vision seen through a style that is uniquely her own. Paul Bowles has spoken of her "wonderful elliptical way of seeing things," and her elliptical glances are evident in the following exchange between Miss Goering and Arnold's father in *Two Serious Ladies*:

> "What kind of men come in here [a bar]," he asked her.
> "Oh," said Goering, "all sorts of men, I guess. Rich and poor, workers and bankers, criminals and dwarfs."
> "Dwarfs," Arnold's father repeated uneasily. (165)

It is the final line of this exchange, almost as peculiar as the clientele of the bar, that identifies the dialogue as that of Jane Bowles. We hear this same elliptical voice in Miss Goering's reflections on a particular community she visits:

> "Why, people have been living here for years," she said to herself. "It is strange that I hadn't thought of this before. They're here naturally, with their family ties, their neighborhood stores, the sense of decency and morality, and they have certainly their organizations for fighting the criminals of the community." She felt almost happy now that she had remembered all this. (130)

But yet when we try to identify the source of this uniqueness and the delight that her writing so often gives us, we find ourselves in that predicament Dillon describes:

> What she said was often puzzling and at the same time hilarious. If asked, "what did she say that was so funny," no one can give an exact answer. Her wit was in her words, of course, but it was also in her timing, in the play of voice against gesture. (*Life* 141)

But then again, the world with which she presents us is similarly ambiguous and puzzling, not lending itself to easy description or understanding by those who try to come at it directly. Toward the end of *Two Serious Ladies*, one of the work's male characters writes to Christina Goering, referring to a scene that has taken place earlier in the novel:

> I will always remember the story you told me when we first met, in which I always felt was buried some strange significance, although I must admit to you now that I could not explain what. (182)

This particular vignette does indeed have, as Arnold suggests, special significance, some larger meaning "buried," as it were, within it, for it gives us not only a metonymical image of that world we confront in Bowles's art, one that has been dismantled, torn apart, and wounded, but also a haunting image of that human subject who must inhabit such spaces, gazing upon its holes and gaps. The story that Arnold has in mind is told to him and Mrs. Copperfield by Christina Goering, quite early in the novel, as she recounts a scene she had just recently witnessed:

> From my window I could see the room of this building, as the wall opposite me had already been torn down. . . . I finally felt rather sad watching this and I was about to go away when a man came into one of these rooms and, walking deliberately over to the bed, took a coverlet which he folded under his arm. . . . Then he walked around the room aimlessly for a bit and finally he stood at the very edge of his room looking down into the yard with his arms akimbo. I could see him more clearly now, and I could easily tell he was an artist. As he stood

there, I was increasingly filled with horror, very much as though I were watching a scene in a nightmare. (17)

Jacques Lacan has spoken of the image of the fragmented body, the *corps morcelé*, finding variations of this image in our dreams, our nightmares, and our art. He suggests in his essay on the mirror stage that this image has its origin in the infant's bodily sense of itself as fragmented, insufficient. And, Lacan theorizes, just as the infant seeks in the mirror-image an ultimately illusory relief or escape from such fragmentation or insufficiency, so too do we as adults seek throughout the rest of our lives for similarly illusory or fictitious images of totality, completion, looking for them in what Lacan will identify as "the lure of spatial identification [and] . . . succession of phantasies" (See *Écrits* 4). The fragmented body, bruised and in pain, searching for a sense of wholeness or unity, haunts the landscapes and cityscapes of Bowles's world; but her world itself is also a fragmented body, that which has been torn apart, Bowles suggests, by the death of myth and the withdrawal of God from it.

And Bowles's strongest or most compelling figures are those who attempt to resist those fantasies and illusory spaces of wholeness or totality that might make us forget the inescapable condition of the human experience. Lacan locates some of the most eloquent expressions of the *corps morcelé* in the paintings of Hieronymus Bosch—"we must turn, he writes, "to the works of Hieronymus Bosch for an atlas of all the aggressive images that torment mankind" (*Écrits* 11)—and like a scene from one of Bosch's canvasses, Bowles's world is often inexplicable, grotesque, phantasmagoric, and within it her characters are always on the move, trying to flee from that which they cannot flee or attempting to overtake that which forever eludes them. Only temporary reprieve from this condition is possible—Bowles's characters inevitably awaken, after their fitful naps and troubled sleep, into a world that forces itself upon them while at the same time it denies them access to it. It is a world of impenetrable surfaces, hard, opaque, often rough, permitting only fleeting moments of clarity that must finally die, aborted perceptions untranslated into action. For some of her characters, such as Christina Goering, partial reprieve from this world seems at times possible:

> "A guardian angel comes when you are very young and gives you special dispensation."
> "From what?"
> "From the world." (12)

Yet, like the man she saw in the apartment, her world too remains torn apart, watched over at best by a guardian angel who has nodded off to sleep.

Bowles's characters exist, however, not only in loneliness and homelessness, but in a perpetual state of guilt as well. In a world from which God has withdrawn, but is insistently present by virtue of His absence, there is no source of salvation, no myth that might allow one to find a sense of place and belonging. The first time we meet Christina Goering, she is a young girl baptizing one of her sister's playmates:

> If you don't lie down in the mud and let me pack the mud over you and then wash you in the stream, you'll be forever condemned. Do you want to be forever condemned? This is your moment to decide.(6)

And throughout the rest of the novel, she tries to work out her own plan of salvation, attempting to redeem sins, the specific nature of which she cannot know.[1] "The hardest thing for me to do," she confesses, "is really move from one thing to another" (158), and thus she is constantly moving, forcing herself into a series of situations that are either distasteful, frightening, or difficult for her. "You could perfectly well work out your salvation during certain hours of the day without having to move everything," a friend tells Christina, but she replies that "that would not be in accordance with the spirit of the age" (29). We must, Christina tells her friend, "change first of our own volition and according to our own inner promptings, before they impose completely arbitrary changes upon us" (29).

But in Bowles's world, those same inner promptings that make our gestures of freedom possible also urge us to accept that easeful and comfortable nature against which her greatest creations—such as Christina Goering and Mrs. Copperfield of *Two Serious Ladies* and Gertrude Eastman of *In the Summer House*— constantly struggle. For in succumbing to such promptings, we conceal those aspects of our existence that are more terrifying and more real than most of us can bear. As Mrs. Constable of *In the Summer House* observes,

> They say that people can't live unless they fill their lives with petty details. That's people's way of avoiding the black pit. I'm just a weak ordinary, *very ordinary* woman in her middle years, but I've been able to wipe all the petty details from my life. . . . (Bowles, *Works* [1978] 269)

For those who have the courage to descend into this "black pit" redemption seems possible, and thus Bowles's figures thrust themselves into it, seeking out that God Who might be hiding at the bottom. "There are certain people," says Miss Gamelon, a friend of Christina Goering's, "who turn peace from the door as though it were a dragon breathing fire out of its nostrils and there are certain people who can't leave God alone either" (33). The safety and comfort of this world must be shunned, fought against, in much the same way that Miss Goering resists the lure of property:

> It gives me a comfortable feeling of safety. . . . However, in order to work out my own little idea of salvation I really believe that it is necessary for me to live in some tawdry place and particularly in some place where I was not born. (28)

In "Going to Massachusetts," one of Bowles's unfinished stories, a character by the name of Bozoe Flanner expresses similar sentiments to Janet, her lover and friend:

> I don't feel that I can allow you to sink into the mire of contentment and happy ambitious enterprise. It is my duty to prevent you from it as much as I do for myself. . . . Don't accept social or financial security as your final aim. (Bowles, *Works* [1978] 457–58)

For Lionel of *In the Summer House*, homes especially create a dangerous illusion of well-being: "To me, this place is a fake, I chose it for protection, and it doesn't work out" (272). Such places entrap one and thus exclude the outside world. "What interests us most, certainly," says Mrs. Copperfield, "is finding out what we are like" (71), and by fleeing from the world, we also turn our back on those chances of self-definition that it makes possible: "Suppose," asks Lionel,

> I kept on closing that door against the ocean every night because the ocean made me sad and then one night I went to open it and I couldn't find the door. Suppose I couldn't tell it apart from the wall anymore. Then it would be too late and we'd be shut in here forever once and for all. (272–73)

Bowles's major characters, however, continue to seek for a proper home, even as they flee or attempt to flee from that which might impede their search for salvation. They seek spaces that will fulfill rather than diminish self, that will make possible an authentic harmony between them and the world they inhabit. Such quests, however, are doomed to the failure described by Gertrude Eastman of *In the Summer House*:

> . . . sometimes I wake up at night with a strange feeling of isolation . . . as if I'd fallen off the cliffs and landed miles away from everything that was close to my heart . . . Even my griefs and sorrows don't seem to belong to me. Nothing does—as if a shadow had passed over my whole life and made it dark. I try saying my name aloud, over and over again, but it doesn't hook together. (210)

This shadow that passes over one's life, darkening it and making it impossible to find connections, to "hook things together," is for Bowles evidence that we inhabit a world fallen from God's grace and a self fallen from the grace of childhood. Thus most of Bowes's central figures are either in pursuit of a God Who continually evades them or a childhood that similarly cannot be found. In their various wanderings and driftings, Bowles's figures search for a home in a world from which God has withdrawn and, in doing so, has taken all homes with Him. Mrs. Copperfield observes:

> . . . when people believed in God they carried Him from one place to another. They carried Him through the jungles and across the Artic Circle. God watched over everybody, and all men were brothers. Now there is nothing to carry with

you from one place to another, and as far as I'm concerned, these people might as well be kangaroos; yet somehow there must be someone here who will remind me of something . . . I must try to find a nest in this outlandish place. (40)

By the end of the novel, Mrs. Copperfield has found, or so she tells us, her happiness, but she is still "only a step from desperation all the time" (199). Befriended by a whore, Pacifica, whose name and apparent resilience conceal the darkness of her vision, Mrs. Copperfield enjoys her companionship and friendship as the novel ends, but it is a relationship strained by Mrs. Copperfield's desperate and possessive clinging to Pacifica. Like that temporary euphoria Mrs. Copperfield seeks in gin, Pacifica both threatens and comforts, a source, by virtue of the fact that her continued presence is always in doubt, of both solace and anxiety for the woman who loves her.

Vacillating between fulfillment and emptiness, Mrs. Copperfield, in her attempt to live within a world "of happy moments," is able to find some transient but intensely experienced fragments of happiness. Such fragments for Bowles arise from fleeting moments of human contact and, in this respect, resemble that beauty Mrs. Copperfield once found in the face of an older woman:

"I was once in love with an older woman," said Mrs. Copperfield eagerly. "She was no longer beautiful, but in her face I found fragments of beauty which were much more exciting to me than any beauty that I have known at its height." (49)

All of her figures move toward a death they carry within themselves and because they are for the most part acutely aware of this reality, they are, as one of her character's says, "so lost and so far away and so frightened" (60). Moments in her art that provide temporary reprieve—there is no escape—from this anxiety can best be characterized as repetitions or approximations of childhood, moments in which her characters can recreate, or have recreated for them, a sense of well-being and wholeness, enclosed within spaces that recall a time prior to their "voyage into the world." But such spaces are precarious, fragile precisely because they are fantasies; depending upon an oblivion of the world itself, they are incapable of being sustained for long. Pacifica speaks of such a moment to Mrs. Copperfield:

When you wake up in the morning and the first minute you open your eyes and you don't know who you are or what your life has been—that is beautiful. Then when you know who you are and what day in your life it is and you still think you are sailing in the air like a happy bird—that is beautiful. That is, when you don't have any worries. (47–48)

But Pacifica is not so serene as her name might suggest. Like Alva Perry, the central figure of "Plain Pleasures," the title story of Bowles's volume of short stories, Pacifica's pleasures are anything but plain. Mrs. Quill, the proprietor/madam of the hotel/brothel where Mrs. Copperfield and Pacifica live, hints to Mrs. Copperfield that some rather peculiar sadomasochistic dynamics are possibly at the heart of the attraction between Pacifica and Meyer, her sailor boyfriend. For in response to Mrs. Copperfield's remark that Pacifica "wouldn't allow him [Meyer] to hurt her . . . before she went to bed with him," Mrs. Quill tells her, "Sure she would . . . but I don't know anything about such things" (55). But more than Pacifica's erotic life is troubled or ambiguous. Mrs. Quill also tells Mrs. Copperfield, for example, of how Pacifica "is always looking on the darkest side of life. She's the gloomiest thing I ever knew" (58), and of how she, although much younger than Mrs. Quill, has "been out in the world much longer than I have," that "the Lord has spared me more than He has spared Pacifica" (79).

Pacifica seems to have survived more or less intact her entrance into the world, however, regardless of Mrs. Quill's rather dark pronouncements on her attitude. She is one of Bowles's few characters who seems capable of confronting the world on its own terms. For most of her characters, the voyage into the world is violent, traumatic, and wrenching, a birth into an arena of knowledge and death that recapitulates our original Fall. In "Camp Cataract," one of Bowles's finest stories, Sadie, a middle-aged woman, has been playing at being grown up throughout her life: she "certainly yearned to live in the grown-up world that her parents had established for them when they were children, but . . . she did not understand it properly" (Bowles, *Works* [1978] 368). But shortly before her death she discovers the nature of this experience during the moment that is both unanticipated and unsought:

> She opened her mouth to speak and doubled over, clutching at her stomach as though an animal were devouring her. Sweat beaded her forehead and she planted her feet wide apart on the ground as if this animal would be born. (396)

This moment in which she gives birth to herself or to a permanently transformed perception of herself is a painful and irreversible recognition: "Sadie knew then that this agony she was suffering was itself the dreaded voyage into the world—the very voyage she had always feared Harriet [her sister] would make" (396). The enclosures of her apartment and her previous innocence collapse, and Sadie is thrown into the world, ultimately responding to it, as we discover in a twist that provides this story with one of Bowles's most innovative closures, by committing suicide. Her sister, on the other hand, is "a great admirer of the nomad, vagabonds, gypsies, seafaring men . . . the old prophets [who] roamed the world . . . and most of the visionaries" (361). Yet by the end of the story, she is still within Camp Cataract, where she has gone "to imitate the natural family roots of childhood . . . long enough so that I myself will feel: Camp Cataract is *habit*, Camp Cataract is life, Camp Cataract is not escape" (363).

Those of Bowles's characters who do not retreat into themselves reach out, thrusting themselves against a world that is cold and impenetrable, in an attempt to become enfolded by a sense of themselves as part of a larger community of selves that will make it possible for them to retain or regain what they have lost, forgotten, or are fearful of not finding. Whether it be the salvation of a Christina Goering, the "nest" sought by Mrs. Copperfield, or those happy moments Lionel is afraid of having forgotten, the object of their desire, however vaguely defined it might be, is always in front of them, capable of being approached only asymptotically and thus never grasped. Thought only makes one more acutely aware of the limitations of reflection and introspection, of its final ineffectuality in a world and self that remain unknowable. "If you could only stop me," says Mrs. Copperfield, "from thinking, always" (72). Mrs. Constable of *In the Summer House* confesses that "I don't want any answers. It's too late for answers. Not that I ever asked much anyway. . . . I never cared for answers. You can take your answers and flush them down the toilet" (247). Christina Goering comes to a similar recognition during a conversation she has with an old man:

> "Well," said the old man, lifting his arm and making a vague gesture which included the river and the sky, "you can see where it is impossible to know anything." Mrs. Goering looked around her and it seemed to her that there could be nothing hidden from their eyes, but at the same time she believed what the old man said to her. She felt both ashamed and uneasy. (135)

Within Bowles's skewed and fallen world, contexts and verbal constructions go astray, moving from sense to non-sense and from the tragic to the comic, and then back again, with little if any recognition on the part of the characters of these shifts. In this respect, Bowles's dialogue often reminds one of Dickens (thus Mrs. Copperfield?), where we also find language taken to its furthest extreme, stopping short of—while at the same time revealing—that chaos and desperation behind the words. Christina Goering is reprimanded by a train conductor, after she has been reported to him by another passenger who is, although herself much more peculiar than Goering, nevertheless convinced that Christina Goering is a lunatic:·

> "the next time you're on this train, stay in your seat and don't molest anybody. If you want to know the time you can ask them without any to-do about it or you can just make a little signal with your hand and I'll be willing to answer all your questions. . . . Remember also," he added, "and tell this to your relatives and your friends. Remember also that there are no dogs allowed on this train and people in masquerade costumes unless they're all covered up with a big heavy coat; and no more hubbubs," he added, shaking a finger at her. (129)

Bowles's language, like her world, consists of hard, impenetrable surfaces. Words are flat, disconnected. Trapped within a self that is isolated and frightened, Bowles's characters try through language to force their way through those barriers that isolate them, only to be reminded again and again by language itself of their separateness. Monologues are ubiquitous in such a world, revealing those whose solipsism is disclosed even as they try to crash through it. Language does not so much liberate Bowles's figures as bury them. The insignificant phrase is picked up, the real drift or meaning is missed, and the possibility of isolation being diminished is lost, denied by the very attempt to overcome it. As in Flannery O'Connor, the grotesque abounds, closely aligned with the comic and the horrible, for in Bowles's art, the comic moment is aligned not against the chaotic and alienated, but serves rather to reinforce their presence:

> LIONEL. . . . . I won't let it happen. We're going away—you and me. We're getting out of here. We're not playing cards in this oyster cocktail bar until we're old.
> MOLLY. (*Turns and looks up the stairs and then back to Lionel*) If we had a bigger light bulb we could play in the bedroom upstairs.
> LIONEL. (*Walking away*) You're right Molly, dead right. We could do just that. We could play cards up there in that God-forsaken bedroom upstairs. (273)

The grotesque in Bowles's art is aligned with comedy insofar as the comic impulse, as Freud reminds us in *Jokes and their Relation to the Unconscious*, enables the repressed to escape censorship. Aggressively insistent in its right to be politically incorrect, the comic impulse is in fact dangerous and subversive, for it, by its very nature, threatens to undermine or circumvent coercive and repressive forces. The comic moment, like the dream, enables the repressed to find expression, and makes it possible for us to transgress those boundaries of the taboo.[2]

We see this particular transgressive or subversive alignment of the comic and the grotesque in a powerfully rendered scene in *Two Serious Ladies*, in which a newly acquired lover of Christina Goering, who has propositioned her by suggesting that "it would please me in the midst of all this horror to go to bed with you" (146), tells her of an incident from his past involving a young woman with neither arms or legs:

> "She was already in her chair the next night when we got there; nicely made-up and wearing a very pretty clean blouse pinned in front with a brooch shaped like a butterfly. . . . Then right away I began to wonder what she would be like: the rest of her, you understand—without any legs. . . . "
> "It came into my mind like an ugly snake, this idea, and curled there to stay. I looked at her head so little and delicate against the grimy wall and it was the apple of sin that I was eating for the first time." (150)

He finally does sleep with the young woman, contracting, as we discover, a "beautiful case of syphilis" (151). And although he begins to hate himself, actually giving himself the secret name of "Citizen Skunk," he also tells Christina Goering that "you can have some fun in the mud, though, you know, if you just accept a seat in it instead of trying to squirm around" (152). Nevertheless, he does not tell his fiancée about this experience, because "I wanted the buildings to stay in place for her and I wanted the stars to be over her head and not cockeyed. . . . I didn't want her to have to lock something up inside of her and look out at the world through a nailed window" (151).

This "apple of sin" assumes various shapes and tastes in Bowles's art, but once having partaken of it, our world becomes disjointed, askew. But this world must be lived in, not looked at through nailed windows, for however cockeyed it may be, it can yield up pleasure and beauty. As Lionel of *In the Summer House* asks Molly:

> Did you ever worry about running away far from sad things when you were young, and then later getting older and not able to find your way back to them ever again, even when you wanted to? (260)

When asked why he would want to remember sad things, Lionel replies that "you might have lost wonderful things too, mixed in with the sad ones" (261). Mrs. Copperfield is also a person of memories:

> "Memory," she whispered, "Memory of the things I have loved since I was a child. My husband is a man without memory." . . . For her, all that which was not already an old dream was an outrage. (40)

However, Mrs. Copperfield only partially understands her husband. He and Lionel are two of the most fully realized male figures in a world otherwise dominated by Bowles's women. As Dillon observes, Mr. Copperfield "seems to stand outside [the] interweaving" that connect the two main women (*Life* 102), but he survives and is at home in the world by virtue of his capacity to be entranced by the commonplace and then to see through it into the beauty and life within it. He has little need of that memory of which his wife speaks, for his world is in some respects created anew each day by him. His present is continually renewed: "For God's sake," he writes to his wife, "a ship leaving port is still a wonderful thing to see" (111).

Most of Bowles's characters are, however, not only beset by memories, but entrapped within them, incapable of moving beyond their fixation on certain images, frozen, as it were, in front of specular images of wholeness and completion. Such, for example, is the case with Harriet of "Camp Cataract":

> I will clarify my statement by calling Camp Cataract my *tree house*. You remember tree houses from your younger days. . . . You climb into them when you're a child and plan to run away from home once you are safely hidden among the leaves. (362)

Her attempts to "imitate the natural family roots of childhood" fail, however, and at the end of the story, she is yanked out of her "tree house" and confronted by the reality of her sister's suicide. She too, the story implies, must embark upon her own horrible voyage into the world.

One of Bowles's figures observes that "life is tragic," and the first tragedy is that we must lose our tree houses, our roots of childhood. In a passage that Dillon suggests comes the closest "to revealing what Mrs. Copperfield—and Miss Goering— are at the mercy of" (*Life* 102), Mr. Copperfield writes to his wife, telling her that

> Like most people, you are not able to face more than one fear during your lifetime. You also spend your life fleeing from your first fear towards your first hope. . . . I believe sincerely that only those men who reach the second stage where it is possible for them to combat a second tragedy within themselves, and not the first over again, are worthy of being called mature. (110–11)

It is, he suggests, our shared fears and pain that make tenderness and sympathy possible:

> Your first pain, you carry with you like a lodestone in your breast because all tenderness will come from there. You must carry it with you through your whole life but you must not circle around it. You must give up the search for those symbols which only serve to hide its face from you. (111)

This "first pain" of which he speaks can, as he realizes, give rise to an emotional or spiritual paralysis, can become the object of a fixed or frozen gaze that either paralyzes us or compels us to return to it again and again in compulsive patterns of repetition. "You must not circle around it," he warns his wife. It is the "black pit" of Mrs. Constable and the shadows that haunt Mrs. Eastman, transforming love into a paralyzing fear and tenderness into a destructive possessiveness. For most, this pain is unendurable, as Lionel observes:

> I dread being a minister because it brings you so close to death all the time. You would get too deep in to ever forget death and eternity again, as long as you lived—not even for an afternoon. I think that even when you were talking to your friends or eating or joking, it would be there in the back of your mind. Death, I mean . . . and eternity. (233)

Most of Bowles's figures are either in search of salvation from this condition or for a forgetfulness of it. Their efforts ultimately fail, however, for in Bowles's world, there is no place to hide. Mrs. Eastman of *In the Summer House* tries to create such spaces for herself and her daughter, haunted by the desperateness and precariousness of her need to believe that her father, whom she adored, indeed worshipped, loved her better than her sister, while all the time knowing (but not admitting) that such a belief is an illusion, a lie. Molly, her daughter, is in turn destroyed by her mother, the central figure of her dreams. "Molly," Mrs. Eastman observes, "is a dreamer," another of Bowles's figures of innocence and childlike simplicity. And although by the end of the play she has murdered the girl she fears is stealing Mrs. Eastman's love, even this act does not destroy her innocence.

By the end of the play, her innocence shattered, her dreams violated, Molly leaves that false paradise her mother has attempted to create for the both of them, while her mother, on the other hand, moves toward the remembered or created enclosures of an imaginary childhood in which she, and not her sister, was her father's favorite child. But her journey is also a futile one, betrayed by dreams that will not repress the emptiness of her life and love:

> I opened it up and took out a macaroon and I gave it to Molly. . . . When she began to eat, I saw that it was hollow, just a shell filled with dust. Molly's lips were gray with dust. Then I heard him . . . I heard my father. He was laughing. He was laughing at *me*! . . . I loved him so. I don't know what's happening to me. I've never been this way. I've always thrown things off, but now even foolish dreams hang over me. (281)

"I have nightmares all the time," she admits, "I've lost my daily life . . . I've lost my Molly" (282). And as the curtain falls, we hear from deep within the shadows of the stage Mrs. Eastman's closing words, "When I was a little girl" (295).

If fear, loneliness, and dread are givens in Bowles's world, there are moments of reprieve from this condition, those that approximate at least the emotional spaces we seek. And for Bowles, these moments most often are erotic, occurring between two women more often than between a man and woman. Such, for example, is the case when Mrs. Copperfield snuggles up close to a whore who has propositioned both her and her husband, or an even more extensive and eroticized scene involving Mrs. Copperfield and Pacifica, after they have been swimming together naked in the ocean:

> [Pacifica] helped Mrs. Copperfield to her feet and led her back to the beach, where Mrs. Copperfield collapsed on the sand and hung her head like a wilted flower. She was trembling and exhausted as one is after a love experience. She looked up at Pacifica, who noticed that her eyes were more luminous and softer than she had ever seen them before. (98)

This experience reminds Mrs. Copperfield of a recurrent dream she had of climbing a hill and finding a mannequin on top. As she clung tightly to it:

> they fell off the top of the hill and continued rolling for quite a distance until they landed on a little walk, where they remained locked in each other's arms. Mrs. Copperfield loved this part of the dream best; and the fact that all the way down the hill the mannequin acted as a buffer between herself and the broken bottles and little stones over which they fell gave her particular satisfaction. (98)

To survive in Bowles's world it is necessary to keep a proper perspective toward it, to make necessary distinctions, as does Miss Goering in the closing lines of *Two Serious Ladies*:

> "Certainly I am nearer to becoming a saint," reflected Miss Goering, "but is it possible that a part of me hidden from my sight is piling sin upon sin as fast as Mrs. Copperfield?" This latter possibility Miss Goering thought to be of considerable interest but of no great importance. (201)

Bowles's world consists of people too human not to be lost and lonely, and too honest and courageous to deny, even though they often attempt to, those truths that they know about themselves. It is inhabited by those who are incapable of being, in Mrs. Copperfield's words, "only interested in a bearable life" (112). Dominated by women who wander, seeking that concealed truth that might emerge out of a moment snatched from a life moving toward eternity, Bowles's art both perplexes and haunts those fortunate enough to come upon it.

Within it we are shown those figures who are interested in "finding out what we are like" (*Two Serious Ladies*, 71), for the self, radically problematized, is at the center of her fiction: it is "always the starting point for everything: yourself" (*Two Serious Ladies*, 145). And in the midst of her art stands the artist, aware, it would seem, of the horror and grotesqueness of the world, yet regarding it nevertheless with compassion, humor, tenderness. In the passage from *Two Serious Ladies* referred to above, Miss Goering is asked by Mrs. Copperfield whether the artist who looks out of his destroyed apartment jumped, and Miss Goering replied: "No, he remained there for quite a while looking down into the courtyard with an expression of pleasant curiosity on his face" (17–18). Bowles provides us here with an oblique glance at herself as an artist and at her own unique way of looking at things, for like her artist, she too regards the world with "an expression of pleasant curiosity," at once bemused by and sympathetic toward her women and men. Hers is a world of decrepitude, haunted memories, and frightening spaces, and yet it is, her literature reminds us, the only world we have. And while the mud is always there, the lying down in it, she suggests, need not be wholly bereft of pleasure.

Notes

1. Compare Dillon's remark about how "from the time she was a child Jane had a sense of sin—a sin that she could never define except to say that it was hers and original, that which separated her from others" (*Life* 414).

2. Dillon's biography suggests that the joke or comic impulse was also implicated in Jane's attempts to expand or test the boundaries of the taboo or forbidden in her own life as well, as in the story she told to her friend, Ira Yeager: "She said she was once in Arizona and went to a carnival. There she saw a 'freak,' a half-man, half-woman. She said she flirted with the man-woman and they went out to dinner together. She told the story as if it were a great joke" (*Life* 46).

10

The Unfinished Jane Bowles

Gena Dagel Caponi

J ANE BOWLES'S LIFE was filled with tragedy, from childhood illnesses that left her partially lame to her later struggles with alcohol, prescription drugs, a terrible stroke, and with private demons most of us will never understand. Some of her appeal as an American writer comes from this strange and sad life, and it is hard not to make a symbol—or a signifier—of the life itself. In Jane Bowles's turmoil we see the distresses of the artistic woman in American society, where the decision to become an artist or to pursue an artistic profession is not usual, is not encouraged, and will not be supported.

Neither can it have been easy for her to be married to a writer, particularly when Paul Bowles's success seemed to come so quickly and easily. For a few weeks in 1950, Paul Bowles's first novel was a bestseller, and although he slowed down in later decades, during his first ten years of writing fiction he published twenty short stories and three novels.[1] He was a steady worker (some might say compulsive) who revised relatively little and then usually to a minor degree. Jane, on the other hand, wrote slowly and with great labor. She revised everything many times and started more pieces than she finished. Her husband wrote in his autobiography that he had only an "inkling" of what Jane meant "when she remarked, as she often did, that writing was 'so *hard*' " (Bowles, *Without Stopping* 287).

While it may be futile to determine the exact effects of such struggles on Jane Bowles's work, it is not an idle exercise, and it is relevant to understanding both the work that exists and that which might have come to completion. Jane was a Francophile and a member of a generation awash in existentialism, a philosophy understood to be a way of life. Its foremost proponent, Jean-Paul Sartre, wrote that a person is "nothing else than the ensemble of his acts, nothing else than his life" (32). To act in a certain way is to proclaim that such an action is right, and thus each action becomes a moral statement. For Bowles each decision was intensely moral, "and that was so even if the choice was between string beans and peas," Paul told her biographer Millicent Dillon (*Life* 119).

The act of writing was also a moral act, demanding countless decisions. For Jane the process was even more difficult than making decisions in her own life. In addition, Dillon concluded that Jane drew so deeply from her own unconscious world in her writing that she eventually became fearful that she might remain submerged there. It is impossible to separate the life and the work in studying Jane Bowles, and tragedy in one translated quickly into the other.

For her readers, the greatest tragedy of Jane Bowles is that she published such a small amount of her work. In her papers at the Harry Ransom Humanities Research Center in Austin are several typescripts and eighteen notebooks, numbered 22–39. Most contain drafts of works she never finished. Much more than outlines for stories or novels, these fragments might have been pulled from finished works, so detailed are they, even in their incompleteness. The notebooks tantalize the reader with possibilities. They also chart the bleak course of Jane's initial recovery and then gradual decline following her stroke: a few pages of incoherent description that she wrote for her therapist, a notebook full of startings and stoppings, wondering, wandering, and agonizing over the direction she might take in works she never really began.

The complete list of Jane Bowles's manuscripts in the Paul Bowles Collection at the HRHRC is as follows:

Unidentified fragment re medical treatment
Tms/fragment [1 p]
n.d.

Untitled Red O'Shaugnessy play
Ams/notes and fragments with A revisions [14 pp]
n.d. [1953]

Notebook 32
Untitled Red O'Shaugnessy play
Tms/misc. pages with A revisions [5 pp]
n.d.

Untitled Rita play
Ams/draft fragments and notes with A revisions [51 pp]
n.d.

Notebook 33
Untitled Rita play
Ams/scenes and fragments with A revisions [34 pp]
n.d.

Notebook 28
Untitled Rita play
AmsS/scenes and fragments with A revisions [82 pp]
n.d. [1956]

Notebook 29
Untitled Rita play
Tms/notes and fragments of dialog [4 pp]

Tms/scenes and fragments with A revisions and one A page [71 pp]
n.d.

Untitled story [Doro and Murray Sitwell]
AmsS/drafts and workings with A revisions [29 pp]
n.d.

Notebook 30
Untitled work
Ams/draft/ with A revisions written in notebook [76 pp]
n.d.

Notebook 27
Camp Cataract
Ams/original draft with A revisions [104 pp]
n.d.

Notebook 26
Camp Cataract
Ams/draft fragments with A revisions [10 pp]
n.d.

Notebook 27
Compositions written during her illness
2 Ams/inc [2 pp each]

1 Tms/inc with A telephone numbers included [2 pp]
3 n.d.

A Day in the Open
TccmsS [15 pp]
n.d.

Draft fragments and notes for unidentified stories
Ams/fragments and notes [35 pp]

Notebook 22
Everything is nice
Ams/draft fragments with A revisions [33 pp]
n.d. [1950]

Notebook 22
Folle de Chaillot [by Jean Giraudoux, tr. Jane Bowles]

Ams/draft fragments with A revisions [13 pp]
n.d.

Notebook 26
In the summer house
Ams/draft fragments with A revisions [21 pp]
n.d.

Notebook 30
In the summer house
AmsS/draft fragments with A revisions [25 pp]
n.d.

Notebook 38
In the summer house
Ams/draft fragment [3 pp]
n.d.

In the summer house
Composite Tccms and mimeo with A inscription S to Andreas Brown [75 pp]
1952 November [date revised]

In the summer house
Mimeo play script S with A notes on verso of final page [77 pp]
n.d.

In the summer house: Act II
Ams/draft fragments with A revisions with A note laid in [36 pp]
n.d.

Notebook 32
In the summer house: Act III
Ams/S new script with A revision [25 pp]
n.d.

Notebook 34
In the summer house (Ann Arbor version)

Duplicated TmsS with several T pages [80 pp]
n.d.

Once by fire, once by wind; a play and opera by Jane and Paul Bowles
Tms signed by both Jane and Paul Bowles, with A deletions [50 pp]
n.d.

Out in the world
Ams/draft fragments, sections and workings with A revision and workings
   [418 pp]
n.d.

Notebooks 23, 24, 25, 31, 35, 36, 37, 38
Out in the world
Ams with A revisions
n.d.

Notebook 26
Out in the world
Ams with A revisions
n.d.

Notebook 34
Out in the world
Ams with A revisions
n.d.

Notebook 39
Out in the world
Tms/draft fragments and workings with A revisions [27 pp]
n.d.

Plain pleasures
Ams/draft fragments with A revisions [16 pp]
n.d. [1946]

Notebook 27
A quarreling pair (puppet play)
TmsS with A revisions [8 pp]
n.d.

A stick of green candy
Tms and Tccms/inc with A emendation and deletions [9 pp]
n.d.

Two fragments
2 Ams [2 pp each]
2 n.d.

In addition, the HRHRC holds a substantial collection of materials Millicent Dillon amassed during her research for the Jane Bowles biography *A Little Original Sin*. Within this collection are two long, significant manuscripts:

Unpublished autograph manuscript of untitled novel and poetry.
18 July 1946

Unpublished autograph manuscript, with autograph notes by Millicent Dillon.

The unpublished manuscripts of Jane Bowles bear significance for the Bowles scholar for a number of reasons. First, and most obvious, is the fact that since Jane Bowles wrote so little, any addition to the existing material increases our ability to understand her work. No less idiosyncratic or brilliant than her available work, the unpublished writings provide compelling confirmation of the talent Bowles revealed in her published pieces.[2]

Second, as ideas recur and repeat from one manuscript to another, the worldview that seemed unique to Jane Bowles becomes even more clear. These manuscripts add contours to the imagination that Bowles revealed in her published works. As Bowles states her concerns and, more often, her fears, their importance confirms itself.

Finally, to read these manuscripts in a sort of chronological order, difficult to do with precision because most are undated, is to follow the growth and deterioration of a writer. Peculiar though her gifts or process may have been, the mere existence of so many unpublished pieces tells us something about that process. In Bowles's case it was a frustrating and frustrated one, in which her anxieties and problems with writing increased in geometric proportion to her successes.

While reading the manuscripts mainly confirms the published career, there are a few surprises. Chief among them is discovering that several of the manuscripts are fragments of plays. Bowles wrote terrific dialogue, and these play-fragments suggest her pleasure and prowess in writing conversationally. Bowles also loved play-acting. Writer Christopher Wanklyn said:

Jane especially delighted in the sort of people who might turn into characters in her plays. Sometimes she found them ready-made but sometimes she had to coax them into their roles, to mould them a little until they became her own inventions and could pretty much be counted on to perform, all unsuspecting, in a fashion that their playwright was designing for them. Sometimes these comedies, while amusing in retrospect, were torture for the captive audience who might find himself swept into the drama.[3]

Among the plays Jane left in the HRHRC was the completed manuscript to "Once by Fire, Once by Wind," a one-act opera on which she collaborated with her husband. This work shares characters and setting with the excised portion of her novel *Two Serious Ladies*, published as "A Guatemalan Idyll" (*Works* [1978] 321–58). We have only the script, or libretto, typed and signed by both writers. Apparently no score has survived. A recording of Paul Bowles's 1943 opera *The Wind Remains* uses the title "Once By Wind" for the finale. Perhaps Paul used music from this opera for the one-act work with Jane. To my knowledge, neither one of the Bowleses has ever mentioned this work in print.

It was not surprising to find references to Jane's needs as a writer, and particularly as a woman writer: needs for a room of one's own, for being heard and understood, for protection. Like so many women writers, Jane Bowles wondered whether it was possible to say the things one really felt, to speak the truth of one's own existence. When writing, was she in her own room where she could speak the truth? In one of the "Untitled Rita" plays (Notebook 29), Bowles alludes to the safety one feels in one's own room and to the fear that lies outside:

> RITA. I'm afraid of Sadie. I wouldn't be so afraid if I wasn't fighting with Claude—or if I was in my own apartment—if I were at home. I can't stay away from normal living too long. I can stand up against world conditions and world tension just the way my neighbors do—but only if my life is normal.[4]

(The fact that Paul Bowles's father was named Claude makes it easy to see the Claude character as Paul.) Although Rita spoke of the safety of her own room, another Bowles character distinguished between a room and a cage and said she would prefer a cage.

> "You can see out and other's can see in even though your protections are as strong as the silver wires of a cage," she said. "But in a room you're really shut off."[5]

To speak the truth was to be a serious person, to have a serious life. A fragment of writing from one of the Dillon notebooks suggests how important that was to Jane:

> She had a very sweet voice and only experienced people recognized the tension behind it. She was hysterical and original but not a very serious person.[6]

Another astonishingly consistent concern is that of food. Painter Maurice Grosser said that he once asked Jane how her play was coming along, and she gave him a menu describing what each of the characters was having to eat. Most of the HRHRC manuscripts contain major scenes set in restaurants or involve food as an important element of the plot. The "Untitled Rita play" takes place at the "Jumping Bean" restaurant, which serves bean-burgers and side orders of jumping beans. The "Everything Is Nice" notebook pauses between fragments to discuss a juke joint called the "chicken coop," where one can order very small chicken dinners at a reasonable price. A character in the 1946 Millicent Dillon manuscript is repulsed by men eating at the counter of the restaurant across the street and by the people eating in their homes behind her. "She felt a deep hostility toward other human beings— and therefore hated most of all to see them eating or making the necessary preparations for a meal."[7]

Eating is life-support. We have to eat in order to survive, and Jane Bowles was deeply concerned with how people survive day to day. In the 1946 Dillon notebook she wrote, "Life is chaos and happiness is a system—imposed on chaos—. You must move about within your own happiness system—as if in a very delicately wrought but strong cage—while the life chaos remains outside."[8] Food, for Jane Bowles, was one way of ordering the chaos, of forging the bars of one's cage.

A third striking motif through these manuscripts is that of twins and doubling. The 1946 Dillon notebook involves several sets of sisters. In the "Red O'Shaugnessy" manuscripts, Bowles discusses a true and false self, a true and false heart. In one of the several "Rita" plays, as well, a character struggles with opposing feelings:

> The wind was blowing around my head and the air was full of salt but I felt more like I was standing inside a closet. Maybe I'm getting a quirck. I felt like too men. One strong minded man who stood watching birds and the other one shivery and scared.[9]

One often thinks of an obsession with doubling as arising from a personality that is split. With Jane Bowles, it is more likely that she was in some ways undifferentiated, unable to define boundaries between herself and others or within herself. In her biography, Millicent Dillon came to this conclusion: "For her there was no need to dredge up from the unconscious: its terrors existed side by side with and [were] interwoven with ordinary events" (*Life* 93).

One of the earliest of the manuscripts is the notebook from the Millicent Dillon Collection dated "18 July 1946." That summer Paul and Jane Bowles lived at the Southampton home of their friend John Uihlein, a well-to-do beer executive. Paul Bowles began his *Concerto for Two Pianos, Winds, and Percussion* there, while Jane worked on the novel contained in this notebook. The hardbound composition book consists of twenty pages of false starts and seventy-seven pages of continuous narrative followed by three pages of poetry and two pages with Bowles's notes on the unfinished novel and ideas for further work. Most of the manuscript is in ink, with a few pages in black or red pencil, suggesting Bowles worked in the notebook at different times. Many additions, deletions, word substitutions, and rephrasings show Bowles's laborious writing process.

A few loose pages titled "Lesson XII" also came with this notebook. The bookseller's description states that they were translations of French lessons Bowles gave to duo-pianists Robert Fizdale and Arthur Gold in 1947. No one but Jane Bowles could have assigned for translation phrases such as these:

> They are all monstruous.
> Who?
> The aunties.
> But they are clean.
> Often but not always.
> Are all Lesbians dirty?
> Most of them.

The novel in the notebook is set in Camp Cataract, the short story scene to which Bowles returned in many of her manuscripts. Two camp residents, Laura Seabrook and Sally McBride, visit an Italian restaurant in town near the camp and enter into various unsuccessful conversations with the two sisters who run it, Rita and Berenice Cassalotti.

Jane Bowles created several sets of sisters before she settled on the Cassalottis. In one of the early versions, she describes a pair who could have been modeled on herself and her husband or on Helvetia Perkins, with whom she was involved at the time. (Inside the back cover of this notebook she wrote "Jane Bowles loves Helvetia.") This first set of sisters, Katharine and Gizella, are emotional opposites. Like Paul or the eminently practical Helvetia, Gizella detaches from any problem. Like Jane, Katharine takes up residence in the center of her emotional storms:

> There are many persons who as far back as they can remember have felt frightened and depressed at nightfall to change from one place to another—even if only to spend the evening at the house of a neighbor is often enough to dispel this kind of mood. The stimulating effect of a scene change is never of course a very lasting one—. New friends and lovers—as well—serve to relieve the disagreeable contraction of the heart—but these too only for a while—. Fortunate persons busy themselves in intellectual pursuits and are thus able to treat their moods—as foreign bodies—quite incidental to life itself. Others examine these same moods—very closely—and in spite of a seemingly assiduous fight against them—they come in the end to worship them—.
>   The former at times end up in lunatic asylums—or resthomes—as easily as the latter. A mood will grow whether the person looks into it or away from it.

Katharine Giacometti looked into hers—all of the time but her sister Gizella did not. Katharine at the time this story begins was beginning to feel sad in the afternoon as well as in the evening. So she felt she has reached a dangerous if interesting turning point in her life—. She was a person of depth—and with a tremendous desire for sincerity but she possessed neither a well trained mind—nor any culture—.[10]

Gizella Giacometti is thirty-five years old (about the age of Helvetia Perkins):

She had a middle-aged taste in clothing—preferring rather complicated silk dresses to sport clothes. She had no respect for any childlike quality in a grown woman—.[11]

Katharine corresponds with Gizella in language that is pure Jane Bowles:

Wherever I look people are busy—which is I suppose the natural state of affairs—in this century. Perhaps now only old ladies—and sick people have time to lead a serious life—. If this is so I am wrong to run back home—just so I can—have long empty hours and days to myself. I should stay here and find my depth right in the middle of a thousand distractions—and occupations. But I am too literal—: the outside and the inside are much the same for me—alas. I am frightfully uneasy because I am not quite certain of what to do. I seem evil to myself whichever way I choose—. Naturally a great deal attracts me here. I shall miss the French bread and all the garlic but I can buy garlic at home, I think.[12]

Later Bowles writes again about the outside and inside, inability to separate herself from others, to find herself. Her characters are always people at the mercy of their moods.

"My heart is not light, Laura," Sally said. "I have to spend many hours in my cabin alone—. I'm going there now—I had a fit of nervous irritability this afternoon—and I want to think about it."[13]

Laura is equally vulnerable.

"Oh God—" thought Laura— "I had almost forgotten for a moment—I wish I could be really here—having the kind of fun I think it is to be here." She was quite accustomed to this cold fright that gripped her heart whenever her pleasure was acute but it was not the fright itself that interested her. . . , Should she consider the anguish to be the natural underlying side of life itself—that side which gives depths and gravity to the sense of living from hour to hour and which is to be endured simply and accepted—or was it on the other hand—a signal for a departure—a signal for a decision? It was this last possibility that she found so upsetting—For she was actually—in her thinking at least a very conscientious person.[14]

Decisions between peas and string beans again. It is impossible to read fragments like these without putting them in the context of the existential philosophy that so dominated the literary world of the late 1940s. To be a serious person, to make the right decision, to get inside of the life one was living: these were the issues of the day, and Jane Bowles took them on in everything she wrote.

Jane first published her story "Everything Is Nice" as a nonfiction article for *Mademoiselle* in April 1951 under the title "East Side: North Africa." One spiral-bound notebook contains Jane's original notes for this piece, as well as notes for other works never published (Notebook 22). According to Dillon, Paul had revised "Everything Is Nice" from the *Mademoiselle* piece, changing the first-person narrator to the third. However, this notebook contains fragments of both third- and first-person versions, suggesting that Paul might simply have used an alternate version for the short story.

Bowles began the "Everything Is Nice" notebook with a smattering of conversation between a Bostonian named Emmanuel Cook and his sister Lottie, whom he lectures, as Paul might Jane: "Nobody is going to love you just because you can stand outdoors in the wintertime without a coat."[15]

Following this pronouncement are a couple of stabs at a piece involving a woman named Alice sitting at a table in a boardinghouse, four pages in all. Then Bowles begins a story about a young boy arriving at a seaside establishment called the Fish and Tackle Inn (eight pages). Each of these sections is so well developed that it is perplexing and frustrating to reach the end and discover that it goes nowhere. It is as if Bowles had fully imagined a particular scene but only that one scene, and then had nothing else with which to connect it.

Other pages in the notebook involve later versions of Mr. and Mrs. Copperfield, the couple who first appeared in *Two Serious Ladies*. In this notebook the travelers have reached Morocco, and they argue about going into the desert and about the disintegration of civilization (published posthumously as "The Iron Table" in *Works* [1978] 465–67). Here Bowles wrote one of her most stunning pronouncements on her marriage and on the impossibility of communication in general:

It would happen some day surely. A serious grief would silence their argument. They would share it and not be able to look into each others eyes. But as long as she could she would hold off adopting his grievances. . . .
But as long as she could she would hold off this moment.[16]

Jane Bowles returned to this thought in another manuscript in the HRHRC, the "Untitled Red O'Shaugnessy play" on which she was working in New York during the 1953 rehearsals for her play *In the Summer House*":

(he looks at her with a certain wistfulness You never mind that, night coming on, I know—sometimes I wish you would— . . . just so we would both feel something alike once—at the same time—. and yet I've been afraid that if we did—it would spoil it all—.[17]

It was a realization that Paul Bowles had woven into conversations between Kit and Port, the characters he loosely based on himself and Jane, in his 1949 novel *The Sheltering Sky*. There he also wrote that Port "was unable to break out of the cage into which he had shut himself, the cage he had built long ago to save himself from love" (100). Jane wrote:

She speaks of her other heart which she says is behind her heart which is her true heart and someday she expects to experience everything with that heart— but now she is shut away from it—[18]

At the least, the fact of Paul and Jane Bowles's marriage affected their writing. Perhaps similarities between their works grew out of conversation. Perhaps one unconsciously drew from the other. On at least one occasion, they collaborated on a work. The manuscript for "Once by fire, once by wind; a play and opera by Jane and Paul Bowles" is typed and signed by both Jane and Paul Bowles. It is not dated, and it is difficult to guess more than that it predates Jane Bowles's 1957 stroke. The inside cover sheet describes it as a "Miniature play in 3 Scenes and Epilogue." Yet the play itself consists of three short acts and an epilogue, with Acts 2 and 3 each containing two scenes. All take place "in the patio of the Pension Espinoza in a distant town in Central America." Instructions state that there is to be no intermission and that the scenes are to be joined by music or silence.

The entire play is a recycling of the excised Guatemalan portion of *Two Serious Ladies* (or perhaps *Two Serious Ladies* recycled this play). The characters include: a traveler, a child with a shaved head, Espinoza, Lilina and Consuelo Ramirez, Señora and Señor Ramirez, Maria, two young male boarders, an English lady, a musician, Señorita Córdoba, and an old lady. The first two acts and the epilogue come directly from "A Guatemalan Idyll." Act 3 is the excised Señorita Cordoba portion of *Two Serious Ladies* (Dillon, *Life* 107).

Beyond the major characters familiar from other works and discussed at length in the Dillon biography, even the minor characters take on attributes of Jane Bowles. The midwestern traveler doesn't see the sense in traveling: "I don't see what you're supposed to get out of traveling." In the midst of a chaotic scene between Sr. and Sra. Ramirez, their daughter Consuelo, and Srta. Cordoba, the traveler says petulantly, "What about me? Don't I count in this at all?" One remembers Jane getting lost in the goings-on of the Moroccans in Tangier, despite or perhaps because of her intense involvement with them.

Excepting the unpublished novel, *Out in the World,* the remaining major manuscripts are also plays. There exist two versions of the "Untitled Red O'Shaugnessy play" (Notebook 32 and typescript) and four versions of the "Untitled Rita play" (Notebooks 28, 29, 33, and typescript), portions of which can be found in the published "At the Jumping Bean" (Bowles, *Feminine Wiles* 39–47).

In the first of the two "Red O'Shaugnessy" manuscripts, only five pages long, Red is a girl who wants to be the twin brother of her brother, also named Red. "I should have been a man," she muses. "Twins maybe."[19] Red is shy and awkward and speaks only out of a compulsion to do so. "She speaks out of a boiling heart."[20] The second version (Notebook 32) begins with a description: "Both girls are called Red—the other Red is a quiet girl with a boyish voice—'Red' Cooper."[21]

The great issue of this manuscript is dividedness—from oneself and from life. This is the play in which Bowles wrote of her "other heart." Here she describes a "great longing to be whole hearted to find the other half of herself to throw everything out of her life and not just hang on to half of her life."[22] She says:

> It is because she believes she has this second heart—or spirit—that she commits herself to false trust—to her loneliness is more unbearable than false trust—and to find her true heart would be to endure loneliness—love takes her away from herself.[23]

On the back of a page from the "Summer House" section of this notebook, Bowles reaches the still center of the matter, the truth behind all of the wonderfully whimsical play-acting, desperate depressions, and inability to finish more than half of what she wrote:

> Maybe because I'm never sure where my life is—except that I know I feel separated from it—as if it was going on somewhere else—always in some other place where I've never wanted to go—but where I must go—I know[24]

The "Untitled Rita" plays probably date from the mid-1950s. We do know that Bowles was working on a play in 1956. The four notebooks and more than seventy typed pages of at least twelve different scenes are full of completed fragments and hilarious Jane Bowles moments. Among the different typed pages grouped as the "Rita" plays, the characters include: Rita, Katie, Ida, Berenice, Beryl Jane, Claude, Sadie, John, Sylvia, Harriet, Beryl, Barbara, and Gabriel. Most of the scenes seem to take place at the Jumping Bean restaurant or at Camp Cataract. This conversation from one of the typed sections shows the slippage and ellipsis that made Bowles's work so funny:

IDA. I was trying to take your mind off normal living.

RITA. You're going to speak to me about world conditions and tension. (chewing on her gum rapidly, with a ferocious expression) Do you want me to turn into a bum just because there's world tension? Gabriel doesn't think people should be bums just because there's world tension . . . and he went to college You didn't go to college at all.

IDA. Gabriel went to Ohio state.

RITA. I know he did but that's not the point of this argument.[25]

Between such dialogue slip moments of deep despair, as when Rita talks about her mother:

> She told me my heart had a hole in it, like my aunt Sadie's . . . she said it was small but when I grew up it was going to be big and black like my aunt Sadies . . . and no money or sunlit fields or oceans or mountains would ever fill it up.[26]

The characters Ida and Rita in this notebook are twins, and this is the version in which the character Claude feels he is becoming two men, one who watches and one who acts. Here, too, a character named John feels split between two hearts:

> I thought my heart was not my real heart . . . and that anything I loved too much I was robbing from my self . . . from my other heart the true heart still locked away from me but the heart that would blossom someday when I went away . . . I didn't know where I was going but I was going far away . . . and then I was going to find my real heart and I was going to love the forest without pain.[27]

Bowles resumes her discussion of Rita's Aunt Sadie with a conclusion only she could have mustered.

RITA. I'm afraid . . . I don't want to be like Aunt Sadie—.

IDA. She's the only one in our family who has beautiful diction.[28]

A second notebook (Notebook 33) grouped with the "Rita" plays contains complete sections of dialogue among characters at Camp Cataract: Beryl, Jeanie (Bozoe) Flanner, Barbara, and Phoebe (Jeanie's sister). Among their conversations is a hilarious discussion of the appeal of indigenous cultures:

BERYL. Don't you love these feathers.

BARBARA. No I don't love them. I don't love anything savages make—, Savages—give me the willys.

BERYL. (staring at her candidly): Even American Indians—

BARBARA. I don't like snake dances or feathers or Blue Beads—Savages give me the willys—. . . .

BERYL. I think that most of us have a longing for a more primitive life—. That's why we love camping. You know, bonfires, marshmallows.

BARBARA. Did savages eat marshmallows—?

BERYL. Well . . . figuratively speaking. I was trying to emphasize the bonfire aspect of things—.

BARBARA. (popping a lozenge into her mouth): What's the bonfire aspect of things—.

BERYL. Well . . . we can leave out the marshmallows if they got you mixed up—and use groupe [*sic*] singing instead. Groups singing and gathering together at night—out of doors—. Just leave out the marshmallows—. The early American Indian by the way was not a savage—the————tribe for instance had a culture that we might be proud of emulating—. Note: (look up a tribe)

(Beryl is visibly pleased with this pronouncement)

BARBARA. He can keep it—I'll keep my atomic age. I feel at home in it. I'd rather be frightened of the atomic bomb than of leprosy. When I was little I always had nightmares about leprosy—now they can cure it—at least they can arrest it before your nose drops off. I really hate leprosy.[29]

A final notebook (Notebook 28) is quite fragmented, beginning with a scene between Katie and Rita. A nostalgic monologue from Gabriel sounds much like Paul Bowles or Port Moresby in *The Sheltering Sky*:

I feel now that a beautiful spring day is nothing more than a tribute to some other spring day—maybe not—maybe not even my own spring—But springs that belonged to real years—if I was an old man I'd see they belonged to my youth—. It's as if they'd worn it out worn out the universe before I could loved it—[30]

A few more incomplete scraps of dialogue or description, then this letter to Paul:

Dear Bubble—

I have not been able to get to work yet! isn't it awful—mostly my own lackadaisical mood—and the fact that I have reached a difficult and perhaps impossible point in my play. I feel some *drama* is required—and to generate the heat—that drama requires well—I don't know if I be able to. I will be free until about 8 o'clock—should we see—[31]

Several fragments of writing from the period immediately following Bowles's stroke record her struggles with the neurological damage that made writing difficult. One catalogued as "Two fragments," consists of two pages, one of which describes her room and the other an elevator ride with her mother. The labored feel of the prose is as excruciating to read as it must have been to write.

I went out on the street with my mother in the elevator on the way down I noticed the door man—elevator man-he had on gloves. I don't know how many doormen there are—but they none of them seem to make any impression on me—. They are none of them very young. they do not seem to be either angry or friendly—except one of them a doorman actually who is a more colorful than the others who seem grey. the elevator men are pail and old. No dequripet at least I don't feel that they are going to pass away quietly leaving the elevator stuck—between two floors—. I have the uncomfortable sensation that they waiting to be tipped but I don't know which one of them to tip—and how much.[32]

The manuscript catalogued as "Composition written during her illness" is more literary and more chilling, quoted at length in Dillon, beginning, "There are three people in here. Mother. my mother myself and a monster."[33] The second page, quoted entirely in Dillon, begins:

I cannot write a composition. If I could I would. I don't think I have been able to for years anyway. and this time it is completely impossible. If it is a failure of the will—then my will is sick—it is not lazyness.[34]

In this fragment, Bowles made the existential conclusion regarding her condition and that of humanity, "One is alone finally and there is no doctor for the soul."[35]

Probably the latest of the HRHRC manuscripts is the second of the two notebooks in the Millicent Dillon collection. One can see in it the progress Bowles made in the years following her stroke, but this notebook shows little of the concentrated writing Bowles was able to do in earlier times. Where earlier notebooks contain unfinished chunks of narrative or dialogue, this one holds page after page of musings over different plots, characters, and combinations of plots and characters. Such hesitations go beyond Bowles's earlier indecisions and questions about literary presentation. Now it seems as if she couldn't make any decision that would get the writing going. Early in the notebook Bowles writes, "Try various combinations until you get the right one."[36] The notebook testifies to that effort.

Set at Camp Cataract, the play involves Hortense (age nineteen or twenty), Miggie, with whom Hortense is in love, Loretta, Beryl, and Tommy. Bowles describes Miggie as, "a kind of Helvetia driving Bonzoe to leave her. . . . Tommy is the God in Loretta. Loretta thinks that she is closer to God when she chooses Tommy." Of Tommy, however, she says:

Tommy falls in love or confuses love with a spiritual experience.— He has love completely confused with God if it is a confusion. He has it so confused that he kills himself.[37]

As was the case in much of her work, the women represent different aspects of one person. Trying to solidify them, Bowles writes:

All four women love images and not people.
Each character has his own conception of when he is pleasing God.
Hortense must be rewritten. . . . But she must be pathetic and a wild tyrant at
the same time—.[38]

Where before decisions were a test of her philosophy, now they became an emotional
impossibility. Where before she labored among different versions of the same scene,
trying to see the whole thing at once from as many points of view as possible, now she
worried a sentence at a time. She tried various combinations:

Every twig was frozen and coated with ice. Every twig and every branch was
coated with ice. Every branch on every tree was coted with ice—[39]

For the first time in these notebooks, Bowles wandered in her writing between
personal thoughts and her creation, blurring the distinction between herself and her
characters while she wrote about the walls between them.

The play has no ending no solution—there is a wall between myself and my
life—she tried to break through the wall with Miggie but it seems even more
futile.[40]

She repeated the phrase "wall between myself and my life" several times in different
passages, different scenes, throughout the pages of this notebook: "this is about people
who build up an artificial destiny or life through which nothing can pierce."[41] Finally,
with characteristic humor and bleakness, she wrote, "I know that destiny isn't what it
used to be."[42]

Perhaps in the end Jane felt it was not her destiny to publish in her lifetime more
than a small portion of what she actually wrote. Certainly editors, readers, and her
husband disagreed. In 1964, Paul suggested to his London publisher Peter Owen
that he revive Jane's 1943 novel *Two Serious Ladies*. He recorded Jane's objections
to the project in a letter to Owen:

It all seemed so simple, a reprint, twenty years after publication. But for her it
assumed tremendous proportions. She was sure it would be reviewed, and
would everyone understand it was an early work, and they would be sure to
loathe it, and she couldn't bear reading adverse reviews, and having the whole
thing raked over once again, and the first publication was already a traumatic
experience, and did I want her to have a nervous breakdown or what? . . . She
also made a remark, only once, but one to which I attach some importance,
which was: "And anyway, why should it be your publisher? Why does it have to
be yours? Why can't I have my own publisher? He only wants it because of
you."[43]

Such anxiety, over a work already published! Fear of failure, fear of rejection, jealousy, and a longing for autonomy. Added to her terror of making the wrong decision, perhaps these emotions also explain the notebooks of unpublished material in the HRHRC. The manuscripts hold the record of Bowles's creative process and magnify the forces that might have kept her from bringing more work to public inspection. Whatever else they reveal, they establish one point unequivocally: although the body of Bowles's published work is slight, it wasn't for lack of trying.

Notes

1. Jeffrey Miller's *Paul Bowles: A Descriptive Bibliography* (Santa Barbara: Black Sparrow, 1986) lists two short stories published in periodicals in addition to the seventeen included in Paul Bowles's short story collection *The Delicate Prey* (New York: Random, 1950). The London short story edition, *A Little Stone* (London: Lehmann, 1950), contained one story not published in the United States.

2. By far the largest group of manuscripts is that of the unfinished novel *Out in the World*, which Allen Hibbard discusses in his 1994 *Library Chronicle* essay. Jane Bowles, Notebooks 23, 24, 25, 31, 35, 36, 37, 38, 39, Paul Bowles Collection, Harry Ransom Humanities Research Center, The University of Texas at Austin (hereafter HRHRC; unless otherwise noted, all manuscripts are contained in the Paul Bowles Collection, and are quoted by permission of Paul Bowles and the HRHRC).

3. Christopher Wanklyn, letter to the author, 28 May 1991.

4. Jane Bowles, Notebook 29, HRHRC.

5. Jane Bowles, Unnumbered notebook, 18 July 1946, Millicent Dillon Collection, HRHRC. I have not corrected any quoted passages for spelling, punctuation, or grammatical errors. Ellipses are those of Jane Bowles.

6. Jane Bowles, Unnumbered notebook, 18 July 1946, Millicent Dillon Collection, HRHRC.

7. Jane Bowles, Unnumbered notebook, 18 July 1946, Millicent Dillon Collection, HRHRC, 6.

8. Jane Bowles, Unnumbered notebook, 18 July 1946, Millicent Dillon Collection, HRHRC, 5.

9. Jane Bowles, Tms, HRHRC.

10. Jane Bowles, Unnumbered notebook, 18 July 1946, Millicent Dillon Collection, HRHRC.

11. Jane Bowles, Unnumbered notebook, 18 July 1946, Millicent Dillon Collection, HRHRC.

12. Jane Bowles, Unnumbered notebook, 18 July 1946, Millicent Dillon Collection, HRHRC.

13. Jane Bowles, Unnumbered notebook, 18 July 1946, Millicent Dillon Collection, HRHRC, 7.

14. Jane Bowles, Unnumbered notebook, 18 July 1946, Millicent Dillon Collection, HRHRC, 35.

15. Jane Bowles, Notebook 29, HRHRC.

16. Jane Bowles, Notebook 29, HRHRC.

17. Jane Bowles, Notebook 32, HRHRC, verso of 32.

18. Jane Bowles, Notebook 32, HRHRC, 9.

19. Jane Bowles, [Untitled Red O'Shaugnessy play] Tms, HRHRC.

20. Jane Bowles, [Untitled Red O'Shaugnessy play] Tms, HRHRC.

21. Jane Bowles, Notebook 32, HRHRC, 1.

22. Jane Bowles, Notebook 32, HRHRC, 1.

23. Jane Bowles, Notebook 32, HRHRC, 9.

24. Jane Bowles, Notebook 32, HRHRC, verso 18.

25. Jane Bowles, [Untitled Rita play], Tms, HRHRC, 2–3.
26. Jane Bowles, [Untitled Rita play], Tms, HRHRC.
27. Jane Bowles, [Untitled Rita play], Tms, HRHRC.
28. Jane Bowles, [Untitled Rita play], Tms, HRHRC.
29. Jane Bowles, Notebook 33, HRHRC.
30. Jane Bowles, Notebook 28, HRHRC.
31. Jane Bowles, Notebook 28, HRHRC.
32. Jane Bowles, Two Fragments, HRHRC.
33. Jane Bowles, Composition written during her illness, HRHRC.
34. Jane Bowles, Composition written during her illness, HRHRC.
35. Jane Bowles, Composition written during her illness, HRHRC.
36. Jane Bowles, Unnumbered notebook [1960], Millicent Dillon Collection, HRHRC.
37. Jane Bowles, Unnumbered notebook, Millicent Dillon Collection, HRHRC.
38. Jane Bowles, Unnumbered notebook, Millicent Dillon Collection, HRHRC.
39. Jane Bowles, Unnumbered notebook, Millicent Dillon Collection, HRHRC.
40. Jane Bowles, Unnumbered notebook, Millicent Dillon Collection, HRHRC.
41. Jane Bowles, Unnumbered notebook, Millicent Dillon Collection, HRHRC.
42. Jane Bowles, Unnumbered notebook, Millicent Dillon Collection, HRHRC.
43. Paul Bowles to Peter Owens, 26 January 1964, HRHRC.

11

Toward a Postmodern Aesthetic

Indeterminacy, Instability, and Inconclusiveness in *Out in the World*

Allen E. Hibbard

I F THE POSTMODERN is described as containing qualities of decenteredness, schizophrenia, wit, and indeterminacy, then surely much of Jane Bowles's work could fit within this classification. Perhaps nowhere in her *oeuvre* are these postmodern impulses felt so keenly as in her unfinished novel, *Out in the World*. The pages of her notebooks, in which she struggled to put the story together, are filled with evidence of flightiness, indecision, unwillingness to settle on one single version of a story, and discomfort with the notion that identity is permanently fixed and stable. Bowles's involvement with these issues is what makes her an important writer, one whose work has somewhat prematurely registered the fissures and cracks of consciousness and culture so acutely felt in the latter part of the twentieth century. Indeed, her literary vision is very much in line with the contemporary philosophical agendas underpinning postmodernism—the attack on logocentrism offered by Derrida; Michel de Certeau's plea for acknowledging and preserving cultural heterogeneity; Foucault's inquiry into the institutional configurations of power affecting the nature of our discourse; Deleuze and Guattari's rejection of "striated space" (and the political and intellectual fascism it engenders) in favor of "smooth space"; and, the varied feminist challenges to the dominance of "phallocentric" culture offered by such critics as Hélène Cixous, Luce Irigaray, Elaine Showalter and others—all of which challenge hegemonic interpretation and provide explanations for the character of our times.

The term *postmodern* has become a capacious umbrella under which a host of often dissimilar items of various genres and mediums have been hustled. The traits characterizing the postmodern are various as well. In Bowles's work we do not find the clever metafictional indulgences or parodic devices associated with Borges, Barth, and Nabokov. Nor do we encounter the generic blurrings found in, say, Doctorow and Coover. Nor is there the playful plagiarism or discursive melange marking the work of Kathy Acker and Ishmael Reed. There are, though, other ways of characterizing the postmodern. More broadly the postmodern has been seen by a good many critics, including the likes of Jean-François Lyotard, Linda Hutcheon and Ihab Hassan, as involving a "problematic," examining, confronting and sometimes challenging our accepted notions of power, identity, and "the real." In a recent discussion of the postmodern novel, Molly Hite ably sums up some of these concerns, speaking of "a kind of radical undecidability" in these works:

> a suspicion that the question "What's the real story here?" cannot be answered in any satisfying way—satisfying, that is, in terms of the sorts of expectations bred by realist and modernist fiction. The "real story" is unavailable in the face of contradictions or divergent accounts, not merely because it is unknowable . . . but because there is no single "real" in the story, no sanctioned reality with reference to which other stories can situate themselves as distorted, fictionalized, partial, biased, hallucinated, or simply lying. (703–4)

This kind of undecidablity, this inability to settle on one particular version of a story is a salient feature of Bowles's unfinished novel. Hite notes as well how "characters in postmodern novels are also likely to be fragmented or multiple" (706). Though these latter remarks are made in connection to Pynchon's *Gravity's Rainbow*, Russ's *The Female Man*, and Coover's *The Universal Baseball Association*, they just as well describe the nature of characters in *Out in the World*.

In the following pages I shall take up the ways in which Bowles tangles with and problematizes acceptable patterns of relationships between the sexes, ethnocentric assumptions, the nature and construction of human identity, and the meaning and implications of conventional configurations of narrative. Before doing so, however, it is necessary to introduce *Out in the World*, and talk about the fascinating narrative threads Bowles was spinning in that perturbingly unfinished novel.

I first came across Jane Bowles's notebooks in the Harry Ransom Humanities Research Center, The University of Texas at Austin, when I was going through material related to Paul Bowles's short fiction. I had prior knowledge of her unfinished novel through the short scenes and fragments published in *Feminine Wiles*, *My Sister's Hand in Mine: The Collected Works of Jane Bowles*, and Millicent Dillon's edition of Jane Bowles's letters, somewhat misleadingly titled *Out in the World*. These references, fragmentary and unordered as they were, scarcely hinted at the breadth of Bowles's project, the extent of her labors on the work, and the tremendous frustration she undoubtedly experienced with the novel. During my time in Austin I began reading through the notebooks, amazed at how much of the novel there was, and became so enthralled that I began to transcribe the fragments and think about how they might ultimately have taken shape, should she have been able to complete the task. I became convinced that this work, unfinished as it was, deserved a wider audience.[1]

Within the eight notebooks containing material related to *Out in the World* (roughly 418 pages total) four basic stories emerge. The first, a portion of which appears as "Andrew" in *The Collected Works* (1978), is of a young man named Andrew Mclean, the "son of family whose mills had ceased to function in his fathers youth."[2] Andrew, evidently searching for his place in the world, enters the army as a young man. Bowles writes:

> He had lost his sense of the worlds density in the army—and he was waiting to recapture it. It was not that his life had been in danger. On the contrary, he had enjoyed the army. He liked working with other men more than he liked to talk with them and the anonymity of his uniform suited him perfectly. (Notebook 23)[3]

Bowles devotes a number of scenes to Andrew's conflict with his parents in his search for identity. This conflict is at the heart of one of the central scenes (one which Bowles wrote and rewrote a number of times, never arriving at a definitive version) involving Andrew's first meeting with Tommy, a fellow soldier. At once, as Andrew approaches him "through the pine grove surrounding the camp" he feels a keen and powerful attraction to the young man, alone in the outdoors:

> The boy was beautiful, with an Irish-American face and thick curly brown hair. His cheeks were blood red from the heat of the flames. Andrew looked at his face and fell in love with him. Then he could not look away. (Notebook 36)

Here and elsewhere are clear suggestions that the two young men are struggling to map out the nature of their sexual feelings toward one another, and toward men and women in general. In one notebook (No. 23) Bowles lays out a possible conversation between the two young men, in which Tommy registers his feelings toward women, suggesting, albeit in a somewhat masked and guarded fashion, a homosexual or homoerotic undercurrent:

> "I don't care for girls." Tommy told [Andrew]. "I don't like much about the material they wear. . . . silk. I like this better. He fingered his own rough trousers. I like guys and being out of doors."

The scene might remind one of the campfire scene in Gus Van Sant's *My Own Private Idaho* where the two male hustlers probe the nature of their desires and feelings toward one another and the shape they might take.

Andrew and Tommy, jittery and seemingly uneasy, never pass through that slight opening to pursue the nature of their homosexual desires. In scenes apparently meant to be placed later in the novel, Bowles shows the two young men interacting with women. Andrew meets a young woman with the wonderful name of Agnes Leather, and Tommy takes up with a girl named Beryl Jane (sometimes referred to as Hazel in Bowles's notes). These new liaisons do not, however, totally eclipse the boys' feelings toward one another. Agnes realizes Andrew's interest in Tommy. At one point in her notebooks Bowles makes a note to the effect that "Andrew hides his obsession about Tommy . . . but Agnes, with feminine canniness recognizes his love" (Notebook 35). In another note Bowles elaborates on the dynamic she intended: Agnes "sees Tommy and Andrew as a union . actually of course she is terribly jealous of them—" (Notebook 35). Toward the end of Notebook 35 Bowles sketches a scene where the two young men go to the Chicken Coop (yet another of the wonderful names, such as the Jumping Bean, the Blue Bonnet, the Green Mountain Luncheonette, and so forth, Bowles gives to her gathering places) where Tommy meets Beryl. Elsewhere she indicates a possible course of the narrative:

> Beryl Jane (or Hazel) and Tommy go to bed on a river bank. Beryl Jane has recognized Tommy as a true lover of nature—He loves her and Andrew. She cries afterwards—suddenly begs him with tears sliding down her cheeks not to make fun of her ideas on farming or keep her from them when they lived together—He had not actually thought of living with her anyway.

A second narrative thread, intersecting with Andrew's story, focuses on the life of Emmy Moore. (Portions of this story have been published under the title "Emmy Moore's Journal" in *The Collected Works*). Approaching middle age, Emmy Moore (who in many ways resembles her author), locked into a marriage with Paul, "a very serious lawyer . . . of North Irish descent," runs away to the Hotel Henry where she writes defending her actions (Bowles, *Works* [1978] 443). Emmy's struggle is meant to parallel Andrew's. At one place in the notebooks Bowles writes that both were "trying to develop philosophies away from home" (Notebook 35). Apparently both of them land in the Hotel Henry, and Emmy Moore is "delighted" to find a young man from her home town.

Emmy Moore's desire to connect with other human beings outside her marriage takes her to the home of an Italian-American family, the Cassalottis. These scenes at the Cassalottis have the wildness and wit of the picnic scenes in *In the Summer House* and the zany and surprising qualities of those between Arnold and Mrs. Goering in *Two Serious Ladies*. By chance Emmy comes upon Cassalotti's fish market where Mr. Cassalotti, seeing her outside the window, pulls her in from the cold. Once inside the family, she witnesses Mrs. Cassalotti's jealousy, and ultimately is drawn to their eighteen-year-old daughter Berenice, a scout leader.

It seems as though Bowles wanted the lives of these various people to become more and more intertwined. In her notebooks she refers, at times, to the "renovated cabin group," associated with Andrew's new home, and to various picnics (of course!) and parties that would bring the characters together and heighten tensions, strains, and desires.

Portions of two other story lines are found in Bowles's notebooks, yet it is not entirely clear whether or not they were meant to be woven into the narrative, or whether they were experiments, fragments, or germs of other discrete stories. One line takes up the relationship between Agnes Leather and Cissy Mcavoy; the other deals primarily with Bozoe Flanner and Janet Murphy (a portion of which has been published as "Going to Massachusetts" in *The Collected Works* [1978]). Both of these stories dwell on the possibilities and problems involved in relationships between women.

The Agnes-Cissy narrative includes the story of their meeting.[4] Just as in Andrew's meeting of Tommy, there is a discernible air of romance as Agnes finds Cissy at the Greek Candy Shoppe and Ice Cream Parlor where Cissy is working as a waitress. Bowles tells us that Agnes, home from school in order to be with her sick father, "developed a habit of driving into the nearest town—, East Clinton, every afternoon to drink hot chocolates and eat cakes—."

> It was here she met Sister Mcavoy—who waited on her daily in a dress with short sleeves. Sister was a raspberry blond with mottled pink and lavendar skin on her arms—: She soon became an obsession with Agnes Leather—who was seeing no one else at that time in any case. (Notebook 37)

At their first meeting, as it is pouring down rain outside the parlor, Agnes tries to connect with Cissy by drawing the waitress's attention to her truck outside, at the same time trying to elide her own wealthy background. "Your hobby is trucks and mine is ice skating," Sister Mcavoy concludes.

As the story continues in another notebook, Agnes is inviting Cissy and her eleven-year-old daughter, Laurie, to live with her:

> Her plan was to suggest that she move into one of the houses in town or near it—at least no farther than the dams were—or the falls—which were only 7 min beyond the town limits—and to invite both Sister and her daughter Laurie to come live with her. (Notebook 39)

The plan apparently works, for Bowles sketches out another scene in which the two women are living together, experiencing claustrophia and restricted possibility: "Sister Mcavoy—the woman with whom Agnes Leather—was living—had said to Agnes that they could not possibly stay in the house day and night—: Agnes, afraid that sister would go out—offered at once to go to the Green Mountain Luncheonette—every day and eat there or untill their life was better organized.—" (Notebook 39) It seems Bowles wanted in the story to capture the anxieties and the insecurities surrounding the love relationship and the impulse to try to possess and control one's lover.

The Bozoe Flanner story also features two women trying to put their lives together. Here, too, we see a lopsided battle for control, in which each woman struggles to assert her own identity in the face of the other, rather like that between Sadie
and Harriet in "Camp Cataract." "This novel is about Bozoe Flanners [sic]," writes
Bowles in Notebook 25. "Janet Murphy must disappoint her—and so in the end
must Harry. Sister Mcavoy is her bitter enemy. Both Agnes and Janet—Protect her
more than they do Bozoe." Bowles goes on to sketch the course of the story: "Janet
Murphy—whole world is spoiled By. Sister Mcavoy who tries first to destroy Bozoe
than [sic] Janet—when Janet crumbles—Bozoe Flanner realizes that she never loved
Bozoe—as a matter of fact. But she has loved functioning in society as a man—."
By the end of this narrative thread we were to have seen

> the utter dissolution . . . of Bozoes struggle—the women No longer have any
> Power over her—writes that she walks through the state forest and tells her in
> the letter how she realizes there is no one at the other end.

The Bozoe Flanner story line is the most sketchy of those Bowles develops in her notebooks. She does, however, devote considerable space to the character of Janet, a lesbian who runs her own automotive garage and for eleven years manipulates the pa-
thetically dependent Bozoe:

> During the first years of their life together and of Janets early struggles with the
> garage. Janet had Pleaded with Bozoe—to reserve all personal discussions—for
> the evenings which they so often spent alone in their apartment: she had sug-
> gested in fact that she keep out of the garage altogether—unless some urgent
> matter should come up—that required Janets immediate—

Bozoe, however, would not stay within the bounds Janet would keep her in.
The drama of the relationship swells with the sudden force of a flash flood in
the "Going to Massachusetts" segment. In Notebook 24, we read: "Janet's inviolate
calm—and her absorption in her garage—were driving—Bozoe—to Massachusetts—where she thought she was going to seek her spirit—and the isolation for
such an undertaking." In the published portion of this narrative segment we see
Bozoe crying at the bus station, where Janet is bidding her good-bye. Bozoe is flus-
tered because she cannot remember why she is going away.
Once Bozoe is off the scene, Janet picks up with Sis Mcavoy whom she terms
"such a relief after Bozoe . . . Alive and full of fighting spirit. She's much more my
type, coming down to facts" (*Works* [1978] 461). An evening, during which Janet
trashes Bozoe, ends with a rather heated reaction from Sis: "I know what kind of
couple you are. The whole world knows it. I could put you in jail if I wanted to. I
could put you and Bozoe both in jail" (*Works* [1978] 460).

These scenes show how Janet does indeed demolish Bozoe, by refusing to recognize her needs, and by insisting on her own control in the relationship, and how
Sis takes both of them on.

This abbreviated account of *Out in the World* should suggest how the novel
registers a number of concerns that we now associate with the postmodern. Most
obvious, perhaps, is the problematizing of gender. Though perhaps not as radically
as Alfred Chester in *The Exquisite Corpse*, or Kathy Acker in *Empire of the Senseless*,
or Taher Ben Jelloun in *L'enfant de sable* (*The Sand Child*) and *La nuit sacrée* (*The
Sacred Night*), Bowles's fiction probes the boundaries of gender. Intent upon showing a whole range of ways in which men and women can relate to one another, she
challenges the hegemony of heterosexual marriage and its exclusive claims for social legitimacy. While there are indeed marriages in *Out in the World*, such as the
one between Emmy and Paul, they are not wholly conventional. Much of the interest in the novel, moreover, seems to be in exploring the possibilities of homosexual
desire and interaction. The Andrew/Tommy story, for example, quite nicely bal-
ances the Agnes/Cissy and Bozoe/Janet stories. Bowles's conception of gender
seems akin to the kind of multivalent bisexuality Hélène Cixous presents in "The
Laugh of the Medusa," where desire, ever-shifting and free, is not bound by specific
gender identifications and can adhere variously and multiply. Taken as a whole, *Out
in the World* could even be thought of as an experiment in articulating various forms
of human desire.

The gender-related issues in the novel are scarcely separable from ones Bowles
dealt with in her own life. Bowles's fictional sketches can seen as an effort to live
several lives at once—her life with Paul, and her life with various women, chief
among them Cherifa, the grain saleswoman of the Tangier souk whom Jane pursued
for more than two decades. Jane's own lesbianism, it has often been suggested,
manifested itself more outwardly and intensely after Paul developed an intimate
association with the young Moroccan painter, Ahmed Yacoubi, in the early fifties.
Something of this dynamic, certainly, can be felt in the connections between Agnes
and Andrew, each of whom, at some point in the novel, is involved in a form of
same-sex romance. Neither in fiction nor in life was Bowles able successfully to
reconcile or represent these competing desires and interests in a fulfilling or complete manner. Rather, the various attachments remain, until the end, unresolved and
ill defined.

Jane's status as a woman writer is, of course, another important dimension of
the gender issue, affecting the practical business of writing this novel. Bowles lived
conspicuously in the shadow of the patriarchy, much like the nineteenth-century
women writers Gilbert and Gubar make their central focus in *The Madwoman in
the Attic*. Her struggle must be seen within the context of the anxieties produced by

the compulsion to measure up to standards and practices established and perpetu-
ated by the patriarchy. Common is the view that Paul's presence exerted a not alto-
gether salutary effect on Jane's work. By all accounts, no matter the reason, Jane
often looked to Paul as the daughter is prone to look toward the father, seeking not
only affection and love but praise and approval for her work.

So long as Paul's primary identity was that of a composer, Jane was able more
or less comfortably to claim and hold on to her identity as a writer. When, in the
late 1940s and early 1950s, Paul's identity as a writer overtook that of composer, she
simply felt she could not compete. These anxieties can be keenly felt in a letter Jane
wrote to Paul in October 1947, at the time she was working on "Camp Cataract"
and Paul was working on *The Sheltering Sky*, his first novel:

> I hope maybe to have done enough writing by [February] so as not to be com-
> pletely ashamed and jealous when confronted with your novel. At the moment
> I can't even think of it without feeling hot all over. And yet if you had not been
> able to do it I would have wrung my hands in grief. . . . However little I have
> done I am pleased with but shall probably throw it in the rubbish heap when I
> see yours. (*Letters* 63)

This tone—one of deference, anger, depression, confusion, and admiration for Paul—
is common in Jane's private correspondence and conversations. Millicent Dillon, for
example, writes:

> She'd say to others, "I must write, but I can't." Paul urged her to work, but she
> would say to him, "What's the use of my working? You're so much more suc-
> cessful than I." Then to other people she would say, "Paul's the writer in the
> family, not I." (*Life* 253)

Michelle Green cogently sums up Jane's condition during the same period: "Paul's
orderly stack of notebooks was a painful counterpoint to her own fitful efforts, and it
was increasingly difficult to dispel the morbid wife-of-a-writer fantasy" (96).

The point to be made here is that these complex and painful psychological
responses coincide with the time during which Jane was trying to write *Out in the
World*, and no doubt had a great deal to do with her restlessness and wavering sense
of confidence. She was acutely aware of the fact that the body of work she had
produced was slim. *Two Serious Ladies* had been published in 1943, when she was
in her mid-twenties; ten years passed before she saw *In the Summer House* reach
the stage. *Out in the World* was a casualty (and product) of Jane's internal turmoil.
Suffering from a kind of colonization of the mind, she seemed to lose sight of what
it was she was doing and found no region sufficient for the retrieval or stabilization
of her purpose.

The relationship between Paul and Jane and its bearing on Jane's writing problems must be viewed within the context of a culture that attached more value to men's work than to women's, and adhered to fairly rigid gender roles. Paul might be seen merely as a manifestation of the cultural forces Jane was up against. It must be remembered that Jane Bowles was working in the forties and fifties, prior to the swelling of a feminist consciousness, in the post-WWII days of early television situation comedies and programs featuring women in their homes cooking and caring for children. In fact, it could be argued that Paul sought ways to encourage Jane and himself became frustrated with his inability to erase or counteract the tremendous pressures of the culture that had produced Jane.

Just as Jane struggled in her life and fiction to break through traditional, constricting boundaries imposed by gender, she also explored the space in which cultures abut and overlap one another. Jane was doubly marginalized—first, as a woman writer, then, with her move to Morocco in 1948, as an expatriate. Both conditions presented her with opportunities and obstacles that, depending upon her mood, circumstance, and capacity, she alternately rose to or was defeated by. Fascinated by other cultures and the romantic possibilities thus afforded, Bowles, even in material predating the Moroccan experience, inscribed encounters between characters from different cultures. We certainly might recall Mrs. Copperfield's infatuation with Pacifica, a young Panamanian, in *Two Serious Ladies*; the Lopez and Solares families in *In the Summer House*; "A Guatemalan Idyll"; and so on.

In Tangier, Jane Bowles lived more intensely than ever before in the often ambiguous and confounding region where cultures meet. The effects of her Moroccan experience can be felt in *Out in the World*, which she worked at, in fits and starts, during this period. "Out of this world of multiplicity and fragmentation into which she had thrown herself she struggled to construct a novel," Millicent Dillon suggests in her piece "Jane Bowles: Experiment as Character" (144).

While most would agree that Morocco nourished Paul, giving him the very stuff of his fiction, many have suggested that the move irreparably damaged Jane. While certainly the result of a complex set of factors, Jane's decline as a writer does correspond to her migration to and continued residence in Tangier. Jane, more socially gregarious and dependent than her husband, no doubt suffered the loss of sources of support and sustenance she had found in New York. In Morocco her writing floundered and sputtered. She continued to work, with occasional hard-won success, on plays and fiction set in America, including *In the Summer House* and *Out in the World*, and managed to set just one story, "Everything Is Nice," in Morocco.

Even though Jane was not, like Paul, able to make much literary capital out of North Africa, she—as much if not more than he—threw herself into the culture. Evidence of Jane's serious engagement with Moroccan culture is found, among other places, in the portions of her notebooks in which she diligently wrote down

Arabic words along with their pronunciation and English meaning. Of the period just after her arrival in Tangier, Millicent Dillon writes in her biography of Jane:

> She had not expected to be so intrigued by the medina, by the deviousness of its streets, by the small scale and the secrecy of its houses, closed off from the street. In the lives of the people she saw things that made this world of special interest to her, the separation of the lives of the women from the men, the slow pace of personal relationships—it might take hours for the sharing of a cup of tea, yet in that sharing were hundreds of nuances of behavior to be observed and wondered at. (*Life* 155)

As this passage suggests, a good deal of Jane's interest focused on Moroccan women. Attractive because of her very elusiveness, the Moroccan woman held out a tantalizing challenge to Jane, a desire that Millicent Dillon has interpreted as an attempt to recover her own childhood and an essential creative power:

> Jane is also, in trying to break into the world of the Arab women, going back to her earliest years, trying to break in there—to force a change there. The source of her own talent and power has become hidden from her and it is in the Arab world, through the Arab women, that she hopes to find it again. (*Life* 163)

That, certainly, is part of the story, but it does not tell the ending, seemingly a tragic failure of romantic aspirations. Cherifa came to represent a kind of impossible, self-defeating love. Jane's letters to Paul reveal a passionate obsession with the Moroccan woman, so strong that it distracted her from work and contributed to her already high level of anxiety. So vast was the gulf created by linguistic, cultural, and personality differences that Jane simply could not in the end establish a stable, trusting relationship with Cherifa.

A number of scenes in *Out in the World* take place in that ambivalent region between two cultures. In her tale, Emmy Moore wrestles with the meaning of the "Oriental woman"—what she terms "the Turkish problem"—and her words are interesting if not completely sensical. To her husband Paul she writes:

> As for the Turkish problem, I am coming to it. You must understand that I am an admirer of Western civilization; that is, of the women who are members of this group. I feel myself that I fall short of being a member, that by some curious accident I was not born in Turkey but should have been. Because of my usual imprecision I cannot even tell how many countries belong to what we call Western Civilization, but I believe Turkey is the place where East meets West, isn't it? (*Works* 445)

Emmy goes on to construct a theory in which Western women, on one side of the spectrum, and Far Eastern women "(I refer to the Chinese, Japanese, Hindus, and so on)" are "independent and masculine," while the "ones living in-between the two masculine areas would be soft and feminine" (446). Morocco could well be substituted for Turkey in this formula.

The scenes at the Cassalottis also inscribe a cross-cultural experience of sorts, even though it involves an American ethnic group. In Notebook 38 Bowles describes Fmmy Moore as trying "to get first hand insight into—Italian Family Life in America." As Emmy steps across the threshold into the Cassalotti family it does indeed seem to be a foreign land with bizarre manners and outlandish behavior. Mr. and Mrs. Cassalotti even resort to speaking Italian at one point, in order to talk freely and directly about their guest. Emmy herself listens on, able only to distinguish English words such as "Rolls-Royce." The scene is full of comic irony. Clearly Emmy has, in her wanderings, sought out this new cultural scene and—like Jane in Morocco—is thrilled by the tantalizing opportunity for radically breaking through the boundaries of her previous experience.

At the core of Bowles's aesthetic is an insistence on keeping various possibilities open, and a resistance to fixed, settled meanings—whether it be with respect to questions involving gender and culture, as just seen, or in matters concerning the nature of identity and narrative. In describing postmodernism, M. H. Abrams refers to its "irresolvable indeterminacies" (110). Even more useful and to the point in a consideration of Jane Bowles is Ihab Hassan's observation that those indeterminacies are part of "a vast, revisionary will in the Western world, unsettling/resettling codes, canons, procedures, beliefs" (xvi). This describes quite well what Bowles is up to.

The very stability of individual identity seems at stake in *Out in the World.* Not only does Bowles have trouble settling on her characters' names, a primary means by which identity is fixed, she also seems frequently to ascribe strikingly different natures to characters whom we have come to know in other portions of the narrative. The Agnes Leather of the Andrew sequence, for example, seems almost an entirely different quantity from the Agnes of the Cissy Mcavoy/Agnes sequence. Cissy Mcavoy (whose name is variously Sister, Sis, and so forth) figures not only in the Agnes narrative but in the Bozoe Flanner story as well. Are we to assume that she is the same Cissy Mcavoy in each? These instances, on the one hand, may simply reflect Bowles's penchant for recycling characters' names, especially when she found one she liked. But, whatever the reason, the practice calls our attention to the way in which identities are formed and the integral connection between name and identity. Identity, we assume, develops as a series of more or less consistent qualities attach themselves to a particular name. I am Allen Hibbard. Those who know me can talk about my qualities. Yet, perhaps, as a lot of postmodern art and theory suggests, identity is a more fluid thing than we have ordinarily assumed. You put one thing beside another and it looks one way; its character can be radically altered when we put it beside something quite different. The Allen Hibbard colleagues in the English Department know may not be the one his in-laws know, or the one his Syrian friends know, and so on. We are, in Whitman's terms, large, and contain multitudes! Jane Bowles certainly was playing with questions of identity, and seeking ways—both in her life and her art—to reflect the multiplicity, the sometimes alarmingly schizophrenic nature of the self. She seems determined that the actions of her characters, at any point in time, not be limited by their previous moves.

A substantial degree of indeterminacy exists, too, on the level of narrative. Bowles almost compulsively rewrites certain scenes (such as the meeting between Andrew and Tommy) over and over again, altering the course of action each time, and never seeming to be able to decide upon a definitive version. "In the notebooks," as Millicent Dillon puts it, "you can see her turning, twisting, feinting, holding off, telling, retracting, telling again" ("Experiment as Character" 145). In fact, she seems even to resist the very notion that there must be only one single narrative sequence, firm and unalterable. At times we are left with two competing versions of events. Does Agnes, who, Bowles writes "is all made up of death" (Notebook 35) finally commit suicide? "She has a suicide plan" we are told at one point (Notebook 36). And, later in the same notebook she says "she does kill herself," but then goes on to say "Later they [her mother and sister Lalla] feel embarrassed to see her because she isn't dead—but her interest in them is dead." Given the unfinished state of the novel, it is often impossible to say with any certainty just what does happen in any given scene.

It is precisely this problematic, this perceived necessity to choose and settle upon a single, unitary version of events, that in large measure must have frustrated Bowles's intentions to write a novel "classical—nineteenth century—in style and in structure" (Dillon, Introduction, *Letters* 5–6). The central structural problem in the novel involves the business of linking all the narrative threads together in traditional form. That is, the work seems to resist the strictures of the Victorian formula employed by Dickens, Trollope, or even George Eliot. Neither Bowles nor her characters seem naturally to stay on traditional narrative tracks, as seen, in *Two Serious Ladies*. While Bowles herself most often viewed the fragmentary, repetitive qualities of her prose as a kind of "failure" of her own literary powers, Millicent Dillon has quite rightly asserted in "Experiment as Character" that her experiment should rather be seen "as a mode of expression that was attempting to manifest itself through her but that she could not accept" (140). Value, thus, can be ascribed to a style at once fragmentary and repetitious. "If it is true," Dillon writes, "that her work was psychically blocked, it is also true that had she been able to view this fragmentation as a valid expression of her own narrative vision, the fragmentation could have led her to further development—which may say something about the nature of 'blocks' " (140). Had Bowles had in front of her clear models of a distinctly postmodern aesthetic, she might have been content simply to let the fragments stand, relieved of the concern for wrapping them together in a neat, tight narrative with no loose ends. We might then have had (as perhaps we do in its unfinished state) a work displaying, as Victor Burgin has dubbed postmodernism, "a complex of heterogeneous but interrelated questions which will not be silenced by any spurious *unitary* answer" (163–64).

The disruption of traditional narrative structure has sometimes been seen (for example by Julia Kristeva and Philippe Sollers in the sixties and seventies) as presenting a challenge to established political ideologies. Bowles's resistance to a totalizing and predictable narrative can be thought of as being consistent with Deleuze and Guattari's conscious designs to break down fascist structures wherever they exist. She seems on some level to have been aware, as Teresa de Lauretis has put it, of how "narrative and narrativity . . . are mechanisms to be employed strategically and tactically in the effort to construct other forms of coherence, to shift the terms of representation, to produce the conditions of representability of another— and gendered—social subject" (*Technologies of Gender* 109).

Here Jane Bowles is on the cutting edge. Her characters are always seeking ways to break through into previously unexplored realms of experience, despite the psychic and cultural obstacles standing in the way. That concern takes on a powerful metaphoric quality at one point in Andrew's story:

> . . . he was walking along the road to his grandmother's house. It was in the summertime and he had not been to visit his grandmother for a year. The stone wall at his left was high enough to prevent his seeing over it. It was warm near the wall and the air was still, though across the road a cool wind was making the grass wave. He would reach out frequently as he always had to touch the warm stone. He was barely conscious of his surroundings when he reached for the wall and felt the wind blowing through his fingers. Automatically he turned and looked at his hand. There was a breach in the wall. He could see fields and blossoming orchards that he had never known existed. In the distance there were cows standing in the pastures and blue oats curving in the breeze. Some of the cows were in the shadows and others flamed red in the sun. The fields of oats and the pasture land too flashed in brightness and then darkened as he watched. Only the blossoms close to him remained brightly in the light of the sun.
> He stood still: The breach had not existed the year before. (Included in *Letters* 215.)

It is unlikely that Jane Bowles was consciously or purposefully postmodern, at least in the writing of *Out in the World*. Her aesthetic seems as much a product of her instability than a result of a clearly delineated, consciously developed program. Unconsciously, unwittingly, she was a fly caught in the ointment. In trying desperately to write a species of nineteenth-century, Victorian multiplot novel, she inevitably failed because those structures could not adequately contain her distinctly postmodern impulses or the kinds of material she was dealing with. It is as though she continually subverts herself by letting things get out of control, or a least by not insisting on control. Perhaps Paul was right in blaming her problems on her method. Yet, too tight a program would fly in the face of the spontaneity that so thoroughly imbues Bowles's work. As she put it to Jane Howard, "The way I write I never know what is going to happen, which is probably what gives my work its quality of surprise, as if the reader and I were finding it out together" ("A Talk in the Casbah" H3).

Of course all of this, including this mess of an unfinished novel, leaves Jane Bowles open to charges that she is simply a flawed or unsuccessful writer, for is not the discipline she so obviously lacked precisely what transforms scribblings and inchoate ideas into works of art? Once again a postmodern critique assists in establishing a place for Bowles, in particular a place for *Out in the World*, for the postmodern carries in it a critique of the autonomous work of art, and encourages ways of seeing all that goes into the process of making. It urges us, moreover, to rethink the nature of discipline—how it is imposed and the price of its imposition. We have tended, in the wake of modernism, to value the monolithic, discrete aesthetic object—whole and distinct—the urn of Keats's ode, Joyce's *Ulysses*, Yeats's finely tuned lyric, and so on. Postmodern criticism, given its shift of attention toward the cultural context of the work, allows us freshly to entertain the status of the fragment—or the unfinished product—by posing such questions as: What interests and concerns does the fragment hold? What psychological, cultural pressures might account for their fragmentary nature? Might there even be an aesthetic embracing the fragment or the unfinished work?

As a last gesture in arguing the value of *Out in the World*, I invoke the words of Peter Brooks whose assessment of our (postmodern) human condition seems so precisely to speak to the topic at hand: "We live immersed in narrative, recounting and reassessing the meaning of our past actions, anticipating the outcome of our future projects, *situating ourselves at the intersection of several stories not yet completed*" (3, emphasis mine).

Notes

1. In my article *"Out in the World*: Reconstructing Jane Bowles's Unfinished Novel" in the the *Library Chronicle of the University of Texas at Austin* 25.2 (1994): 121–69, I fairly comprehensively present the various narrative fragments and lay out a plausible design for the novel.

2. In order to preserve the essential flavor of Bowles's style, including her troubles with spelling and other quirks, I have chosen to present portions of Jane Bowles's notebooks unedited, except for those portions that have already been edited and published, as citations will indicate.

3. Notebook numbers correspond to those used by the Harry Ransom Humanities Research Center, The University of Texas at Austin, to classify and account for Bowles's work. Quotation from Jane Bowles's notebooks by permission of Paul Bowles and the Ransom Center.

4. The principle of undecidability applies as well to Bowles's spelling of characters' names. She variously refers to "Cissy," "Sis," and "Sister" Mcavoy (which also has its variants in spelling!). My own inconsistency in the following discussion, thus, simply reflects the inconsistencies in Bowles's style.

Bibliography

Contributors

Index

Bibliography

Primary Sources

The Collected Works of Jane Bowles. Introd. Truman Capote. New York: Farrar, 1966. London: Owen, 1984.

Feminine Wiles. Introd. Tennessee Williams. Santa Barbara: Black Sparrow, 1976.

My Sister's Hand in Mine: An Expanded Edition of the Collected Works of Jane Bowles. Introd. Truman Capote. New York: Ecco, 1978.

Out in the World: Selected Letters of Jane Bowles 1935–1970. Ed. and introd. Millicent Dillon. Santa Barbara: Black Sparrow, 1985.

Plain Pleasures. London: Owen, 1966. *Plain Pleasures and Other Stories.* London: Arena, 1985.

The Portable Paul and Jane Bowles. Ed. and introd. Millicent Dillon. New York: Penguin, 1994.

Two Serious Ladies. New York: Knopf, 1943. London: Owen, 1965. New York: Dutton, 1984. London: Virago, 1979, with introduction by Francine du Plessix Gray.

Secondary Sources

Abrams, M. H. *A Glossary of Literary Terms.* 4th ed. rev. New York: Holt, 1981.

Acker, Kathy. *The Empire of the Senseless.* New York: Grove, 1988.

Adorno, Theodor. *Minima Moralia: Reflections from a Damaged Life.* Trans. E. F. N. Jephcott. London: Routledge, 1984.

Allen, Carolyn J. *Following Djuna: Women Lovers and the Erotics of Loss.* Bloomington: Indiana U P, 1996.

Ashbery, John. "Up from the Underground." Rev. of *The Collected Works of Jane Bowles,* by Jane Bowles. *New York Times Book Review* 29 January 1967: 5+.

Atkinson, Brooks. "At the Theatre." Rev. of *In the Summer House,* by Jane Bowles. Playhouse, New York. *New York Times* 30 December 1953: 17.

Austin, Gayle. *Feminist Theories for Dramatic Criticism.* Ann Arbor: U of Michigan P, 1990.

Bachelard, Gaston. *The Poetics of Space.* Trans. Maria Jolas. Boston: Beacon, 1958.

Barlow, Judith E., ed. *Plays by American Women: The Early Years.* New York: Avon, 1981.

———. *Plays by American Women 1930–1960.* New York: Applause Theatre, 1994.

Bassett, Mark T. "Imagination, Control and Betrayal in Jane Bowles's 'A Stick of Green Candy.' " *Studies in Short Fiction* 24.1 (1987): 25–29.

Benjamin, Walter. *Illuminations.* Ed. Hannah Arendt. Trans. Harry Zohn. New York: Schocken, 1968.

———. *Reflections.* Ed. and introd. Peter Demetz. Trans. Edmund Jephcott. New York: Harcourt, 1978.

Benstock, Shari. *Women of the Left Bank: Paris, 1900–1940.* Austin: U of Texas P, 1986.

Bentley, Eric. "The Ill-Made Play." Rev. of *In the Summer House*, by Jane Bowles. Playhouse, New York. *New Republic* 11 January 1954: 20–21.

Bernal, Martin. *Black Athena: The Afroasiatic Roots of Classical Civilization*. New Brunswick: Rutgers UP, 1987.

Betsko, Kathleen, and Rachel Koenig. *Interviews With Contemporary Women Playwrights*. New York: Beech Tree, 1987.

Birns, Beverly, and Niza ben-Ner. "Psychoanalysis Constructs Motherhood." *The Different Faces of Motherhood*. Ed. Beverly Birns and Dale F. Hay. New York: Plenum, 1988. 42–72.

Bowles, Paul. *The Collected Stories of Paul Bowles, 1939–1976*. Introd. Gore Vidal. Santa Barbara: Black Sparrow, 1979.

——. *The Delicate Prey*. 1950. New York: Ecco, 1972.

——. *In Touch: The Letters of Paul Bowles*. Ed. Jeffrey Miller. New York: Farrar, 1994.

——. *Let It Come Down*. 1952. Santa Barbara: Black Sparrow, 1980.

——. *A Little Stone*. London: Lehmann, 1950.

——. *The Sheltering Sky*. 1949. New York: Ecco, 1978.

——. *Their Heads are Green and Their Hands are Blue*. 1963. New York: Ecco, 1984.

——. *Up Above the World*. 1966. New York: Ecco, 1982.

——. *The Wind Remains*. Leonard Bernstein conducting the C.B.S. Symphony Orchestra. Noncommercial phonodisc recorded in the studios of G. Schirmer, Inc., 3 East 43rd St., New York. n.d.

——. *Without Stopping: An Autobiography*. 1972. New York: Ecco, 1985.

Briatte, Robert. *Paul Bowles: 2117 Tanger Socco*. Paris: Plon, 1989.

Brooke-Rose, Christine. "Illiterations." Friedman and Fuchs 55–71.

Brookner, Anita. "Going to Pieces." Rev. of *Collected Works of Jane Bowles*, by Jane Bowles. *Books and Bookmen* January 1984: 22.

Brooks, Peter. *Reading for the Plot: Design and Intention in Narrative*. New York: Random, 1984.

Bryer, Jackson R., ed. *Conversations with Lillian Hellman*. Jackson: U of Mississippi P, 1986.

Burgin, Victor. *The End of Art Theory: Criticism and Postmodernity*. Atlantic Highlands, NJ: Humanities, 1986.

Butler, Judith. "Against Proper Objects." *Differences* 6.2–3 (1994): 1–26.

——. *Gender Trouble*. New York: Routledge, 1990.

"Candidates for Prizes." *Vogue* 1 May 1954: 137.

Caplan, Paula J. *Don't Blame Mother: Mending the Mother-Daughter Relationship*. New York: Harper, 1989.

Caponi, Gena Dagel, ed. *Conversations with Paul Bowles*. Jackson: UP of Mississippi, 1993.

——. *Paul Bowles: Romantic Savage*. Carbondale: Southern Illinois UP, 1994.

Chadwick, Whitney. *Women Artists and the Surrealist Movement*. New York: Thames, 1985.

Chandler, Marilyn. *Dwelling in the Text: Houses in American Fiction*. Berkeley: U of California P, 1991.

Chester, Alfred. *The Exquisite Corpse*. New York: Carroll, 1967.

Chinoy, Helen Rich, and Linda Walsh Jenkins, eds. *Women in American Theatre: Careers, Images, Movements*. New York: Crown, 1981.

Chodorow, Nancy. *The Reproduction of Mothering: Psychoanalysis and the Sociology of Gender*. Berkeley: U of California P, 1978.

Cixous, Hélène. "The Laugh of the Medusa." Trans. Keith Cohen and Paula Cohen. *Signs: Journal of Women in Culture and Society* 1 (1976): 875–93.

Coates, Jennifer. *Women, Men and Language: A Sociolinguistic Account of Sex Differences in Language*. London: Longman, 1986.

Collins, Jack. "Jane and Paul." Rev. of *A Little Original Sin*, by Millicent Dillon. *Threepenny Review* (Winter 1982): 8.

Cummings, Katherine. "Sexualities." *Oxford Companion to Women's Writing in the United States*. Ed. Cathy N. Davidson and Linda Wagner-Martin. New York: Oxford UP, 1995. 794–96.

Dace, Trish. Review of *In the Summer House*, by Jane Bowles. *Soho Weekly News* 4 June 1980: 78.

Davidson, Cathy N., and E. M. Broner. *The Lost Tradition: Mothers and Daughters in Literature*. New York: Ungar, 1980.

DeKoven, Marianne. "Male Signature, Female Aesthetic: The Gender Politics of Experimental Writing." Friedman and Fuchs 72–81.

Delaney, Shelagh. *A Taste of Honey*. New York: Grove, 1959.

de Lauretis, Teresa. "Queer Theory: Lesbian and Gay Sexualities: An Introduction." *Differences* 3.2 (1991): iii–xviii.

——. *Technologies of Gender: Essays on Theory, Film and Fiction*. Bloomington: Indiana UP, 1987.

Deleuze, Gilles, and Felix Guattari. *Kafka: Toward a Minor Literature*. Trans. and introd. Dona Polan. Minneapolis: U of Minnesota P, 1986.

——. *A Thousand Plateaus: Capitalism and Schizophrenia*. Trans. Brian Massumi. Minneapolis: U of Minnesota P, 1987.

D'Erasmo, Stacey. "Regarding Jane: The Passion of the Other Bowles." *Village Voice Literary Supplement* June 1994: 23–24.

Dictionary of Modern English. New York: Greenwich, 1983.

Didion, Joan. *Salvador*. New York: Simon, 1983.

Dillon, Millicent. "Jane Bowles: Experiment as Character." Friedman and Fuchs 140–47.

——. *A Little Original Sin: The Life and Work of Jane Bowles*. New York: Holt, 1981.

——. "The Three Exiles of Jane Bowles." *Confrontation* 27–28 (1984): 72–74.

Duggan, Lisa. "Making it Perfectly Queer." *Socialist Review* 22.1 (1992): 11–31.

Fernea, Elizabeth Warnock. *Guests of the Sheik*. Garden City, NY: Doubleday, 1969.

——. *A Street in Marrakech*. Garden City, NY: Doubleday, 1980.

Ford, Charles Henri, ed. *View: Parade of the Avant-Garde 1940–1947*. Foreword Paul Bowles. New York: Thunders' Mouth, 1991.

Foster, Hal, ed. *The Anti-Aesthetic: Essays on Postmodern Culture*. Port Townsend, WA: Bay, 1983.

Foucault, Michel. *Power/Knowledge: Selected Interviews and Other Writings*. Ed. and Trans. Colin Gordon et al. New York: Pantheon, 1980.

Freitag, George H. "Fine First Novel Probes Deep into the Human Mind." Rev. of *Two Serious Ladies*, by Jane Bowles. *Book Week* 16 May 1943: 3.

Freud, Sigmund. "The Economic Problem of Masochism." 1924. *Standard Edition*. Vol. 19. 157–70.

——. *Group Psychology and the Analysis of the Ego.* 1921. *Standard Edition.* Vol. 18. 67–143.

——. *Jokes and Their Relation to the Unconscious.* 1905. *Standard Edition.* Vol. 8.

——. *The Standard Edition of the Complete Psychological Works of Sigmund Freud.* Ed. and trans. James Strachey et al. 24 vols. London: Hogarth, 1953–74.

——. "The Uncanny." 1919. *Standard Edition.* Vol. 17. 217–56.

Friedman, Ellen G. "What are the Missing Contents? (Post)Modernism, Gender, and the Canon." *PMLA* 108 (1993): 240–52.

Friedman, Ellen G. and Miriam Fuchs, eds. *Breaking the Sequence: Women's Experimental Fiction.* Princeton: Princeton UP, 1989.

Gentile, Kathy Justice. " 'The Dreaded Voyage into the World': Jane Bowles and Her Serious Ladies." *Studies in American Fiction* 22.1 (1994): 47–60.

Gilbert, Sandra M., and Susan Gubar. *The Madwoman in the Attic: The Woman Writer and the Nineteenth-Century Literary Imagination.* New Haven: Yale UP, 1979.

Goodman, Charlotte. "The Foxes' Cubs: Lillian Hellman, Arthur Miller and Tennessee Williams." Schlueter 130–42.

——. *Jean Stafford: The Savage Heart.* Austin: U of Texas P, 1990.

Gray, Francine du Plessix. "Jane Bowles Reconsidered." *New York Times Book Review* 19 February 1978: 3+. Rpt. in *Adam and Eve in the City.* New York: Simon, 1987. 286–90.

Green, Michelle. *The Dream at the End of the World: Paul Bowles and the Literary Renegades in Tangier.* New York: Harper, 1991.

Grosz, Elizabeth. *Space, Time, and Perversion.* New York: Routledge, 1995.

Hall, Edward T. *Beyond Culture.* Garden City, NY: Doubleday, 1977.

——. *The Hidden Dimension.* Garden City, NY: Doubleday, 1969.

——. *The Silent Language.* Garden City, NY: Doubleday, 1959.

Harrell, Richard S., and Harvey Sobleman, eds. *A Dictionary of Moroccan Arabic: Moroccan-English, English-Moroccan.* Washington, DC: Georgetown UP, 1963.

Harvey, David. *The Condition of Postmodernity.* Cambridge: Blackwell, 1989.

Hassan, Ihab. *Postmodern Turn: Essays in Postmodern Theory and Culture.* Columbus: Ohio State UP, 1987.

Haynes, Muriel. "The Toughness of Jane Bowles." Rev. of *My Sister's Hand in Mine*, by Jane Bowles. *Ms.* April 1978: 33+.

Hellman, Lillian. *The Autumn Garden.* Hellman, *Six Plays.* 394–494.

——. *The Little Foxes.* Hellman, *Six Plays.* 147–226.

——. *Six Plays by Lillian Hellman.* New York: Vintage, 1979.

Henry, O. *The Complete Works.* Vol. 1. Garden City: Doubleday, 1953.

Hibbard, Allen. "*Out in the World*: Reconstructing Jane Bowles's Unfinished Novel." *Library Chronicle of the University of Texas at Austin* 25.2 (1994): 121–69.

Hicks, Emily D. *Border Writing: The Multidimensional Text.* Minneapolis: U of Minnesota P, 1991.

Hite, Molly. "Postmodern Fiction." In *The Columbia History of the American Novel*, ed. Emory Elliott. New York: Columbia U P, 1991. 697–725.

Howard, Jane. "A Talk in the Casbah." *Washington Post Book World* 19 March 1978: H1+.

Howe, Tina. *Painting Churches. Plays From the Contemporary Theatre.* Ed. Brooks McNamara. New York: New American Library, 1988. 353–410.

Hutcheon, Linda. *A Politics of Postmodernism: History, Theory, Fiction.* New York: Routledge, 1988.

Jacoby, Susan. "A Literary Cult Figure." Rev. of *A Little Original Sin,* by Millicent Dillon. *New York Times Book Review* 13 September 1981: 11.

Jameson, Frederic. "Postmodernism and Consumer Society." Foster 111–25.

———. *Postmodernism or the Cultural Logic of Late Capitalism.* Durham, NC: Duke UP, 1991.

Jefferson, Margo. "Who Killed Jane Bowles?" *Soho News* 11 August 1981: 15–16.

Jelloun, Taher Ben. *The Sacred Night.* Trans. Alan Sheridan. New York: Harcourt, 1989.

———. *The Sand Child.* Trans. Alan Sheridan. New York: Harcourt, 1987.

Kaplan, Robert B. "Cultural Thought Patterns in Inter-Cultural Education." *Language Learning* 16 (1966): 6–10.

Kerr, Walter. *How Not to Write a Play.* Boston: Writers, 1955.

———. Untitled essay on Jane Bowles. *Pieces at Eight.* New York: Simon, 1957. 154–56.

Knapp, Bettina. *Archetype, Architecture, and the Writer.* Bloomington: Indiana UP, 1986.

Koch, Stephen. "Jane Bowles's Plain Pleasures." Rev. of *Collected Works of Jane Bowles,* by Jane Bowles. *Book Week* 12 February 1967: 4+.

Kristeva, Julia. *Strangers to Ourselves.* Trans. Leon S. Roudiez. New York: Columbia UP, 1991.

Kronenberger, Louis, ed. *The Best Plays of 1953–54.* New York: Dodd, 1954.

Labov, William. *Language in the Inner City.* Philadelphia: U of Pennsylvania P, 1972.

Lacan, Jacques. *Écrits: A Selection.* Trans. Alan Sheridan. New York: Norton, 1977.

Lakoff, George, and Mark Johnson. *Metaphors We Live By.* Chicago: U of Chicago P, 1980.

Lakritz, Andrew M. "Jane Bowles's Other World." *Old Maids to Radical Spinsters: Unmarried Women in the Twentieth-Century Novel.* Ed. Laura L. Doan. Urbana: U of Illinois P, 1991. 213–34.

Landau, Rom. *Moroccan Drama, 1900–1955.* San Francisco: American Academy of Asian Studies, 1956.

Lerman, Leo. "Three Quite Different Spring Novels." Rev. of *Two Serious Ladies,* by Jane Bowles. *New York Herald Tribune Weekly Book Review* 15 April 1943: 10.

Rev. of *A Little Original Sin* by Millicent Dillon. *Booklist* 77 (1981): 1383.

Rev. of *A Little Original Sin* by Millicent Dillon. *Choice* 19 (1981): 378.

Rev. of *A Little Original Sin* by Millicent Dillon. *Kirkus* 49 (1981): 710.

Rev. of *A Little Original Sin* by Millicent Dillon. *Library Journal* 106 (1981): 1223.

Lougy, Robert E. "The World and Art of Jane Bowles (1917–1973)." *CEA Critic* 49 (1986–87): 157–73.

Lyotard, Jean-François. *The Postmodern Condition: A Report on Knowledge.* Trans. Geoff Bennington and Brian Massumi. Minneapolis: U of Minnesota P, 1984.

Maier, John. "Asia under the Sign of Woman: The Feminization of the Orient in *The Aeneid.*" *Works and Days: Essays in the Socio-Historical Dimensions of Literature and the Arts* 9 (1991): 91–116.

Masterson, James F. *The Narcissistic and Borderline Disorders.* New York: Brunner, 1981.

Meade, Marion. *Dorothy Parker: What Fresh Hell Is This?* New York: Viking, 1989.

Melville, Herman. *Typee.* 1846. Evanston: Northwestern UP, 1968.

Mernissi, Fatima. *Beyond the Veil: Male-Female Dynamics in a Modern Muslim Society.* Rev. ed. Bloomington: Indiana UP, 1987.

Miller, Jeffrey. *Paul Bowles: A Descriptive Bibliography.* Santa Barbara: Black Sparrow, 1986.

Moi, Toril. *Sexual/Textual Politics: Feminist Literary Theory.* New York: Methuen, 1985.

Moore, Honor, ed. *The New Women's Theatre: Ten Plays by Contemporary American Women*. New York: Random, 1977.

Nagele, Rainer. "The Scene of the Other: Theodor W. Adorno's Negative Dialectic in the Context of Poststructuralism." *Postmodernism and Politics*. Ed. Jonathan Arac. Minneapolis: U of Minnesota P, 1986.

Nice, Vivien E. *Mothers and Daughters: The Distortion of a Relationship*. Hammondsworth: Macmillan, 1992.

Norman, Marsha. *'night Mother. Stages of Drama*. Eds. Carl H. Klaus et al. 2nd ed. New York: St. Martin's, 1991. 1132–54.

Olausen, Judith. *The American Woman Playwright: A View of Criticism and Characterization*. Troy, NY: Whitston, 1981.

Owens, Craig. "The Discourse of Others: Feminists and Postmodernism." Foster 57–77.

Palmer, Richard. "Hermeneutics and the *Postmodern*." Paper delivered at the 1978 Meeting of the American Academy of Religion, 20 November 1978.

Parker, Dorothy, and Arnaud D'Usseau. *The Ladies of the Corridor*. New York: Viking, 1954.

Parker, Dorothy, and Ross Evans. *The Coast of Illyria: A Play in Three Acts*. Introd. Arthur F. Kinney. Iowa City: U of Iowa, 1990.

Paul Bowles: The Complete Outsider. Prod. and dir. by Regina Weinreich and Catherine Warnow. First Run Features, 1993.

Pearlman, Mickey, ed. *Mother Puzzles: Daughters and Mothers in Contemporary American Literature*. New York: Greenwood, 1989.

Polizzotti, Mark. *Revolution of the Mind: The Life of André Breton*. New York: Farrar, 1995.

Porter, Dennis. *Haunted Journeys: Desire and Transgression in European Travel Writing*. Princeton: Princeton UP, 1991.

Probyn, Elspeth. "Queer Belongings: The Politics of Departure." *Sky Bodies: The Strange Carnalities of Feminism*. Ed. Elizabeth Grosz and Elspeth Probyn. New York, Routledge, 1995. 1–18.

Rich, Adrienne. *Of Woman Born: Motherhood as Experience and Institution*. New York: Norton, 1976.

Rich, Frank. "Mothers, Daughters and Tangled Emotions." Rev. of *In the Summer House*, by Jane Bowles. Beaumont, New York. *New York Times* 2 August 1993: C11+.

Richards, David. " 'In the Summer House' Preserves Its Riddles." Rev. of *In the Summer House*, by Jane Bowles. Beaumont, New York. *New York Times* 8 August 1993: 5+.

Roditi, Edouard. "The Fiction of Jane Bowles as a Form of Self-Exorcism." *The Review of Contemporary Fiction* 12.2 (1992): 182–94.

Rorem, Ned. *Knowing When to Stop: A Memoir*. New York: Simon, 1994.

Rothman, N. L. "The Dream Freedom." Rev. of *Two Serious Ladies*, by Jane Bowles. *Saturday Review* 1 May 1943: 20.

Said, Edward. *Orientalism*. New York: Pantheon, 1978.

Samuels, Charles Thomas. "Serious Ladies." Rev. of *The Collected Works of Jane Bowles*, by Jane Bowles. *New York Review of Books* 15 December 1966: 38.

Sanborn, Helen. *A Winter in Central America and Mexico*. Boston, 1886.

Sartre, Jean-Paul. *Existentialism and Human Emotions*. New York: Philosophical Library, 1957.

Sawyer-Lauçanno, Christopher. *An Invisible Spectator: A Biography of Paul Bowles*. New York: Weidenfeld, 1989.

Scarry, Elaine. *The Body in Pain: The Making and Unmaking of the World*. New York: Oxford UP, 1985.

Schlueter, June, ed. *Modern American Drama: The Female Canon.* Cranbury, NJ: Associated University, 1990.

Schott, Webster. "A Shriek from Wasted Women." Rev. of *The Collected Works of Jane Bowles,* by Jane Bowles. *Life* 16 December 1966: 17.

Sciolino, Martina. "Kathy Acker and the Postmodern Subject of Feminism." *College English* 52 (1990): 437–45.

"A Serious Lady." Rev. of *Plain Pleasures* by Jane Bowles. *Times Literary Supplement* 30 June 1966: 579.

Shattuck, Roger. *The Banquet Years.* Rev. ed. 1958. New York: Vintage, 1967.

Sievers, E. David. *Freud on Broadway.* New York: Hermitage, 1955.

Spoto, Donald. *The Kindness of Strangers: A Life of Tennessee Williams.* Boston: Little, 1985.

Squier, Ephraim. *Waikna; Adventures on the Mosquito Shore.* New York, 1855.

Stein, Arlene. "Sisters and Queers: The Decentering of Lesbian Feminism." *Socialist Review* 22.1 (1992): 33–55.

Stewart, Jan. "Into the Ocean of Family Alienation." *Newsday* 2 August 1993: 45.

Stone, Laurie. "Jane Bowles: Blockbusted." Rev. of *A Little Original Sin,* by Millicent Dillon, and *My Sister's Hand in Mine,* by Jane Bowles. *Village Voice* 19 August 1984: 35–37.

Sullivan, Victoria, and James Hatch, eds. *Plays By and About Women.* New York: Random, 1973.

Tannen, Deborah. *You Just Don't Understand, Women and Men in Conversation.* New York: Ballantine, 1990.

Tashjian, Dickran. *A Boatload of Madmen: Surrealism and the American Avant-Garde 1920–1950.* New York: Thames, 1995.

Thoreau, Henry David. *Walden and Civil Disobedience.* New York: Penguin Classics, 1986.

"Two Empty Ladies." Rev. of *Two Serious Ladies,* by Jane Bowles. *Times Literary Supplement* 4 February 1965: 81.

Rev. of *Two Serious Ladies,* by Jane Bowles. *New Yorker* 24 April 1943: 79.

Vidal, Gore. Introduction. *Collected Stories.* By Paul Bowles 5–9.

Vidler, Anthony. *The Architectural Uncanny.* Cambridge: MIT P, 1992.

Wagner, Geoffrey. Rev. of *The Collected Works of Jane Bowles,* by Jane Bowles. *Commonweal* 85 (1967): 493–94.

Walton, Edith H. "Fantastic Duo." Rev. of *Two Serious Ladies,* by Jane Bowles. *New York Times Book Review* 9 May 1943: 14.

Warner, Michael. "From Queer to Eternity." *Village Voice Literary Supplement* February 1992: 18–19.

Wasserstein, Wendy. *Isn't It Romantic? The Heidi Chronicles and Other Plays.* New York: Vintage, 1990. 73–154.

Waugh, Patricia. *Feminine Fictions: Revisiting the Postmodern.* New York: Routledge, 1989.

Weales, Gerald. *American Drama Since World War II.* New York: Harcourt, 1962.

Wheeler, Kathleen. *"Modernist" Women Writers and Narrative Art.* New York: New York UP, 1994.

Woolf, Virginia. *A Room of One's Own.* 1929. New York: Harcourt, 1957.

Wylie, Philip. *Generation of Vipers.* New York: Reinhart, 1942.

Yorkey, Richard. "Practical EFL Techniques for Teaching Arabic-Speaking Students." *The Human Factors of ESL.* Ed. James E. Alatis and Ruth Crymes. Washington, DC: TESOL, 1977. 68–82.

Young-Mallin, Judith. "The Tibor Nagy Puppet Company: Tibor de Nagy and John Bernard Myers." *Gallery News* (Brooklyn College) 19 April 1990. n.p.

Contributors

Carolyn J. Allen is an associate professor of English and an adjunct associate professor of women's studies at the University of Washington. She publishes on feminist literary and cultural theory and on twentieth-century women writers. She is the author of *Following Djuna: Women Lovers and the Erotics of Loss* and is the coeditor of *Signs: Journal of Women in Culture and Society*.

Stephen Benz is an assistant professor of English at Barry University in Miami. He publishes on American and British writers in Latin America and is the author of *Guatemalan Journey*, his account of two years as a Fulbright Scholar in Central America, and of the forthcoming *Teaching and Testimony: Rigoberta Menchu and the North American Classroom*.

Gena Dagel Caponi is an assistant professor and director of American studies at the University of Texas at San Antonio. She has published *Conversations with Paul Bowles*, *Paul Bowles: Romantic Savage*, and is the author of the forthcoming *Paul Bowles*.

Peter G. Christensen is an adjunct lecturer in English and comparative literature at the University of Wisconsin-Milwaukee. He has published articles on Paul Blackburn, Marguerite Young, Truman Capote, John Rollin Ridge, Washington Irving, and John Hersey. He is currently at work on a book on historical fiction dealing with classical civilization.

Charlotte Goodman is a professor of English at Skidmore College. Her publications include *Jean Stafford: The Savage Heart*, "The Lost Brother/The Twin: Women Novelists and the Male-Female Double Bildungsroman" in *Novel: A Forum on Fiction*, the afterword to *Weeds* by Edith Summers Kelley, and essays on Harriette Arnow, Lillian Hellman, Alice Munro, and Margaret Walker. She is currently at work on a study of mothers and daughters in fiction.

Allen E. Hibbard is an associate professor of English at Middle Tennessee State University. He has published *Paul Bowles: A Study of the Short Fiction* and "*Out in the World*:

Reconstructing Jane Bowles's Unfinished Novel." He is presently collecting material for a biography of Alfred Chester.

Robert E. Lougy is an associate professor of English at The Pennsylvania State University at University Park. His publications include *Charles Robert Maturin, An Annotated Bibliography of Martin Chuzzlewit, The Children of the Chapel* by Algernon Charles Swinburne and Mary Gordon, which he edited, and numerous other publications on nineteenth- and twentieth-century literature, including work by Jane Bowles. He is currently completing a book on hidden narratives and the presence of the textual unconscious in some major nineteenth-century British texts.

John Maier is a professor of English at SUNY College at Brockport. He has coedited *The Bible and Its Literary Milieu: Contemporary Essays* and coauthored *Gilgamesh, Translated from the Version of Sin-legi-unninni* and *Myths of Enki, The Crafty God.* He had published numerous essays on ancient and modern literature, including work by Paul Bowles, and he is the author of *Desert Songs: Western Images of Morocco and Moroccan Images of the West* and *A Gilgamesh Reader.*

Carol Shloss is a professor of English at West Chester University. She has published *Flannery O'Connor's Dark Comedies: The Limits of Inference, Gentlemen Photographers: The Work of William and Loring Underwood, In Visible Light: Photography and the American Writer.* The author of numerous essays on literary modernism, narrative theory, and biography, she received the Pew Foundation's award for literary nonfiction prose writing in 1994. She is currently working on *To Dance in the Wake: Lucia and James Joyce,* the first of a trilogy on modernism's daughters.

Jennie Skerl is associate dean of the College of Arts and Sciences at West Chester University. She has coedited *William S. Burroughs at the Front: Critical Reception, 1959–1989* and authored *William S. Burroughs* as well as essays on Burroughs, the Beats, Beckett, Joyce, and narrative theory. Her current research includes American writers in Tangier and women of the avant-garde.

Regina Weinreich is on the faculty of The School of Visual Arts. She has published *The Spontaneous Poetics of Jack Kerouac;* essays on Kerouac, the Beats, and Paul Bowles; as well as numerous essays on the arts in *Paris Review, New York Times, Washington Post, American Book Review, Village Voice,* and many other publications. She produced and directed the film biography, *Paul Bowles: The Complete Outsider* (with Catherine Warnow), which premiered at the Hamptons International Film Festival and at the Museum of Modern Art in New York City. She is currently working on a film on the Holocaust.

Index

Abrams, M. H., 163
Adorno, Theodore, 107–10, 113, 115
Akalaitis, Joanne, 15, 65, 66
ambiguity, 49–50, 55, 62–63, 121
American Woman Playwright, The (Olauson), 15, 52
Anderson, Judith, 9, 65
Arab-Muslim society (*see also* "Everything Is Nice"; Tangier): and family, 90–91; hospitality in, 86, 90, 93; seclusion of women in, 88–90, 94; wa-wa cultural style of, 92–93
artist, quest of, 2–4, 14; and avant-garde, 15–17; and bohemia, 3–4
Ashbery, John, 10, 11, 12
Askew, Constance, 77
Askew, Kirk, 77
Atkinson, Brooks, 9
"At the Jumping Bean" (Bowles), 141, 146
Auer, Jane. *See* Bowles, Jane
Austin, Gayle, 15–16, 66
Autumn Garden, The (Hellman), 49, 59–63
avant-garde, 15–17

Bachelard, Gaston, 108–10, 113
Barlow, Judith E., 65
Basset, Mark T., 16
Beckett, Samuel, 6, 17–18n. 2
Ben-Nur, Niza, 51
Bentley, Eric, 9
Betsko, Kathleen, 73
Beyond the Veil: Male-Female Dynamics in Modern Muslim Society (Mernissi), 88
Birns, Beverly, 51
Black Sparrow Press, 13
bohemia, 3–4
Bosch, Hieronymous, 122
Bowles, Claire, 71–72
Bowles, Jane: as avant-garde, 15; as coterie writer, 11; and decision-making, 134–35, 144, 149–51, 153, 164, 167n. 4; early life, 1–2; fear of madness, 5–6; and fragmentation, 7, 16, 164; French influence on, 2;

health of, 4, 10, 148–49; and isolation, 80–81, 119; and justification, 103–4, 112; legend of, 3–4, 11, 13–14; as lesbian, 20, 72, 80, 142; letters to Paul Bowles, 8, 80–81, 83, 116–17, 148; marriage of, 2–3, 72, 81–82, 97, 144–45, 160–61; and moral act, 134–35; and Moroccan women, 83, 116–17, 162; and plays, 139–40; and postmodernism, 16, 165–66; relationship with mother, 71; self-doubt of, 5–6, 8, 79–80; and sin, 132n. 1; and style, 11–12, 49; unpublished papers of, 16, 135–39; writing process of, 5–7, 10, 139
Bowles, Paul, 2–5, 15, 54, 120; as editor of Jane's work, 13, 94–95; marriage of, 20, 38; music of, 65, 140, 141; on Western corruption, 95; as writer, 6, 8, 48n. 2, 77, 134, 160
Breaking the Sequence: Women's Experimental Fiction (Friedman and Fuchs), 16
Broner, E. M., 73
Brookner, Anita, 14
Brooks, Peter, 166
Burgin, Victor, 165
Burroughs, William, 2
Butler, Judith, 26

"Camp Cataract" (Bowles), 4, 5, 14, 16, 104–7, 113, 126, 129–30, 158, 160; manuscript, 141–42
canonization, 10, 12, 17
Caponi, Gena Dagel, 5, 81
Capote, Truman, 10, 13, 80
Céline, Louis-Ferdinand, 2, 47
Central American literature (*see also Two Serious Ladies*): and empiricism, 42–44; and freedom, 46; and imperialism, 43; and involvement with natives, 43–44; and paradisiacal expectations, 39–40; and positional superiority, 43; relationships with natives in, 41–42; and resistance, 40–41; as subgenre, 38; tourism in, 42–43, 46–47
Chadwick, Whitney, 81